The Heroine's Journey

The Heroine's Journey

The Art of Becoming the Heroine of Your Own Life

By Joan Perry

Perrajin Press

MY HEROINE'S DECLARATION

I AM ME

IN ALL OF THE WORLD, THERE IS NO ONE ELSE EXACTLY LIKE ME
EVERYTHING THAT COMES OUT OF ME IS AUTHENTICALLY MINE
BECAUSE I ALONE CHOSE IT – I OWN EVERYTHING ABOUT ME
MY BODY, MY FEELINGS, MY MOUTH, MY VOICE. ALL MY ACTIONS,
WHETHER THEY BE TO OTHERS OR TO MYSELF – I OWN MY FANTASIES,
MY DREAMS, MY HOPES, MY FEARS – I OWN ALL OF MY TRIUMPHS AND
SUCCESSES, ALL MY FAILURES AND MISTAKES – BECAUSE I OWN ALL OF
ME, I CAN BECOME INTIMATELY ACQUAINTED WITH ME – BY SO DOING
I CAN LOVE ME AND BE FRIENDLY WITH ME IN ALL MY PARTS – I KNOW
THAT THERE ARE ASPECTS ABOUT MYSELF THAT PUZZLE ME, AND OTHER
ASPECTS THAT I DO NOT KNOW – BUT AS LONG AS I AM
FRIENDLY AND LOVING TO MYSELF, I CAN COURAGEOUSLY
AND HOPEFULLY LOOK FOR SOLUTIONS TO THE PUZZLES
AND FOR WAYS TO FIND OUT MORE ABOUT ME – HOWEVER I
LOOK AND SOUND, WHATEVER I SAY AND DO, AND WHATEVER
I THINK AND FEEL AT A GIVEN MOMENT IN TIME IS AUTHENTICALLY
ME – IF LATER SOME PARTS OF HOW I LOOK, SOUNDED, THOUGHT
AND FELT TURN OUT TO BE UNFITTING, I CAN DISCARD THAT WHICH IS
UNFITTING, KEEP THE REST, AND INVENT SOMETHING NEW FOR THAT
WHICH I DISCARDED – I CAN SEE, HEAR, FEEL, THINK, SAY, AND DO – I
HAVE THE TOOLS TO SURVIVE, TO BE CLOSE TO OTHERS, TO BE PRODUCTIVE,
AND TO MAKE SENSE AND ORDER OUT OF THE WORLD OF PEOPLE AND
THINGS OUTSIDE OF ME – I OWN ME, AND THEREFORE I CAN ENGINEER
ME – I AM ME AND

I AM A HEROINE

VIRGINIA SATIR

Acknowledgments

Thank you bundles to Ivri Turner for your wisdom, insights, and love — without you, this Book might not have happened. You joined me with heart and soul in the development of this work, that is such a passion of mine, and the two of us became Heroines in the process of this content development too. You deserve so much credit. I'll always love you!

Thank you to my team — Jacob Kenneally and Erin Egan. You believed, and you inspired me, and mostly you kept me on track. So many hugs to each of you!! Your expertise in putting all of the pieces together to bring this big work into the world is monumental.

Thank you to Bill Martorano for your gentle encouragement.

Thank you to Monkey C Media for the Book Cover well depicting The Heroine's Journey. Rob Kojbere at best seller publishing and Bob Bare at best selling experts excellent.

Thank you to all of the circumstances, ups and downs in life, people who made my life so challenging (and miserable at times), and those Angels who showed up to help me — it was all as it should be for me to learn, grow, formulate and deliver this Book now. It was perfect.

Thank you to Heroines before me who have inspired me — those living and those who have gone on. Their wisdom is imbedded in my heart, as I have looked to them to see who I can become.

Thanks for the work of my first Book — 'A Girl Needs Cash, Banish The White Knight Myth and Take Charge of Your Financial Life', and how it impacted Women's Lives. I hope that this new Book will also light up lives, contributions, joy, prosperity, freedom, and more for women all over — that's the payback for me! Tell your best girlfriend to get this Book (or give it to them) — it's the one that I wish that I'd had when I got thrust onto my Heroine's Journey, for sure!

This Book Is Dedicated To: More and More and
More Heroines All Over The World

Contents

Journey Onward!

Introduction

I did realize something deliciously profound that caused me to write this book. It quickly transformed me, and it wasn't what my mother, my women friends, or anyone else had shared with me.

This was a curious realization because I certainly had wanted, studied, and planned for my happy, prosperous, freedom-seeking life, and I got to the top of the ladder, presumably lighting up my life — but then I discovered that while I had put so much effort and dedication into getting to the top of the ladder, the ladder was in the wrong building!

This is not uncommon. After all, we try what we think works. We look around, see what others are doing, and try it out. In retrospect, we all want to live our dreams, but the things we see others do aren't necessarily what gets you and me there. Then poof — we have a life that is ours to love, ours to hate, ours to emulate, ours to parody.

My life suddenly went off the rails and I thought that I had no business claiming any victory for life. I needed a recovery manual for my own heartbreaks and spiritual explorations. I begged, "How was I going to recover?" Writing this book was one of the ways that I pulled myself out of crazy! I learned so much — and so much that were the secrets that I hadn't learned from my sisters or women before me who were hush hush about what they wanted and needed.

I could go so far as to say that I created — which seemed farfetched at the time — the drama and chaos in my life because my soul yearned for more. Chaos is the door to creativity. For so many years I used to write that in the front of my journal to remind myself — or maybe to subconsciously foretell — my upcoming year and life. More me, more opportunity, more growth — that something deep spark in me that wanted to make sure that I got all of life while I have life (even if it was going to be radically uncomfortable).

It's a conundrum to think that finding the well-suited life is not orderly, but quite disorderly. That was the clue. Now, looking back, I see where freedom began — it was in the *mess*.

Messy!!

Everything was in flux. There wasn't anything to hold on to. I was so bloody sad. I was depressed, a showstopper. I sank into shame for my failed marriage and my self-conviction that I had failed at life. I ached from disappointment after disappointment. I felt weak. I didn't trust myself in the least.

And then I had to crawl out of it. I didn't want to live that way.

I needed possibility where there once was only a tightly compressing box pressing in around me. And as a friend once said: 'the directions are on the outside of the box.' And you are allowed to escape the box. You can revive, reinvigorate, and reinvent yourself.

I discovered that there is a Path forward. The Heroine's Journey. And I discovered that while our stories are different, that there is an underlying plot line that is the path forward and available to all women to journey to our Best-Selves. This was deliciously, profoundly worthy.

The plot line serves as a RoadMap to speed your progress.

The Heroine's Journey kindles your knowing that your life belongs to you. You can go from victim to becoming the Heroine of your own life — and there is a step-by-step path for this to happen. It is the adventure of your life — and a journey that all women must take to grow to their Best-Selves.

This memoir recounts a decade of wide-ranging exploration and gut-wrenching introspection to fully shine. And, putting it here is for it to help change the narrative of the sisterhood. For us to inspire our Courage and Strength — to claim our Self-Worth and our Voice. This is the Journey that profoundly changed my life.

And it's not a Hero's journey — no, *NOT*! That was just why the ladder was in the wrong building for me. What I had done is I'd looked around and I'd thought that the male-journey-version of life would get me to the success and satisfaction that I was looking for. I think that this has caused so much misery for women in the last decades because we've not acknowledged that women have their own Journey, which is distinctly and hugely different.

It's a Heroine's Journey that leads a woman to the joy, prosperity, and freedom that lights up her life.

A woman's life is not for her suffering; it's for her to create her Stability, awaken her Authenticity, light up her Expression, and make her Contribution. Thankfully, life has changed for women, and we now can ask powerful questions of ourselves. The Heroine's Journey changes our perspective for the unique Journey of a women's life. Thankfully, we can ask: Do I own my own life and can I change my path? Who am I and what have I come here to do? How can I feel loved and supported and with whom do I want to share my life? Can I speak what I truly believe and how am I divinely connected to do this? I vote for women to step into an expanded sense of their own Self-Worth, their own possibilities, and their own destinies.

Sometimes you must go through the difficulties, get baffled, unnerved, roughed up, undone, then older and wiser — to start the Journey of *You*! Where you become the Heroine of your own life...

That's what it is all about. Onward, on the Heroine's Journey!

1

The Heroine's Journey to True Wealth

EMBRACING THE FEMININE PATH

H e said that — *REEALLLYYY??....*

My body seemed to involuntarily roll into a sparking-deep-blue bowling ball — clunk right off my stadium seat chair and onto the aisle of the bleachers…bounce down to the main arena floor, pitch onto the stage…and plunk right down in front of her in a dead thunk stop.

Was I the only one in the stadium that heard that — why weren't we all clambering down front?

Yikes! It was Liz Gilbert, author of one of the most notable women's books about the journey of her life titled, 'Eat Pray Love.' Liz spoke on the Oprah Winfrey *The Life You Want Weekend stage* in San Jose, California. The big 'Sharks' stadium was packed to the gills with thousands of women, all the way to the tippy top. Liz was stunning in her red dress, claiming her part as the keynote speaker. She described how her book attracted millions of readers to her adventures — eating in Italy, praying in India, and loving in Thailand.

I, too, had read her book and remembered being captivated by the courage and vulnerability she portrayed when she picked herself up from a very messy divorce situation, where she was sobbing and bereft on the bathroom floor, got on a plane and went off by herself on what was a yet-to-be-discovered adventure. I didn't call it this then, but my heart knew she inspired me by her 'Heroine' sense of owning her own life and readying for the possibilities ahead. Her message rang out to women longing for more in their lives, too.

Then, from the stage, Liz told me about a conundrum — that threw me into motion.

Her story is a Heroine's Journey story. But were women hearing this for the first time? Do women have a journey path forward to fully blossoming into their authentic Best-Selves?

We know this. Men do have a Hero's Journey. The prominent Joseph Campbell identified a narrative pattern in all great story-telling works, like 'The Hobbit' and 'Star Wars.' The adventure identifies how a man goes from unrealized to a fully realized human being. It involves being called to adventure, struggle, conflict, and eventual masculine development. It recognizes that a man goes from being a boy to maturing into manhood. It acclaims men who take the journey as heroes and commemorates their skills and innovations to triumph. And society looks up to and honors the mighty men who prevail.

But what about women? Does society view women in this fashion, too? What perspective is there that acclaims the maturity of a woman? What historic movies, stories, examples — or even acknowledgment — speak to the path for women? Liz's book did! But did it attract so many readers because it opened a new doorway for us to consider?

Then, from the stage on that fateful day, Liz said: "I asked Joseph Campbell (father of the Hero's Journey narrative) — do women have the equivalent of the Hero's Journey in a path to becoming their best, most fulfilled selves? Did Joseph Campbell include women in the archetypal journey of the soul that he described?

Here's what she said that he said — that so blew me away: "I spoke with Joseph Campbell, and he said that women don't have the equivalent to the Hero's Journey — they just stay home and cry."

Double, triple Yikes — I heard myself blurt out!! How could this be?

Does this imply that we, the women of the world, don't blossom and mature, aren't contributors, and can't make legendary contributions?... That we shouldn't be looked up to as having prevailed with our wisdom, insights, and intuitiveness? We don't go from being girls to being fully embodied women through our trials, tribulations, and struggles? That our stories are not worth telling? That there is not the wisdom and insight from women who have gone before us as Heroines? That we don't adventure or have lives that matter in our quest for womanhood?

Heroines? That's a bit bizarre, to say the least!

I don't think this is true. But where are those stories written, and how does our culture display them? And how are we regarded in our culture if it's thought that we stay home and cry?

I stayed home and cried for a while, in the immense struggle that I went through as my Journey unfolded. And then I got myself up, dusted myself off, figured out my capabilities — and as Liz Gilbert says: "Ruin is a gift. Ruin is the road to transformation." And, I got started.

Fast forward to now, and all of the thinking that I've done from that stage-present-moment where I wanted to kiss Liz's feet for hitting the nerve, the longing, of women who flocked to her book and said in unison, "We do have a Journey," we recognize a universal path. And I say: "And now we must tell it!"

As for Joseph Campbell's perspective — this is what I've learned...

Joseph Campbell was right in one regard — and wrong in another. Women *don't* have a Hero's Journey. That's where the man goes out and fights the 'lions, tigers, and bears and brings home the bacon.' This is a masculine *external* journey into the world. In fact — there is a problem here. Many women have discovered that having this journey imposed upon them has caused misery and a mid-life yearning to redirect their lives.

However — News flash — by contrast, women have a Heroine's Journey! Women take this *internal* journey to claim their *Self-Worth* and their *Voice*. It's a Journey where we blossom, grow, innovate, restore, regenerate, reinvigorate, and write our own self-discovery stories. This brings a woman to wisdom, leadership, wealth, and legacy. This woman is fully embodied and plays a significant role in our culture and world dynamics. Her wisdom can guide us.

If it were true that women don't have a Heroine's Journey, we would know no Heroines. That would be — no Joan of Arcs, Amelia Erhearts, Rosa Parks, Ayn Rands, Eleanor Roosevelts, Oprahs, or Liz Gilberts. Time to dispel this backward misthinking! These women, true Heroines, have shown us their struggles and revelations in developing their extraordinary lives. They matured, transitioned, and built upon their struggles, failures, and disappointments and evolved into their notable selves. They let their light shine, and we see their accomplishments. Heroines do exist, and the Journey makes them.

The Dalai Lama said, "Western Women will save the World." I hope so for all concerned. It is essential to polish and prepare us to meet his challenge and have the strength to become this Heroine. This is the Heroine's Journey. It brings out our character, spirit, talents, and courage! It lands us squarely in the acceptance of who we truly authentically are.

In the process, The Heroine's Journey awakens you to new questions. Big questions are part and parcel of the essence of our lives. *"What if I own my own life' — not my husband, father, employer, or someone else who otherwise wants to control it?* What if the path I've been taking (when I looked around and thought that the male version of the Hero's path was the one to take) is clearly not working for me? Who am I, and what have I come here to do? What do I like, what energizes me, and what people do I want to surround myself with?"

"And, if I own my own life — what do I want it to be, look like, feel like, and highlight all that I was created to be?" Heroine-esque questions to ask, for sure.

If your life feels like a tight squeeze right now, you might have your sights set too low to think that you can blossom into a life of joy, prosperity, and freedom. And if your life is going along, but you do not believe it's all it could be, you too awaken to the prospect of change, a change that is as natural as a rose blooming — nature unfolding. You unfolding.

Take heart; you are meant to journey onward. If you have ever experienced life falling apart, you feel unsettled, or you have had challenges — you are being called to the adventure of The Heroine's Journey, here and now!

As thought leader, author, and sociologist Brene Brown so candidly points out, "You may not have signed up for the Hero[ine's] Journey, but the second you fell down, got your butt kicked, suffered a disappointment, screwed up, or felt your heart break, it started."

We tend to think that things just happen to us. Truly, our stories follow a plot line, and you are not alone. Truth be told, 87% of all women will have a major life upset by the time they are age 50. This "Crisis" is the impetus that propels you and me onto The Heroine's Journey. It's when you think that you'd like to stay home, all cozy and comfy, and hold on to safety and security — that life shows up with something unexpected, and you are quite likely taken off guard.

It can be really difficult, but this Crisis is an invitation for you to do two things:

1. *First*, surrender your outmoded ways of thinking that have kept you limited and really haven't kept you safe.
2. *Second*, to collaborate with other women so that you can survive, be supported and understand this universal Journey and the beauty it can bring into your life when you stay open to it.

We've all heard someone say, 'Get empowered,' — but this is not the Path of The Heroine's Journey (that's the male success prescription). This Path is about how to blossom to become your Best-Self. Your story is unique, and what can guide you is the wisdom of women who have gone before you.

I'm here to say that there is a proven Path. This Path will show the way, ease your confusion, provide answers, shine a light, put your past into perspective, illuminate your next Step, and give you hope for the future.

Big things!!

It did for me, and it will for you, too. Because you are writing your Story, and it's your Path to victory. You, too, will shine your Heroine!

We Start This Journey Together

So, let's illuminate the Path that takes women forward to become the Heroines of their own lives.

As Women, we are *truly* forging forward on a Heroine's Journey. When I outline the 13 Steps of The Heroine's Journey, life will finally start to make sense to you!

> Have you been through some real ups and downs in your life?
> Have you recently experienced an upset that hit you hard?
> Do you wonder what to do next and how to go forward?
> Do you need to call out your Courage and Strength?
> Do you wonder how you'll make it and who you will become?

If this is you, I'm so glad you are here! This was me, too. The Heroine's Journey is your adventure of a lifetime, and it blessedly brought me to higher ground. Now, I wouldn't trade my Challenges and experiences and how they formed me — so let me tell you why I say this and how it works.

You'll see that the ups and downs you have been through are part of a larger adventure unfolding right before you. While it may be nerve-racking and frustrating for you, take heart — it's all here to serve you. What your life is showing you refines you and shapes you. It's truly bringing you to know yourself more fully and celebrate life with more joy and abundance. And that's a really *good* thing!

This is your RoadMap home to joy, prosperity, and freedom. Your '*freedom is found in the messiness*'!

Crazy — I know, but let's dig in, and I'll walk with you through this Journey.

I often think that life would be so much easier if we just came roaring down the birth canal with a manual for living, clutched tightly in one hand, with our name embossed on the front cover! It would tell us what to do to create our best life and how to meet those unexpected challenges that crop up along the way.

Whether you are frozen and confused or ready for more fullness of life, you will see that consciously applying The Heroine's Journey will guide you gracefully through the challenges of your magical life experience.

Have you ever thought of yourself as a Heroine? Would you like to meet life's challenges with strength in your heart and grace in your step? A Heroine is not just born; she must earn her powers! She gets strengthened by life's adversities and becomes luminous by welcoming more love.

Although each of us has unique circumstances that form our stories, the Journey we Heroines take is universal. This is the odyssey we're on together. Our first Steps are to *Create Your Stability* so that you can sustain the Journey.

The Path forward is to Create Your Stability, Awaken your Authenticity, Light Up Your Expression, and Make Your Contribution — the complete Path of The Heroine's Journey to True Wealth.

Journey Onward!

The Heroine's Journey

You might ask, "What is this Heroine's Journey all about?" *Well*, that is a crucial question!

> *The Heroine's Journey is a **dynamic adventure** every **woman must take** to become her **True Self**. As she progresses through all **13 Steps** on her unique path, **through the Challenges and Celebrations**, she fortifies her **Courage and Strength**. Her calling is **to blossom** into a life of purpose and fulfillment, **her True Wealth**.*

When you understand this universal process and how it will unfold, you can consciously create the most opportunity for magic. This allows you to navigate into a life you cherish.

The Heroine's Journey to True Wealth is a four-part process that enables women to build sustainable Wealth and Well-Being through progressively:

- First, Create Your Stability - which is the topic of this Book.
- Second, Awaken Your Authenticity

- Third, Light Up Your Expression
- and Fourth, Make Your Contribution

Here, we are undertaking the Journey with: Create Your Stability.

What is Create Your Stability?

Creating your Stability is the process of being thrust through life's birth canal. Sometimes, it can feel dark, narrow, and unknown. But through this process, we are born into the bright light of life with legs on the ground and ready to run. This birthing is the necessary first action to experience the fullness of life.

> *Stability takes root in your **life** when you dedicate yourself to developing the **skills, tools,** and **support systems** to create a **solid foundation**. This brings what you need to feel **supported** in this world. This engenders a feeling of **security** and **comfort** that sustains you through life's challenges. **Stability** is the **first Destination** to reach in **The Heroine's Journey**. It is the **gatekeeper** to designing the **rich** and **purposeful life** you desire.*

If your life has ever suddenly been in disarray and the strategies you'd been using no longer work, then you experienced a need for Stability. The good news is that you can rebuild your life in a whole new and better way. Life's turmoil and challenges are usually a positive impetus to consciously align yourself with your highest self and highest good. Sometimes, the Universe (God for me) just comes along and upsets your apple cart on purpose!

Maybe there is something new that you are supposed to do, learn, experience. Off balance, you get more open to change, modification, new ideas, people, plans — it's often an 'eyes wide open' experience.

The Stability you have in place determines how you can handle this upset. Creating Stability in your life increases your balance, flexibility, resiliency, effectiveness and your possibility for good choices.

The essence of Stability is establishing a solid infrastructure in your life.

Your Stability, which fortifies your Courage and Strength — it is the roar of the Woman who has her spirit intact as her life moves through inevitable changes.

Important? — *YES!* Critically!

The Four Cornerstones

So, how do we create Stability? Four quadrants form the foundation of Stability. I call these your 'Cornerstones'. They are the groundwork for moving from survival to *thrival in your life.*

There are 4 Cornerstones to Creating Your Stability, which are your Tasks to complete in order to construct your life on a solid foundation. They are:

1. Cultivating **Beliefs** that produce your Best-Self;
2. Empowering your **Physical** Well-Being to sustain the Journey ahead;
3. Nurturing relationships with **People** who are a support and resource for your new life;
4. Restructuring your **Financial** flow so that your money needs are met with ease.

How to do this becomes the Tasks you face along your Journey. They require that you master each one of these areas on your Journey. This, my Sister, is the basis for creating your Stability!

You can get this! It will take some ingenuity on your part but the reward is *so* worth the effort. It will set you up to soar! From messiness, freedom springs forth — and joy and prosperity along the Journey.

Hey, once you leverage these 4 Cornerstones….WOW!! They will become so fundamental to your thinking and shape your choices that your life will radically change! I know this to be true from my experience and that of other courageous women. We invite you to leap in with both feet and claim this victory for yourself!

As Women, we are best supported by a community that contributes to our Stability, practically and emotionally — a place to learn new strategies and share our successes. Welcome to this community of Women. Find us on our Facebook group and LinkedIn at The Heroine's Journey LLC. Are you ready?

Here we go....

Through the process of Create Your Stability, you fortify these Cornerstones in your life. They are Beliefs, Physical Well-Being, People and Financial. With this Stability comes a sense of peace, security, and self-trust. Groundwork in place, you'll be filled with the joyful ability to hoist your wings on and fly free.

A HEROINE'S STORY — MINE OF STRUGGLE AND DISCOVERY

Yep, that's me. I claim it.

I know this all too well, as I blurted onto my Heroine's Journey and got forged in the process. It's true. I didn't want it — I was thrust forward (kicking and screaming mightily as the Path forward began).

Can I share my own Heroine's Journey Story of Creating Stability with you? Like yours, I'm sure, there have been upheavals and downward belly flops. . .

My Story starts gloriously, or so I thought. I imagined that it would just stay this way forever. My Father said I was born under a 'lucky' star. I thought life was a rose garden — and I 'smelled the fragrant roses,' but I forgot about the prickly thorns that adored them...

I went to Grad School, got my MBA, worked on Wall Street, started my own business, and had money to spare. I did all of the right things at the right time in what I thought was the right way so it would all line up perfectly. Yep, I had perfectly designed my life. After all, I controlled it, right?

I'd moved to California into a big, beautiful house with a to-die-for kitchen. My clothes closet was magnificent, and fine designers lived there. I had jewelry that a princess would covet. My travels took me to exotic locales. I had a really good life. I even had a good-looking husband.

The only clue was that while the outside looked great, the inside of me didn't feel so good. I wondered about that, but didn't pay it much attention. The outside was looking just fine. And the Status Quo was all I knew. What could there possibly be to change? I had it all, right — right? Nothing unexpected could happen, or so I thought, since I was in control.

Then the unthinkable happened, a one-two punch: Divorce and a family betrayal. It happened all so fast that it blinded me. I got dizzy, weak, and truly lost it. In one week, I lost my house, my office building, my business, my income, my future income, my inheritance, my family, my friends, my self-image, my self-esteem, and more. Unthinkable and unbearable. I tanked. My illusion of who I thought I was crumbled. I was numb, confused, frozen, and petrified.

It was my darkest moment. I saw my life crashing all around me, spiraling down. I thought I couldn't survive. I wondered if suicide was my only way out.

I was shocked and betrayed by the people who caused this. People who I had thought loved me. How could they? I felt so profoundly alone and deceived. Anguish and overwhelm engulfed me.

In a moment of sheer frantic desperation, I bespoke God's wisdom, "If it all goes away, what's left?", I pleaded. The answer that I got back was "*YOU.*" This answer startled me.

Me? — God says I get *Me.* Well, that must be a really good thing if it's a promise from God.

At that moment, I felt a fierce life-giving will rise from the deepest parts of my inner being that defied all else. It was a character revelation moment that profoundly emboldened my life. It was — "This '*ME*' is *valuable.*" What a concept!

It jolted me to surmise, and I reflected — "what if?"— If my breath and my being could design a captive life back then — then, "Hello" — now from this new place, I truly must have the gifted will to create a whole new life that is much more heartfelt and purposeful for myself. Just maybe I could have a life that I might love, cherish, and be grateful to live. Maybe (and hopefully) I could be truer to myself, who I am, what I want, and where my joy lives — just maybe.

I felt a flame of hope. This was my chance because I had so yearned to feel good on the inside of me. Maybe it took things falling apart so that new things could emerge in a better fashion. I was so wounded and hurt, but I felt like I had laid claim to my life. I was not going to give up. I was going to show up.

Unfortunately, where I was, the current circumstances were so dire. I had so much to deal with: stuff that could crater me, stuff that I didn't know how to handle, stuff that seemed too difficult, and more blasted stuff that came at me every day. I kept a quote nearby for comfort: 'God only sends you what you can handle.' "Really?", I queried. But I took it one day at a time, slowly at first and genuinely fearing my demise.

Then, *People* started to show up to help. Thank goodness because I could barely help myself. They offered hands-on help and insight — that I could go on and get through. I wasn't a total disaster; some believed in me.

I started to consider what I needed in terms of resources and more. I had to scrounge, but I did it.

I got up my gumption and began doing what I needed to do. It was a long list, and I learned some really important things. I had to do some nerve-racking hard things. But I kept moving.

As I progressed, I was able to reflect on the amazing process and blessings of how I was rising from the ashes. I discovered that I did four different aspects of self-embodiment that helped me get myself out of the big, big, messy muck: First, I created my Stability, then I became more Authentic, which led me to find my true Expression and allowed me to find new ways to Contribute. It sounds like a lot, but it developed quite naturally and led me one step to the next.

Looking back, I'm so glad my life did not remain in that Status Quo of 'the perfect life.' When I describe my life at its end, I want it to be much richer and more fulfilling than what it was at the start! I'm grateful that life pushed me along in new directions! It pushed me along on my Heroine's Journey, where I blossomed and became more of me. Now, I am at peace with my Story, with myself, and with those who impacted my life so dramatically.

I have great wisdom to share with you from this experience and the wealth of the stories that other Heroine women have shared with me. My passage on the Journey is both different from and the same as all Heroines. This Journey has taken me to joy, abundance, and freedom. I want this for you, too. Your's will strengthen and prosper you.

This is the greatest adventure of a Woman's life — mine, for sure!

HEROINE'S PATH TO TRUE WEALTH

We call this Journey The Heroine's Journey to True Wealth. Let's first consider what True Wealth is. "What is it for me, you might ask?"

> **True Wealth** *is the power to cultivate all of the* **Love, Money, Meaning,** *and* **Impact** *you can dream of while being fully aligned with your True Self.*

That's important. Let me repeat it. True Wealth is the power to cultivate all of the Love, Money, Meaning, and Impact you can dream of while being fully aligned with your True Self. That's big stuff! Hurrah! And that's the destination of the Journey.

"But how do we get there, you ask?"

The secret to building True Wealth is to focus on cultivating the True Self. The very process of The Heroine's Journey naturally leads you home to your True Self. Let's be clear about this.

> *Your* **True Self** *is the purest part of you, where your* **wisdom** *and* **power** *reside. In this place, you are clear and* **stable**. *Driven by a deep sense of* **Truth** *and Connectedness, you act from* **Love**.

You own your life. True Wealth is the result of liberating your True Self. True Wealth is a life where you revel in purpose, peace, joy, beauty, connection, and material wealth — and that is the process of traveling The Heroine's Journey! Literally, it takes you from the discomfort, maybe pain, and agony in life as you know it, and you leap to a life you love living.

You Are A Heroine

The archetype of the Heroine embodies the True Self.

Are you a Heroine?
How do you know how to find her?
How does the Heroine view life and its rewards?

Since you are now on The Heroine's Journey, you are in the process of unveiling the Heroine within you!
So, who is she? How will you know her as she arises in you?

*A **Heroine** is a woman who consciously cultivates an inner state of invincible knowingness of **her own Self-Worth** and is enraptured by her **connectedness** to the origin of all life. With perseverance, she aligns her outer actions first to serve her own **Well-Being** to activate her **purpose for the greater good**.*

Let's consider the qualities of a Heroine next. Do you recognize these in yourself and, perhaps, see many that can be cultivated?

Qualities of Your Inner Heroine

Here are the qualities of your inner Heroine. They are alive and well within you as you seek these qualities that will guide your life to more joy, prosperity, and freedom.

The Heroine:

> Heeds the call to adventure
> Possesses the fortitude to address the unknown
> Commits to the quest
> Trusts her own truth
> Follows her own inner knowing
> Embodies her Fierce Feminine
> Stands in the power of her unique self

Possesses courage and strength
Advocates for herself and others
Redeems adversity
Sacrifices wisely and willingly
Serves the greater good
Identifies and acquires what she needs
She is unmovable in her groundedness
Achieves realization about herself
Collaborates with others
Attains freedom
Acts in Love

Yikes, you say! This description of the Heroine certainly sets the bar high! As you think about them, do you feel some of the qualities of the Heroine within you? I promise you they are there. However latent they may be, they long to live fully through you.

And, can it be said that you feel like your life is falling short of the extraordinary life a Heroine can create? The purpose of this Book is to rearrange some of your thinking and how you live your life so that you can coax the Heroine from within. It did its work on my life — and buckle up for the ride of your life!

When the Heroine reigns and directs your life — you will have more power, confidence, clarity, and courage. Your adventures will unfold in new ways, and you'll cross into the life you are meant to live.

How do you actually get there? Heroines aren't born. They are cultivated. It is a bold choice to allow the course of life not to wear you down but rather to exalt you into embodying the inner qualities of the Heroine.

It is the Heroine's Journey that cultivates your inner Heroine. Let's talk about this Journey. It's a Step by Step process that every Heroine must take as she grows herself into her magnificence. . .

Your Heroine's Journey Will Redirect Your Life

One note here is that the Journey likely takes you places you never expected to go. Surprise, surprise!

That's because your truly authentic self may have different plans for you than the reality you previously engineered. At first, we do what we conceive will bring us 'safety' and 'security.' Then, on the Journey when that gets blown wide apart, our travels on the Path can take us where we never thought of going ourselves.

This is because what we used to make our earlier plans may elevate us to the top of the proverbial 'ladder' — but maybe the ladder we climbed has nothing to do with what we were actually sent here or enabled to do in this lifetime. And remarkably, you find that you got to the top of the ladder — BUT, the ladder was in the wrong building!

Stunning!

Mid-life on the Heroine's Journey, you can witness yourself going in a whole new direction. Maybe your skills and talents, your interests and loves, your gifts and inner guidance were previously overridden — and now, suddenly — with upset and crisis unfolding — you might (thankfully, before this life is over for you) — find yourself careened in new ways that were unthinkable before.

Maybe you are granted a new vision to see life in ways that someone or 'something' has bigger plans for you to live into on your Journey. Maybe it all adds up to more than 'what you can control,' that there are bigger ways for you to show up — and that life is an exciting and unpredictable ride going in a purposeful direction.

I wrote this Book because that's just what happened for me. I've been inevitably seeing Heroines' Journeys in many thousands of women now too. Their stories are different, but the Path of travel is the same. For me and others, life has taken on new shapes and dimensions from what I thought when I went off to man-handle and bulldoze the financial world. *Whoa!* My Journey turned into a Heroine's Journey, leaving behind the notion of going out and fighting the 'lions, tigers and bears.' What emerged was that my authentic voice was feminine. This made a big twist in things.

This is a lifetime of dedicated work for me. I am deeply passionate about sharing this with you.

Here's how the funny twist of events went for me…

Early in my professional career, I was curious to learn about myself and the crazy challenges arising in my life. I attended a self-improvement course in Cincinnati about self-esteem with one of the early leaders of personal development, Bill McGrane. Wow, at that time, self-esteem was a whole new concept for me, and I was hungry to learn.

At the end of the course, Bill gave each of us one word that he determined from knowing us — that he said was related to our life's work. He was intuitive in this way. The word that he gave me was 'WOMEN.' It jolted me!

Really??…

Here's the funny part: At the time, I was an Investment Banker working at a Wall Street Firm in a very, very male-centric world. My reaction to Bill's word for me was: — "What, that's freakin crazy?… Why 'WOMEN' as *my* word?"

Because, my brain spit out — "I don't *even* know any of them" (on the financial trading floors)! And, in the uber-competitive world that I was in, I wasn't even sure that I *even* liked any of them! I was bewildered by this mission that I'd been given. It seemed so far from my world at the time. And that *is* the way it often works.

Life unfolds in ways that initially don't seem obvious, but it makes perfect sense later! It's our Path.

I went on from that Wall Street job to establish my own securities brokerage firm. This is exceptional because mine was the very first female-owned investment banking firm in the Country that underwrote municipal bonds for entities like the City of Chicago and the State of California. This meant that I ran a firm and actively traded literally billions of dollars of bonds in the public markets, with my firm taking the market risk. Big! huh?

This was real pressure, and it taught me a lot about money, courage and strength, people, and what I thought about myself — wisdom that I gained and will purposely share with you!

My mission evolved as I was inspired to write my first book, 'A Girl Needs Cash,' with Random House as the publisher, eventually leading me to become a best-selling author. This was the first book ever written to women about money. Writing this book took me to speaking and training in support of women. I've been on national TV and radio and have been published in national publications. I've taught on big stages, including at the Peak Potentials Extreme Wealth Course with T. Harv Eker, coaching with Tony Robbins in his national financial programs, big women's groups throughout the Country, and many podcasts.

I've also co-authored with Lisa Nichols 'Living Proof, Gifts that came wrapped in Sandpaper.' — pretty appropriate groundwork leading to this work, for sure!

Here's what I learned and the twist that reshaped my life: My word is '*WOMEN*,' truly! And I *am* here to serve in shaping women's understanding of their Journeys that lead to True Wealth. I was born to do something very different from what I initially took on in the male-dominated world of securities investment.

Life showed up differently for me when I lost control of my predetermined plans. Now, I see the usefulness of this sometimes rocky terrain I have traveled. These challenges have polished me to be a worthy guide for other women along the way.

This work has been created for *you,* so that you have the support and inspiration you need as you walk the Path of your own unique Heroine's Journey, and maybe your life is majorly inspired again.

Stability Quiz

Now, do you have a Journal? A place where you reflect and record? How about a pretty one with a colorful cover, a favorite quote on the inside page, and a note to yourself about who you really are? You'll need it as you go through this Book. Making notes for yourself will light up your progress. Take a moment to get your Journal ready…then note your reflections and answers in it.

It's time to take the Stability Assessment Questionnaire. It is a process to establish where you are right now in certain areas of your life and be helpful to you on the Journey. You can get this Questionnaire by going to: www.HeroinesBook.com/Free-Resources.

Go get it now and ready yourself for gaining this new understanding about yourself. It's your tool to moving forward to the joy and prosperity that is your birthright.

Go now to get your free resources. Then, record your answers in your Journal.

Please, Please, please, do not judge yourself in this process. Just be honest, vulnerable, and answer the questions with as much clarity as possible. There are no right or wrong answers. It's just a measuring cup for you right now.

Then, after finishing this… read on. There's so much for us to talk about.

THE HEROINE'S JOURNEY ROADMAP

It's here!!

If you are going on a Journey, having a map is helpful, right?

Well, you're in luck. We do indeed have a map. The Heroine's Journey RoadMap gives you direction, inspiration, and hope. You are in good company. Many women have traveled this Path before you and found their way home in the very same Steps.

You'll see that the ups and downs you have been through are part of an unfolding larger adventure. It refines you and shapes you. It's truly bringing you to know yourself more fully and celebrate life more joyfully. That's a really *good* thing!

Here are the Steps of the Journey. And here's the thing — with them — *finally*, life will start to make sense to you! It's the Journey every woman must take!…and better to see where you are going….

There are 13 Steps on The Heroine's Journey RoadMap. (See the RoadMap that you can download in the Free Resources available to you). The first 10 Steps of The Heroine's Journey lead you to Create your Stability. Each of the remaining 3 Steps is an entire discussion filled with the wisdom you need to make it all the way home to True Wealth. Step 11: is to Awaken your Authenticity. Step 12: is to Light up your Expression, and Step 13: is to Make your Contribution.

This Book focuses on traveling together through the first 10 Steps to *Create Your Stability*.

First, I will introduce you to The Heroine's Journey by giving you an overview of each Step. Throughout the Book, we will explore each one thoughtfully and experientially so that you build a solid foundation for an extraordinary life. Here's how it goes . . .

The Heroine's Journey Steps:

Step 1: Status Quo

Living in your comfort zone

You are living comfortably within the known. You have crafted a manageable life to fulfill the appearance of safety and security. You just want to fit in and have it all work. Life is good enough on the outside, even if it feels empty on the inside. You are playing the part of a fictitious persona that you have scripted to impress the outside world. You do not yet realize that there is so much more truth to you that you have not yet discovered. You are in a bubble from which you don't see anything unexpected happening on your horizon. Why would you change anything?

Step 2: Crisis Appears

The unthinkable happens

A life-storm hits. You are caught off guard. You try to hold on to the Status Quo of what life once was. Your old ways of doing things just aren't working. You are numb to the circumstances and you cannot grasp the changes that are occurring so fast. You've been knocked flat, and you feel paralyzed. If you thought someone else was going to take responsibility for your life, that illusion is shattered. Life has a plan for you, but you can no longer control the circumstances.

What you don't know is that this Crisis is the catalyst for your transformation.

Step 3: The Challenge

The darkest moment

Your life seems very perilous — like you're positioned on the edge of a tall cliff, and it's an 'oh shit' moment as you look out. The challenge is you cannot stay on the cliff forever. You're confronted with your choices to fall on the rocks below or to power yourself to rise into the sky. You feel fear. You wonder, "Can I make it? Could I be ruined, die here, fall off the planet?" You question who you are. But, there is no energy to maintain the false self. You are no longer the illusion of what you were before. You are stripping away the old self, and it feels very vulnerable. You are at the mercy of this new reality. It may feel like the darkest moment of your life.

Step 4: Character Revelation

You realize what you're made of

From under this tremendous weight, your Inner Self breaks through. Your True Self is unmasked and reveals itself with conviction. It says: "I Am Worthy. I was not born to be the victim of this circumstance. I have natural inborn assets that I can engage to get me out of this mess." This conviction reveals your essential character. It informs you of the path you are capable of taking. You will find a way. You will go on despite all odds. Here, your commitment shows up from deep within. You know what you're made of. You realize that you are empowered. This part of the Journey calls forth your Courage and Strength and reveals your true Heroine's nature to you.

Stability Cornerstone: *Beliefs* - Believing in your Self-Worth

Step 5: Called to The Crusade

Confront new realities

The circumstances are dire. There is no way out but to go through. You are wounded, hurt, and suffering. And still, you decide not to let it take you out. With primal instinct for self-preservation, you finally take a stand for yourself. You know you must survive and you use this to invoke your perseverance. Like it or not, now, you must deal with your life as it is. You are being forced into new realities. There are some Tasks you just have to get done now, however unpleasant they are. It's big, and it is scary. You do it anyway. Digging deep, you find the fire in your belly. You get Fierce Feminine. You hoist your wings on and muster up Courage and Strength for a Journey into the wild.

Stability Cornerstone: *Physical* - Resourcing your Life-Force energy

Step 6: Angels Show Up

Your support system arrives

Here come the Angels, those who arrive to support you and steady your wings on your back. As your Journey is progressing, People that you never expected come to help as if a universal energy called them to your aid. You thought you were on the path all alone, but now you welcome their help. You can discern who supports and guides you, and you move away from People who impair you. Your Angels have a new perspective for your Journey. They provide critical support and pieces of the solution. You are ready to humbly receive. You are self-revealing. You accept your humanness. Your Angels are there to encourage your flight and give you confidence. They believe in you. There is hope.

Stability Cornerstone: *People* - Engaging your Circle of Love

Step 7: Gathering Your Provisions

Acquire fuel for your flight.

You will need fuel for the flight. In order to get off the ground, it's time to provision yourself for the Journey ahead. You draw in Life-Force energy and all of the resources you require to sustain yourself on the Journey. Your Inner Heroine realizes that she must generate plenty to thrive. It is her birthright to live in abundance. You cannot go on without. You clearly communicate to the Universe what will sustain you for the long road ahead. The Heroine is responsible for acquiring what she needs. Get resourceful to gather resources. From a place of Self-Worth, she asks herself what gifts and talents she can use to produce bounty. There is effort in the hunt, yet some supplies may be hiding in plain sight. There is plenty; go and harvest. You will have ample fuel for the flight as long as you are careful to use only as much as you gather.

Stability Cornerstone: *Financial* - Living within your Means

Step 8: Taking Empowered Action

Spread your wings and fly.

Conscious to calm your fear, you thrust yourself into critical action from a new, empowered place. You release the past in preparation for something new. You ask, "What do I truly want my life to look like?" Consider all good options and make strategic moves to shore up your foundation. You master new skills, tools, and talents. Standing on the cliff, you spread your wings and lift into the clear blue sky. You flap furiously. The hardest part of the flight is the first few moments, and you maintain your Courage and Strength. You don't look back because you are focused on the future. New miracles are showing up in your life now.

Stability: The *foundation* of your Stability is initiated

Step 9: Wind Currents That Test You

Navigate another challenge

In flight, you have a panoramic view and life looks better. You assess how much you got through and how many successes you have had that jettison your flight. You can see the horizon in front of you. Suddenly, another Challenge comes along in the form of a big wind that whips you around, scares and imbalances you. You are tested again in some kind of unexpected or surprising manner. You wonder, "Will this take me out when I have finally come so far?" Because you have been through the narrows of Crisis and Challenge and survived, this time, you hear your Inner Voice call out, 'I Am A Heroine.' From this awakened inner knowing you steady to navigate these challenges with your new compass — pointing you to glorious horizons.

Stability: You are ***being forged*** into Stability

Step 10: Crescendo

You are lifted into freedom.

Finally, the air currents around you become stable. When the wind currents of flight lift you, they lift you fast. You are out of survival and struggle mode and into the freedom of soaring through the air. Spirit runs through you. You are strengthened within. This Journey brought you the gift of wisdom that roots you deeply in your power as a woman. You are no longer wrapped in fear, broke without resources, numbed to your sense of what is good for you, neglectful of your Inner Voice, led by your former impaired Beliefs, tied to external things for your security, wedded to familiarity, impaired by rules of what to be, or armored in your heart. You are free! Now, your heart is open, and you see love in yourself and the world. You have conviction, determination, and focus. Your power is in your wholeness. You proclaim your Stability, and so it is!

Stability: *Stability is created,* and you are ready for what is next

Remember, Step 10 isn't the end of the Journey. There are 3 remaining steps, 11, 12, and 13, which deliver you home to True Wealth, living your True Self. Each of these last 3 steps will be an entire discussion. But it is imperative to create your Stability first, so let's start at the beginning.

The Heroine's Journey has had a profound impact on many women. We begin to understand we are not alone and there is a RoadMap that calls us to develop ourselves in specific ways. This is the Journey we are embarking upon together.

Now…it's your Story….

WRITING YOUR HEROINE'S JOURNEY STORY

Hey, wouldn't clarity about your life help, and how it is developing into your unique Heroine's Journey? In fact, where we're going is for you to take the leap to write down your Heroine's Journey Story next.

You might not have recognized it at the beginning of this Chapter, but I shared with you my Heroine's Journey Story — 'Mine of Struggle and Discovery.' Instead of just random happenings of terror and deceit (for me) — when I wrote my Journey, it started to put things in perspective, give me context, and encourage my progress. I began to see that there was a 'method to the madness.' I was not lost or forgotten. What happened was real, but what I thought was important at the moment became a Story (my unique Story) — that had a bigger life of its own.

The Steps were essential to see where I was emerging and where my struggles were still veiled. It showed me where to engage, dig in, overcome, and carry on. It helped me to celebrate myself, too.

Your unique Journey will also emerge when you write your own Heroine's Story — bigger, fuller, and more understandable.

Why it's important to write your Heroine's Journey Story

Why is writing your Heroine's Journey Story so important? When you understand the Journey and how it is uniquely unfolding for you, you can gain confidence to traverse the Path ahead, and importantly, how to do that and that you will survive! . . . and ultimately, you will thrive!

It is important to allow yourself to be vulnerable to the process of life and recognize that the ups and downs are part of this bigger adventure. Understand that it *all* serves to your advantage, even though sometimes it doesn't seem like that at the moment. But it is true. *Life is designed to serve you.* Nothing is wasted. It's all necessary for your progress.

Making your way and forging the Path in front of you, you'll use your intuition, heart energy, body sensations, and an open mind.

Now, in order to do this, let yourself experience a guided visualization with me. I will walk you through the Steps of The Heroine's Journey. Trust the process even if you don't quite know where it is going yet. We will get there together . . .

Visualization: The First 10 Steps Of The Heroine's Journey

Find a comfortable place where you can be at rest and close your eyes. Enjoy a cup of tea, and get your Journal close at hand.

Take a deep breath with your eyes closed, and settle into your body. Feel a 'knowing' coming from your heart.

You will imagine your own life as it has traveled through these Steps that I lead you through. Let your imagination create the pictures and the feelings that you experienced. Maybe some of these Steps on the Journey feel very familiar to you, and maybe some of them are still part of your process yet to come. Just see what comes as we take this adventure.

You may find that the makings of your Heroine's Journey stem from parts of your childhood or possibly more recently from your adult life. Just sense and notice what comes up for you. Drop into this Journey from your own unique life experience.

Let's begin. Read the Step as it follows below. Then close your eyes, let your senses experience what the Step describes, and see the places, people, smells, and situations that the Step describes for you. Record this in your mind's eye.

Take the first step on The Heroine's Journey.

Step 1. *Status Quo* — Imagine that you are sitting at home in some quiet place when life felt relatively under control. It seems like life is telling you that you don't need to change anything. What is around you here that you see and feel? Who is around you? Maybe you are safely nested and have built a comfortable life. Take a moment to picture this. You might experience being settled and planning for life to just go on like this.

[Pause and see this for yourself]

Step 2. *Crisis Appears* — Now visualize the moment when the unexpected happened. Did it come at you from left field? Maybe it was marriage, job, financial, health, or family-related. What was it that stirred your innermost feelings and appeared as a threat to your world? Can you picture where and how this happened?

[Pause and see this for yourself]

Step 3. *The Challenge* — Now, life feels very perilous. You feel fear. OMG! What could possibly happen now? You wonder, how can I make it? Could I be ruined here? You struggle with your emotions. You don't want it — and it is staring you right in the face. Do you feel paralyzed, confused — at the mercy of the situation? It is forcing you to deal with new realities. See old parts of yourself being stripped away. You find yourself asking, when it all falls away, what will be left?

[Pause and see this for yourself]

Step 4. *Character Revelation* — Under all this pressure, you can feel your Inner Heroine break through. Listen. Can you hear your Inner Self heralding your Self-Worth, enumerating your qualities of goodness? This is the moment when you defend your Worth. You pull your life out of the fire to reclaim your value. Was there something that you said to yourself — something that came from deep within you — that fiercely affirms that you are not going to give up the fight; you deserve more? Was there one sentence that erupted as your rebel yell? It fires back at all the odds that would try to defeat you. What did you proclaim in this moment?

[Pause and see this for yourself]

Step 5. *The Crusade* — Like it or not, it's clear. You have to whip up your will. You literally claw your way forward. You feel the dire thirst for water in the desert of your life. What is your primal instinct for self preservation, your reason for survival? See yourself leaving what you know and stepping into the unknown. Can you see yourself taking the first painful steps? What circumstances can you see?

[Pause and see this for yourself]

Step 6. *Angels Show Up* — Who are your Angles that show up? Did someone serendipitously appear that offers you help when you didn't think you could help yourself? How did they come into your life? Can you see the one, two, or three people that graciously came to your aid at the right moment?

[Pause and see this for yourself]

Step 7. *Gathering Your Provisions* — What resources do you need right now to fuel up for the Journey ahead? Do you have enough, or must you find a new way to generate provisions? What gifts and talents will you need to leverage to responsibly create what you require?

[Pause and see this for yourself]

Step 8. *Taking Empowered Action* — Now your blood begins to flow, and your brain begins to fire. Feel the power of the creative actions that you conjured up to take? Do you know the first, second, and third actions that move you into the new reality of your life? You try something, and then you try something else. You might feel fear, but you have new Courage and Strength to inspire your actions. What do you do to lift off and fly into blue skies? What do you do to lead your life out of the danger?

[Pause and see this for yourself]

Step 9. *Wind Currents That Test You* — You see yourself flying. You've put out some of the fires in your life and leaped hurdles that once seemed insurmountable. Can you feel the gratitude for the stable air? And, when it seems to be 'on the road to peace' again, the winds flare up and send you yet another turbulent situation. Do you wonder, "I made it through all of this, and now will this take me out?" But you remember you are made of new and stronger material this time. You know that you are a Heroine. Can you picture yourself being more resourceful and more pro-actively handling this trial? Is your new compass in your hand pointing you toward a glorious horizon?

[Pause and see this for yourself]

Step 10. *Crescendo* — Finally, the air currents calm around you. Do you feel the currents lift you quickly from survival and struggling to live freely? The challenges are behind you. Who are you now? What do you see in front of you now? Does your flight lift you to new heights, and do you feel Stable in flight?

[Pause and see this for yourself]

Take a moment to acknowledge this Journey. Now, gently move your body. Keep this Journey in mind as you are ready to write.

Write Your Heroine's Journey Story

Use your Heroine's Journey RoadMap from this Book and the descriptions above as you open your beautiful Journal and begin to write your Heroine's Journey Story.

How did you envision it? It's ready to be told from your experience and your current perspective and understanding. These are the events and feelings that have marked your Journey. Begin with Step 1, and write about each Step you've gone through. If you reach an unfamiliar Step, then note that more is coming for you. Write something about all 10 of the Steps.

This is just the beginning. Later, how you write your Story now will be important as we use this journaling to see the changes you make. With further learning, you'll have new insights. Good idea to make sure your responses to each Step are thoughtful and supportive of your process.

After you finish writing your Story in your Journal, take a moment to be grateful for all that you have been through, how you have made your way, and are gifted with life.

USING FEAR AND PREPARING TO PUT YOUR WINGS ON

So now you know that there is a Heroine's Journey, and you are being thrust forward on this Path. The question is: What's your pace? Are you stuck? Or are you rapidly moving forward? In this discussion we're going to cover two critical aspects of propelling yourself forward — using fear as a motivator and how to put your wings on to fly.

The Directions From Fear

As you are on the Path of The Heroine's Journey, do you notice that fear gets triggered over and over? Fear is that unpleasant emotion that tells you that you are in danger of experiencing pain or something threatening. In the Crisis phase of my Heroine's Journey, I experienced fear as a terror that the earth would open up, and I would fall right into the hot molten center and be swallowed alive. I felt on the verge of annihilation. Not a pleasant feeling!

This type of fear can be all-consuming. It can paralyze you as its victim. Here's the problem — If you get stuck here, you are in jeopardy of not finding the will to take the next Step out of the Crisis phase. Truth be told: even if you have traversed further on The Heroine's Journey, fear just comes up on the way and will certainly rear its head again.

When you get trapped in fear, you fall into believing that you have no *options*. Fear is in control and seems to be dragging you toward certain doom.

How do you progress on The Heroine's Journey when fear is an inevitable companion? The answer is: You Create *Your* Stability. This Stability that you are building is the force that keeps you in the middle of the road rather than in danger of veering off into a ditch — or flying from gutter to gutter. It is a matter of aligning yourself with the Cornerstones of Stability — Beliefs, People, Physical and Financial — that insure that you will be protected and safe.

The point of gaining your Stability is to lessen your fear. Fear will diminish as you gain more traction and more Stability in your life.

The quirky thing is, fear is still going to come up . . . because it has a purpose. Its purpose is to alert you that there is something you need to acknowledge, address, or act upon to keep you from being run over by some madness traveling down the road behind you or in front of you.

So, when this fear arises, use it positively; it is a compass on The Heroine's Journey. It can provide direction for you and serve you. You can view it differently.

Once you find a new orientation, you realize:

The Universe is trying to help me, and it is sending this message through the messenger of fear to get my attention and give me direction and impetus.

Fear is a reminder message to do what you need to do in support of your progress right now. Here's the key: Don't let fear stop you; work with it to galvanize you into right action.

There is a process for hearing fear's message. I call it Using Fear.

I'd like to share the process steps with you now:

Using Fear:

1. Feel the sting of 'Fear'.
2. Acknowledge that it has arrived with a very powerful message.
3. Breathe. Get quiet so you can access your inner wisdom.
4. Ask Fear what message it is bringing to you.
5. Accept that the circumstances are a part of your Heroine's Journey.
6. Ask what action is appropriate at this moment to move you forward.
7. Let the Wisdom you receive productively guide your actions.
8. Thank Fear for its service with gratitude in your heart.
9. Invite Fear to go on its way now that it has served its purpose.
10. Embody your Heroine energy now that you have safely used Fear.

It may be easier said than done, but you just gotta do it. Fear is your tool. Don't let it paralyze you. You have a choice to use it to propel you.

Although you may encounter fear on this Journey, it's not your constant companion. Your Courage and Strength are built as you navigate on the Journey. And now it requires building the motivation to elevate your life consciously.

Story: Standing On The Cliff

I want to share a true story about a Heroine who had to face unpredictable fear and then make a courageous choice to rise above the circumstances.

My friend Susan and her husband were celebrating their 24th wedding anniversary. Susan had planned, packed, and anticipated the fun of being in Mexico for a glorious vacation.

They flew from Seattle down to Cabo for a magical two-week celebration at a wonderful resort on the water. The plans had been made for some months. Susan called the hotel and told them it was their anniversary gala.

They cabbed it to the hotel, checked in, and found their room. When they walked in, there were rose petals across the bed and champagne to celebrate what was to be an extraordinary time in their lives.

They changed their clothes and headed down to the dock, where a rowboat was waiting to take them around the bend to the cove where they were headed for dinner. The special restaurant was situated high on top of the cliff overlooking the vista. The water and the evening were marvelous. The boat pulled up, and they scrambled up the steep trail to the plateau of the cliff.

They took a moment to walk to the cliff's edge and enjoy the view. They stood perched over the ocean with the gorgeous blue sky above them. And, a long distance down, the blue-water sea was crashing on the rocks below. Blissfully, Susan soaked in the magic.

In that awe-striking moment, her husband turned to her and said, "I want a divorce." *Wham!* She was devastated! That was the moment that marked the beginning of her Heroine's Journey.

She had two choices. She could crash on the rocks below, allowing the pain with fear to overwhelm her and her life. Or, she could muster her Courage and Strength, dig deep into who she is, and fly into the sky.

This is the quintessential moment when everything shifts out from underneath you. You cannot find the ground. You are overwhelmed by pain and loss. And somehow, you reach deep within, awaken a part of yourself that may have been forgotten, your Heroine-Self, your Fierce Feminine that can and will.

Susan, being a Heroine, blessedly decided from that moment to put her wings on and fly.

Putting Your Wings On

At times we all encounter very difficult situations in life. It is part of the human experience. Your choice is how you will use adversity as fuel for your life and recognize it as a catalyst for your Journey.

Imagine this conundrum: chaos is a great opportunity for you to uplift your life. It presents a choice where you can either decide to be a victim of the circumstances or muster your Courage and Strength in preparation to make radical new choices that lift your life to glorious new heights.

This choice could usher in more love for yourself, vibrant health, nurturing relationships, and financial prosperity. A beautiful awareness that musician Tim McGraw shares in his award-winning song, *Humble & Kind,* is: "Bitterness Keeps You From Flying."

Will you have the Courage and Strength when you are standing on the precipice to put your wings on and get ready to fly? What would your life look like if you decided to put your wings on in preparation to lift off consciously?

Even if you cannot fathom what the Path ahead might look like, if you know in your heart it is time to fly, you are in the right place here, reading this Book and in this Community.

This is 'flight school'.

Support For Hoisting On Your Wings

To facilitate your growth, along with this Book, please consider if your personal Well-Being requires additional professional help. This could be in the form of a therapist, holistic medical consultation, financial advisor, or other therapeutic support.

It's so important to add a note here: If you are in a place right now where you are truly in danger of crashing on the rocks below, stop and reach out for immediate support in the form of a crisis hotline, law enforcement, or local hospital. First, you must be safe, then come back, and together we can co-create *Your* Stability.

If you need the support of camaraderie along your Path, you may want to join a women's, religious, spiritual, or singles group. Just keep connected with those who support you. And remember, you have our Community of Heroines in our Facebook Group.

Once you have the support you need, you will be far more resourced to access the inner strength necessary to hoist your wings on. It is a Journey that we will spend the remainder of this Book discovering with the tools and processes for getting your wings mounted squarely on your back and preparing to fly.

This is really good news; flight instructions are on the way as you keep reading!

Free Resources

We've got you, Sister! We have more to help you on your way!

Go, now to:
www.HeroinesBook.com/Free-Resources

1. Here you'll find the Heroine's Journey RoadMap. It outlines the whole Heroine's Journey.
2. And, here, you'll find a Self Survey that you can take — it's the Stability Assessment Questionnaire. It's the questions to ask yourself so that you can clarify for yourself where you are now.

The Heroine's Journey has had a profound impact on many women. We begin to understand we are not alone and that there is a RoadMap that calls us to develop ourselves in specific ways.

This is the Journey we are embarking upon together — Yahoooo!!!

2
The Archetypal Journey

The Archetypal Heroine

The Wise Woman

The Midwife

The Alchemist

Walking As A Heroine

With Wings You Can Rise Above

THE ARCHETYPAL JOURNEY

In my wildest imaginings, I'd like life just to be a 'rose garden,' but the start of my Heroine's Journey was punitive — truly, life cranked me up and threw me down hard. This is the way it goes. Heroines are forged; yes, it's through painful experiences very often. It's then that you can feel isolated and disoriented.

But you know that you're not alone, right?

Let's say that 'it sucked' from my vantage point — I'll share more of that later on — and then the Journey revealed some blessed help. Hoorah for that! Wise women appear to teach you bigger Wisdom — and you'll see they are there to guide your Journey forward.

They prompted me to start to ask new questions!

How do we challenge ourselves to walk The Heroine's Journey, not with fear and uncertainty (and painful looking back) — but as a head-held-high Heroine, knowing that the Path is leading home to our True Self? These wise women are apparent to say that you are embarking on the best adventure of your life — your unique Heroine's Journey! There are big bonuses that await you.

While that can really feel like it's a stretch, this is the truth. The Journey you are on will open insights for you to understand the events in your life — even those that challenge you — in a purposeful and impactful way. You'll have the opportunity to get a higher vantage point in your life and realize the opportunities that are before you.

Life is not ill-fated. You are not at the mercy of the random events in your life. It may seem this way when you look at circumstances individually. But really, they are interconnected in a grand scheme that teaches you life's lessons, refining who you are for your highest good. This connected pathway is an archetypal adventure called The Heroine's Journey.

There are destination points along the way that, as women, we *all* visit, yet our Heroine's Journey is specially crafted as our own. The plot line is the same, but our stories differ in many ways. Ultimately, we are all headed in the same direction: to be our Best-Selves and a noble contributor in our gifted way to the world.

Once you recognize the fundamental stepping stones on the Journey, you will have the clarity to understand with greater Wisdom what lies behind, remain centered in the moment as you take each Step, and anticipate what lies ahead. This gives you a sense of acceptance that allows you to digest the past and offers hope for your future, a grand place to land.

When you view life through the lens of The Heroine's Journey, life just makes sense. There is reason for hope. And you can identify the gifts coming to you all along the way. You are cultivating a Path to meaning, purpose, legacy, peace, abundance, and connection — True Wealth.

And, ultimately, you come home to yourself. Let's listen to what these wise women say, shall we? They are your guides on this Journey!

THE ARCHETYPAL HEROINE

Whether or not you consciously choose the Journey (or find yourself radically plopped into the start of it), it inevitably begins. There is a universal mistress of ceremonies, a force of nature, a universal law of genesis that ushers you onto the Path of your own blossoming.

What is this force?

Imagine that a great Archetypal Heroine is the creatrix of the wind beneath your wings. She is the collectively inherited identity of the Heroine that guides us along the Path.

We can see the Archetypal Heroine embodied in the great women of past and present. If you reflect upon their achievements, you can feel a spirit of power within them that lifts them to great heights to fulfill their life purpose. They are women who know the way.

As you become a human Heroine, this spirit of power is also alive in you. She is present to give you the hope, help, and support to guide your way home to True Wealth and elevate your wisdom to share.

The Wisdom of the Archetypal Heroine is bestowed via three distinct aspects. Each reveals unique Wisdom to you. Their shared mission is to assist you with each Step of The Heroine's Journey.

They come to you out of the ethers with voices that counsel you. They are your guides on the Path, giving you access to their Wisdom, compassion, and direction resources. They speak to you through intuition. Invite them in and listen carefully.

Let's meet these three aspects of the Archetypal Heroine now. Then, let's ask them to help you navigate your adventurous Journey.

THE WISE WOMAN

First, meet the 'The Wise Woman.' The Wise Woman serves as a guiding internal presence for you.

She is the embodiment of Wisdom. She has experience, knowledge, and insight beyond your own. Accessing her is the timeless, infinite inspiration to awaken yourself. She is here to be your influence on the Journey.

She believes in you and whispers into your heart, "You are so much greater than you imagine." She knows because she sees your grander self.

She reminds you to surrender to the greater Wisdom. This great feminine energy brings knowledge beyond your current circumstances and can help you navigate difficult situations. She delivers significant insights that steer you in the right direction. Sometimes, she asks you to do things outside your comfort zone that ultimately propel you in the right direction. With the 'Wise Woman' at your side, all is revealed in perfect timing.

The embodiment of the Great Mother, 'The Wise Woman' nurtures and protects you. She calls you to trust your inner knowing and make the choices that will keep you safe and secure.

She calls you to trust a higher Wisdom that will evolve into your own Self-Worth.

You will be well served to welcome her into your vulnerable part and receive her direction. You may even want to name her or ask her what she calls herself. Call her to come to you. Maybe give her a place to sit in your imagination and ready her to help you.

Go with me now. Relax into a comfortable position. We're going off on a process of active imagination. Take a few deep breaths. Your imagination will guide you and take you to a place of tapping into greater Wisdom.

Deep breath and let it out. Make some sounds if you wish, like Hmmmmm…

That's it. Now, picture a door swinging open. An older woman comes to sit in front of you. Immediately you sense her warmth, and you relax in her presence.

Looking at her, you see a depth in her eyes that makes you feel like you can drop right into her deep waters. She has a faint smile as she watches you being captivated by her presence. She's not beautiful but appears familiar, gracious, and trustworthy to you as she takes you into her feminine essence.

With an inquisitive look, she asks, "What do you need to know?" You sense that she is coaxing the deepest part of you to answer. And this makes you pause.

She taps your emotions and spirit. What do I need to know right now that will guide my heart and actions in the following Steps on my Journey? Are your questions about your Self-Worth, Money, or the way through a complicated situation?

As you form your question, this Wise Woman drops deeply into a space within her and taps a pearl of Wisdom from an expansive place.

Ask this Wise Woman. Look deeply in her eyes — go ahead. Ask her what you need to know right now that will guide your heart and actions in the next Steps on your Journey.

Listen carefully as she answers. What she has to offer is a piece of Wisdom that will guide your heart. And lead your footsteps.

When you have deeply heard her Wisdom, thank her for her answer. Tell her you will visit with her often because you need her more profound Wisdom.

Now, she will send you to the Midwife.

THE MIDWIFE

Next, meet the Archetypal Heroine known as 'The Midwife.' She has a different calling for you. She brings more skill to your Journey and fosters your progress.

The Midwife serves to usher in the birth of your Inner Heroine and steers you through the entire process of becoming your Truest Self. She is the flow of progress and your growth.

The process of your becoming is the ultimate creative process. Your life is brilliant beyond what you can imagine, and you are met with great beauty when the Midwife assists you. This is your hope for the future.

The Midwife births you into your purposeful life. You do not have to know what it will look like yet. She beckons you to let go of your limited preconceived notions of how life should be so that you can be born into innocence, open to all the mysteries life has waiting for you.

The Midwife makes it safe for you to surrender to this flow of life. When you are moving through the darkness of the birth canal, trust that the Midwife is guiding you out and is there to receive you as your True Self as you enter this glorious new world.

She intervenes in your small self to make way for your bigger self, the self that will bring you to new creations and new joys. When you keep moving forward, you will be led into unfolding your unique gift to bring to the world.

Welcome her into the part of you that desires new creation. Take a deep breath.

Go with me again. Relax and feel your breath flow. Enjoy this process of meeting the Midwife.

See the door in your mind's eye swing open. This time, here's the Midwife. She has a different kind of guidance to offer. She brings the voices that are calling you to show up in some bigger way in life. Bigger than you imagine.

You may feel uneasy as you sit in front of her. That's because she's there to grow your bigger self. You secretly hoped that life would only be that rose garden — filled with sweet smells and beauty. You weren't counting on it being rough and thorny at times. She knows this is true and that you need her capable hands along the way.

What does she look like as you meet her? As you look into her crinkled eyes you ask yourself, "Where am I going? What am I becoming?" She's gentle with you. She's even humored that you need to ask because she knows great things are in store for you. You are on a Journey of self-discovery, and she's there with you.

Ask her — "What do you see for my future? What am I being birthed into? Can I make it through the 'narrows' of my life? What's my hope for the future?" Listen closely to her Wisdom.

As she speaks, allow yourself to surrender and move through into the light of her Wisdom.

Thank her for her answer. And tell her that you will visit with her often too because you need her guidance.

She offers you that ray of hope about what your future will become.

Now, she will send you on to The Alchemist.

THE ALCHEMIST

Now meet the Archetypal Heroine known as the 'Alchemist'. She will stir you up and mix you around to propel you forward. She might even poke you to get you moving. You need her to prod your progress, call her in.

The Alchemist serves as your teacher, instructing you on the practical 'how to' things necessary to take the following steps in transformation. She ignites you to discover the skills, tools, and talents to transform your life from raw and unrefined to brilliant and priceless.

The Alchemist hands us the RoadMap, knowing that each Step on the Journey catalyzes our metamorphosis. Calling upon her skillfulness, she imbibes us with the inner ability to navigate.

She burns away the impurities in your thinking that make you feel less about yourself. She transforms self-doubt into Courage and Strength. She cultivates the strategic and practical steps to forge new circumstances in which you feel better about yourself. The Alchemist transmutes your awareness so you can see your precious worth.

She blends all the elements. She is the leader of our Sisterhood, bringing the tribe together and harkening us into community. She weaves us together to share connections and good ideas that ignite new thinking.

She nudges you with urges to go and do and learn more so that you can deliver more and receive more rewards.

Welcome the Alchemist into that part of you that is ready to take skillful action.

Once more, go with me. See the door swing open, and the Alchemist sits in front of you this time. She giggles as she imagines everything there is for you to do and what you will learn. What new ideas will you awaken to? What resources will you discover in you? What new ways of being are there that will emerge for you?

She is very task-oriented. There are things to do and places to go. She knows you need tools in your pink tool belt and skills to bring to the tasks at hand. She's patient because she understands your frustration when you're confronted with building these new resources within yourself, but she doesn't let you give up. She says, learn this for today because I'll have another learning for you tomorrow. She giggles again as she pokes at you.

There is no rest for the weary when the Alchemist is around. She's sparking all of this for your worthy expression into the world. She will roust you to move onward.

Ask the Alchemist, "What is one skill I need to learn to transmute my life into its highest expression? What is one action I need to take to transform my reality?"

Listen carefully. The Alchemist is whispering Wisdom to you to get the transformational results you deserve.

Receive her guidance with gratitude. Accept her Wisdom.

Thank her for her answer. And tell her that you will visit with her often too so she nudges you forward.

These three — The Wise Women, The Midwife, and the Alchemist — are collectively there for you. Now that you know them you can reach out to them. Deliciously, you can visit with them often and be enriched and enlarged with their elevated visions for you.

WALKING AS A HEROINE

How did it feel asking for the Wisdom of the three aspects of the archetypal Heroine?

Before I realized I was on my Heroine's Journey and life was rocky, I felt impoverished because I was spiritually broken. I needed to commune with these three aspects of the Archetypal Heroine to be uplifted into hope and possibility. This was an active process of surrendering and asking for help.

The guidance I got was:

- The Wise Woman takes our hand and invites us on the Journey.
- The Midwife ensures we make headway through the narrows of our Path.
- The Alchemist gives us the Road Map, instructions, and right actions.

Can you hear them whispering their Wisdom to you?

Your Heroine-Self must travel the Journey I am describing in this Book, and truly *not* from the victim voice within you. Victim will neither be fulfilling nor propel you toward your true destiny. The Victim is stuck — Heroine is on her way.

Maybe when you wrote your Heroine's Journey Story as outlined in the first chapter of this Book, you let your 'inner victim' have some control of your pen. Can you notice that? Victim is one point of view, but there is another far more powerful point of view. . . that of the Heroine!

The Heroine walks the Journey with her heart open, her head held high, and a sense of conviction in her walk.

She:

1. knows the truth of who she is;
2. celebrates her accomplishments;
3. is ready to be flexible in handling whatever lions, tigers, and bears jump out onto her Path.

Each of us is a Heroine. Our task is to let go of the ragged beliefs of the Victim and fiercely claim the power of our Heroine-Self.

WITH WINGS, YOU CAN RISE ABOVE

Here's some magic — adversity can serve you! Imagine that…

Even a Heroine faces adversity. No matter how clear and courageous you are, life sometimes gets messy! A Heroine is still a human, after all.

This messiness is where your growth comes from. In the process, you must surrender your attachment to particular outcomes and things and learn to adapt to new circumstances. Messiness is an excellent thing! It brings new opportunities, new perspectives, and new adventures.

The adversity you face along the Path refines you and serves to help you recognize the innate gifts, of skills, tools, and talents you already possess that want to be expressed. They are looking for a break in your routine so that they have a calling out.

It's astonishing that circumstances that unexpectedly change can be even more rewarding than your prior limited expectations of life.

So how does that work, you wonder?

In my life, I thought the end of my marriage and subsequent moving out of my home was simply awful and life-ending. I honestly believed that it was a disaster and that I was doomed.

Now that I look back on the situation, I feel this was one of the best things that could have ever happened to me. *Surprising!*

What came about was that I moved further along in my Journey to more life-giving circumstances — new, loving people and a new, more supportive residential community. This transition even created the space for me to step into purposeful work that I would not have been able to accomplish in my old circumstances. It was a disruption that made an opening.

The disaster was actually a huge blessing!

It is pretty astonishing that the things I labeled 'the worst' in my life, now looking back at them from the present, are some of the most important gifts I could have received. I even co-authored a book titled Living Proof 'Celebrating the Gifts that Came Wrapped in Sandpaper.' A little nod to the fact that the arrival of a gift can often look terribly rough and uncertain at first!

Once you understand that there are gifts in adversity, everything becomes a teacher.

Ask yourself: "What is the message of good in everything you experience?" It's there. Excellent stuff is there. My Father used to say, "There is horse poop here; there must be a pony somewhere!" Yep, it's truth!

You are the author of your Story. You are the author of your Heroine's Journey Story.

You choose the characters, meanings, feelings, and actions you take.

There is an important skill to render: that's to separate facts and Story. You may be unable to change the facts, but you always author the Story. Here's an example . . .

Fact: I am divorced.

The Story is either:

I am unworthy.

Or, re-written, the Story is:

I am free, I am Me.

As the author of the Story, you get to make your own pick. Isn't that powerful? Did you know how much of the interpretation you have in your power?

Many of us spend decades in the story "I am unworthy." A Heroine chooses the Path and does the work that allows her to author her Story titled "I am free, I am Me!"

Later, you will have the opportunity to re-write your Heroine's Journey Story from the Heroine's point of view. But first, there are many new skills and perspectives to gain in the following Chapters, which will shape your understanding and empower you in the mighty Heroine's viewpoint of your Heroine's Journey.

Let your Journey proceed with hope. That's the necessary ingredient. It's the thing that lights up your Journey, feeds your spirit, and powers your way. Hold on to Hope. The process of the Journey is 'right on,' and hope will take you onward.

Sometimes, the Journey will seem obscure, and you will get bewildered. This bewilderment is meant to shake up your assumptions about who you are, how you see your life, and how you think the world works. It forces you to seek out new ways of gaining clarity. This is part and parcel, 'right on', bringing you to your radical acceptance.

Remember, the Path is of hope and a mixture of faith and trust. I love this definition of HOPE. H-O-P-E: Help One Prosper Everyday. When you reside in HOPE, you prosper.

But, let's concede, Hope can often be ephemeral. If you lose hope, you walk with your head down, and your trajectory is towards falling down. Not a good thing!

When you can wrap your arms around hope, your eyes lift, and your vision is on the horizon. You'll take flight with hope. Hope is vital to your navigation. It's what carries you into the air. Funny fact: there is no aerodynamic reason why a bird should be able to fly. It just does! And with hope, you will, too. Hope is the wind beneath your wings.

Will you claim your Heroine's Journey or waffle in resistance?

Either way, you will be pulled into what is not known to you right now. While your heart may be pounding, you keep moving methodically and purposefully. You stay on the Path when all might be telling you to flee, fight, jump off a cliff — anything to get away — but you continue on your Journey.

When you make this commitment, what's ahead? Well, you snap in! There is an internal urge for growth within you. This urge moves you to be more than you know. At the core, you are many truths. Growth is calling you, and it's magical. The calling feels like an urge deep within that you can't deny. You will help yourself if you follow this urge for your destiny to blossom, which might also allow you to help others on their Paths forward. This is a magnificent part of being human and a Heroine.

What does it take, what's asked of you? Good question.

It takes doing the Tasks that I'm going to teach you. These Tasks are found in developing the 4 Cornerstones of building your Stability to fortify your life. You can rest assured that we're headed to this discussion in this Book — they are *essential*, and I know that you're on your way to your Best-Self and are starting by Creating Your Stability!

Heroines put their wings on. Standing high on the cliff — they escape crashing on the rocks below; they wildly flap their wings and fly. And up in flight, it is sooooo much more fun!

Welcome to the 30,000-foot view. This will take you from a myopic to a panoramic view of the landscape of your life. From here, you can see the bigger picture. This vantage point provides Wisdom, how all things fit together. It allows you to rise above the situation, where previously you might have felt panic. Now you have maneuverability!

Now, you have the perspective in which you can see that your challenges can present opportunities. Within these challenges, there are choices to be made in any situation. A Heroine can recognize that there are always options in front of her that are key to her vitality, and she lives into becoming her Best-Self.

Hey, let's proclaim!

A Heroine doesn't stay home and 'cry' — NO, a Heroine is in the making, and while she may shed a tear, she's on her way to something better. There is a reason she was born, she celebrates that knowing, and her Journey is in the making.

A Heroine knows that the road ahead is the road to living into her True Self, her magnificent self!

Where Are You Now On The Journey?

As you remember, there are 10 Steps to Stability on The Heroine's Journey. Knowing where you are relative to your destination is essential as a traveler. If you are starting in New York, it's good to know you are heading to Oregon versus Louisiana. That's what we are about to do. Let's get oriented to where we are and where we are going.

Now, review The Heroine's Journey RoadMap, which was a free resource in Chapter 1. You can get it again by going to —
www.HeroinesBook.com/Free-Resources

Grab your Journal, too so that you can refer to your personal Heroine's Journey Story that you wrote from Chapter 1.

Take a look at these resources and ask yourself a few crucial questions. . .

1. Where am I in the Journey? What Step am I on?
2. Can I Trust that my Journey is perfect — for who I am genuinely becoming? Are there circumstances that I interpreted as 'bad'? When I look at them now, can I re-interpret them as something that is positive for my growth?
3. Can I find hope in my Journey? Even if I have to dig deep, where is there a light on my horizon?

Congrats, you are on The Heroine's Journey, your very own! You've learned about The Heroine's Journey RoadMap and each Step along the way. You now know that Creating Stability is the critical place to start to ensure success, the gatekeeper to the life you want. You've even written your own Story of your Journey thus far.

It's a great road ahead knowing how to navigate the twists and turns. It's vital to keep going and keep gaining the provisions you need along the way. No matter what obstacles may arise, commit yourself to continuing — Journey Onward!

Hurray! Your Heroine's Journey will bring you necessary lessons, unveil your life purpose, and fulfill your true joy.

Free Resources

Yippeee — more for you!

Go n*ow* to —
www.HeroinesBook.com/Free-Resources

You'll find a PDF for the descriptions of the 13 Steps of The Heroine's Journey.

3

Cornerstone One: Beliefs

I Am The Heroine of My Destiny

What Are My Beliefs?

Beliefs That Work

Your Lighthouse

Heroine's Proclamation

I AM THE HEROINE OF MY DESTINY

hew, that was a lot to cover so far — where you learned about The Heroine's Journey and how it is a universal process for blossoming as Women. The stories of each of our individual lives are different, but The Heroine's Journey plot-line is the same. This is very comforting to know because it shows that there is an underlying RoadMap to follow. Heroines have gone before you and light the way!

And *you* are on The Heroine's Journey, living more of your True Self each Step of the way, no matter what Step you are currently on.

Let's talk about being the Heroine of your Destiny. Carefully choosing 'Beliefs' will lift you into flight. We'll start with a discussion to help you uplift *your* Beliefs. The design is to set you on a course to strengthen your Self-Worth. Because a Heroine knows her Self-Worth is her greatest treasure, and she should protect it fiercely to be her guiding rudder.

Self-Worth is precious to a Heroine — and she makes sure that no one — no one — *no one* —not herself or others — messes with her Self-Worth!

So, let's start here …

'*Beliefs*' is the first Task of the Heroine on the Journey! It is the first of the 4 Cornerstones we'll discuss for Creating Your Stability. This process creates your Stability in light of the foundation of who you truly are — not your past experience, what others say about you, or an unsustainable pipe dream. That's important.

A 'Belief' is something you accept as true or accurate. It is a firmly held opinion or conviction you have about yourself internally or your world externally — and it amply guides your decisions and direction from moment to moment.

Truly, quality Beliefs you embrace for yourself are one of the most important things you take with you on this Journey. Your Task for this Cornerstone is to strengthen your own Beliefs so that they uplift you into flight. *Got it?!*

If your Beliefs about yourself are weak, then you will be siphoning off the fuel for your flight and sabotaging the foundation of the other 3 Cornerstones. If you choose to think poorly about yourself, you are sabotaging your sense of Self-Worth.

What's up with that? That's so not what I want for you! That makes life harder and the Journey slower.

When you value yourself and have generous Beliefs about who you are, you will commit to establishing your Stability.

Your Beliefs add up to your Self-Worth. It's simple really.

This is some big but rewarding work! Are you ready? I look forward to the very best of you: the Heroine with Stability, supported by her Beliefs and Self-Worth. She's headed for glory.

What is your Self Worth?

*Self-Worth is your inner sense of 'knowing' that you are a **magnificent expression of Creation**. This is not your ego speaking; it's your **bigger, better Self** that lives within you. It's your **Heroine-Self**. This **Self** guides you on the Path of The Heroine's Journey to living the life you **truly want**.*

Your Self-Worth is part and parcel of who you appear to be in the world. The world needs you to show up as your Heroine-Self so that you can magnificently contribute your gifts and talents.

The world needs Heroines — more than ever now!

Wake Up to Your Character Revelation

Your Beliefs about yourself show up big time when you face the adversity of the Crisis and Challenge Steps. Remember, these are the beginning Steps on The Heroine's Journey.

Here's what happens: the drama of this chaos awakens the sleeping giants of all your self-sabotaging Beliefs! *Oh*, and that can be ugly! It can make you want to stop in your tracks and doubt that you can be saved.

Even though it can be enormously painful, this incredible pressure of the beginning Steps is exactly what your heart needs to break open and reveal the incredible light of your Being. The Journey purposefully and magnificently awakens before you. Change occurs when chaos is just about to turn into disarray. If this is you, you've got it, and know you are on your way!

See how it works…

This brings you to Step #4, Character Revelation. It is described this way:

Step 4: Character Revelation

You realize what you're made of

From under this tremendous weight, your Inner Self breaks through. Your True Self is unmasked and reveals itself with conviction. It says: "I Am Worthy. I was not born to be the victim of this circumstance. I have natural inborn assets that I can engage to get me out of this mess." This conviction reveals your essential character. It informs you of the Path you are capable of taking. You will find a way. You will go on despite all odds. Here, your commitment shows up from deep within. You know what you're made of. You realize that you are empowered. This part of the Journey calls forth your Courage and Strength and reveals your true Heroine's nature to you.

This is where your Inner-Self speaks to you so loudly that it almost screams your head off. It proclaims boldly your Truth.

When this happened to me, the Fierce Heroine within me shouted, "I am not going to be measured by my fall, but rather by the strength of my Rise!" It was a '*You just watch me*' moment! My Inner-Self was proclaiming that the Crisis and Challenge Steps that I had been through were not going to get me or be the end of my Story!

You know what you are made of in Step #4 of Character Revelation. This Step brings you to the universal realization: "I Am Worthy!" this is clearly one of the most important Beliefs you can cultivate on The Heroine's Journey.

But often, there are layers of limiting Beliefs that get in the way. We must slay these dragons if we are going to make it home to our True Selves and a life we love.

Let's do some self-inquiry.

OK, so here's a moment of disclosure. Let's look at the fundamental Beliefs that reside within you. These messages you tell yourself daily can either 'float your boat' or 'sink your ship.' You already know this. What we believe has everything to do with our Self-Worth, which translates into the results we get in our lives. What you believe is your choice. And the good news is that you can choose Beliefs (in a moment) that will support you to becoming your Best-Self.

The Journey begins with Status Quo, a moment sitting at home feeling that everything is just fine, and *then* the Crisis appears. The natural reaction is to resist it. But this Crisis presents itself on the Journey for a reason, so avoiding it is futile.

Here's my suggestion for you: *Embrace it!* If you surrender to the process, you will realize that the Crisis is really a call from that Inner True Self. While it may suck, it is navigating you to ask the fundamental question of your Being: "Who am I?"

Maybe you were going down the Path of doing one thing, but it wasn't your true expression. The sole goal in life is for the True Self to emerge in this lifetime so that it can express and contribute. You are the rose that feels the sun on her petals and must open.

What arises as you unfold with this beautiful question — "Who am I?" — are the Beliefs that you have internalized about yourself, many of which *falsely* describe you and stand in the way of creating a life of infinite possibility.

Just by being here reading this book, you are already engaging in the process of self-inquiry, which is an important skill on The Heroine's Journey.

Here, at the beginning of the Journey, we ask ourselves these burning questions:

"What are my Beliefs about myself?"

"Do they support, or are they negating, my ability to create Stability and freedom in my life?"

"What can I do to uplift my Beliefs?"

Hmm….Very good questions! Let's do the work to find these answers in a meaningful way.

Have you stopped to think about how Beliefs work?

Beliefs seed your thoughts and your feelings. They are woven into the fabric of your subconsciousness. Your behaviors are a direct result of what you believe about yourself.

Take a moment to sit with two opposing Beliefs and see how they make you feel:

- I can't travel through The Heroine's Journey. I am unworthy.
  Feel that.

Now shift that Belief.

- I can travel through The Heroine's Journey. I am a magnificent expression of Creation.
  How did that feel?

Of course, you *are* a magnificent expression of Creation. When humans come roaring down the birth canal, there is not a spirit standing at the bottom that stamps some babies 'reject' and others 'approved.'

No, No … all babies come fully into the world, *perfect* as they are. You certainly did!

So what happened? Why do you sometimes believe icky things about yourself?

Sometime after day 1, you took on some thinking about yourself that is untrue and does not support you. It didn't come pre-programmed in you. You picked it up along the way. It stuck to you — like bad juju — and messes with your Journey, and there is more…

Then, the Beliefs you harbored informed the direction of your Destiny. Yikes! *Wow*, did you know you were informing your Destiny when you picked up a silly Belief from that sixth-grade teacher? That teacher may have been having a bad day and spouted off about you just because you happened to be standing in front of her at that moment. Did she know anything about the big magnificent you, or was she just wrapped up in her own limiting Beliefs at that moment?

That's the conundrum: nobody knows your bigger, more magnificent, loving Self like you do. Others don't see all of us. They make comments about us that 'stick' to us — and then cause us to see our 'limited' selves. This is yucky! Ick!

Here is the impact of your Beliefs, both the supportive ones and the undermining ones.

The Cycle of Beliefs works like this:

Your Beliefs affect your Feelings.
Your Feelings affect your Thoughts.
Your Thoughts affect your Actions.
Your Actions affect your Results and, therefore, your Destiny.

Here's the positive side of it. I had a Professor in College who said to me: "Joan, you are a beautiful writer." At the time, I didn't see myself that way. I told him, "No, I'm a biology student!" I saw myself as a Biology major. But he touched my heart with his comment, and I felt the warmth and caring of his sharing.

Later, I found myself thinking — "Dr. Consolo said that I was a very good writer and that I thought deeply about literature. He was a very good English teacher, so he must be right." Then, I started to consider writing a book. Wow, that was new territory for me. And I thought — "I can write." I had internalized a Belief that supported my venture on this new Path. I wrote that first book, 'A Girl Needs Cash,' and got a major New York publisher. My Destiny became that I am a Best Selling Author.

What if Dr. Consolo had not taken that moment to shape a Belief I held? What if I'd rejected the value of his comment? What if I'd made up a Belief that made me 'smaller' than my 'bigger' Self? What if I felt that there was something innately wrong with me? I could have derailed the process at so many junctures.

This thinking would surely not have supported my pleasure and enjoyment of life. And it could go either way, depending upon the way decided. We have power when it comes to our Beliefs.

Writing a book and having it published was a life I wanted, and it all started with the Beliefs that supported me as a writer. I had to keep the love for me going. I had to reaffirm to myself that I was born into this life fully approved and capable. This is your Task, too.

Start with your Beliefs to create the wonderful results you want in your life. Polish up those Beliefs so you shine brightly. It's much more fun that way. When you have supporting Beliefs for yourself, it makes everything easier. We work better together, we laugh more, we love more, and we can sustain partnerships to create together.

Why should you punish yourself with Beliefs that get in your way of being your Best-Self? A Heroine holds her head high. She nurtures her internal Being to foster her Courage and Strength on the Journey. Beliefs clearly support a Heroine's Self-Worth. The internal structure of a Heroine is founded in Beliefs, here's how it works:

Let me tell you this wonderful story about my friend Thomas kinkade.

The famous American Painter Thomas Kinkade lived in my town. Tom was a motorcycle-riding tough guy on the outside and a peach of a guy on the inside. I imagine he could not have been the iconic American Painter he was without the big, sensitive guy he was on the inside.

I asked him to paint a picture to raise funds for a charity, and he graciously said he would. Incredible! And more incredible was…

One Saturday, I met him in our quaint little downtown. He laid out his blank canvas on his artist's easel. I sat behind him as he stood at the easel and began. I was so curious to see his technique and watch this amazing artist painting before me. Here I was, witnessing the genius of 'The Painter of Light,' as he is known. I watched very closely, feeling that I had an immense honor sitting behind this glorified Painter and watching him firsthand apply his craft.

What a gift. I bubbled with enthusiasm. I wanted to ask all kinds of questions, and he invited me to please stop talking so he could paint!!

This is what I saw. First, he drew lines with a pencil that roughly formed an outline of his composition. They set the structure of the painting. I could imagine where he was going from these lines. They were clearly forming the subject of his work.

When this was done, he applied some color along the lines all over his canvas. This formed one layer. Next, he went back over the whole picture and applied another layer of color. He applied another layer, not in one particular spot, but again, working the whole canvas and adding an additional layer.

It was wild to watch as if each layer brought the picture sharper into focus. It was like he felt the picture coming to life from underneath, and he was moved to more and more detail.

By the end of the day, the painting was alive. These lines that he started with had blossomed into the full brilliance of the picture. The lines had guided the emergence of more and more beauty.

This turned out to be an extraordinary day of realization for me. We are each the artists of our own lives. And if we are dedicated, we too can paint light, the light of our own Being.

This is what Beliefs are in your life. They are the lines you draw. Your Beliefs determine the picture that emerges. Do you get how powerful that is? And, I might add — your Beliefs show up on your face, which is the canvas of your inner Being.

Do you know that *YOU* can re-draw the lines? Amazing!

Here's the basic work of Beliefs: Start with honestly taking a look at them.

See if the Beliefs you have incorporated support you. If you need to erase some of the lines and re-draw them, now's the time to do it. And I'll give you a process for this later in this Chapter.

Circumstances don't need to control your Beliefs. No matter the circumstances, you can re-draw the lines. You can re-draw the lines because each of us is 'Everything', a pure potential human expression.

What do you choose to illustrate? It's up to *you*! Isn't that fun? You get to construct the Beliefs of who you show up to be. You get to be the artist who paints your life's picture. You can either tap into the Belief of your worst Self or the Belief of your Best-Self. How will you pencil in the lines that will produce the picture of your life?

I love this quote by an unknown wise person, and I put it on the front of my daily planner for many years for guidance;

'I am an artist at living — and my art is my life.'

~Unknown

Building your Stability requires you to frame yourself in Beliefs that are supportive for you to create *your* solid foundation. Let's move on to understanding your current Beliefs and then to your opportunity to re-draw the lines on the canvas of your life. You'll choose the Beliefs that produce the most beauty and freedom.

WHAT ARE MY BELIEFS?

Let's get started on life-changing work together.

Isn't reflecting on your Beliefs about yourself and where they came from fascinating? I had a mishmash of Beliefs about myself until I began to question where I got some stuff, how it added to my thinking, and what effect it had on my life. Jeeemninie crickets!

Hey, good news. I became aware that there were multiple things I could believe about myself. And, sometimes, I was truly getting false information about myself by listening to what others were saying about me. Yikes, I needed to stop listening to them and start listening to bigger voices within me. What a revelation!

When I looked at them, Beliefs I had grasped, I was astounded. I began to see that some of the Beliefs I was holding onto could topple me like I was a 'yard sale' flinging my stuff everywhere. Some Beliefs would keep me planted like a grounded bird with a broken wing, and some would cause me to stand proudly at the edge of the Cliff, look to the horizon, and joyfully take off in flight. It was truly a mishmash.

Once I understood how various Beliefs affected me, I also saw how I have the power to choose them. This was a turning point in my life because it fundamentally shifted my ability to support myself with generous Beliefs.

Let's roll so you can experience how your Beliefs work for you.

Let's start by questioning where Beliefs come from before diving into our psyche.

Where do these crazy things we call Beliefs come from, anyway? Are you surprised to see that they come from within you — things that you make up — and from outside of you — things that others make up about you and tell you or the Culture tells you?

Along the way, you grabbed onto a variety of Beliefs and held them closely to your bosom as truths. Were they truths? Probably not. But you used them as shortcuts to make choices in your life. Here's how they arose in you:

1. They came from past experiences where you decided something about yourself;
2. They came from others who either directly or subtly told you something about yourself, and you took it on and decided it was true;
3. They came from the Culture and its norms, ones you decided to let define you.

When you took these Beliefs in, did you decide which ones you wanted to keep and which ones you didn't? Did your parents say something to you that has restricted your life?

I have a friend whose Mother would tell him: "When people get to know the real you, they will discover the truth." He took that to mean that when people got to know him, they would learn that he was bad and unworthy. Did his Mother mean that? Maybe she was cruel, or maybe that's what she feared for herself, so she said it to him. It's caused him real misery. In any event, is carrying this Belief worth the pain and uncertainty it has caused him? It's taken the bloom off his rose. Sadly!

What similar 'untruths' have you been carrying around? When I took that early personal growth course from Bill McGrane, which I mentioned in Chapter 1, he told me a very striking thing! He said to me: "Joan, you are like a '*Garbage Ship*.'" He was saying that I was loaded up with all the garbage of my negative Beliefs and was toting them around with me on the sea of life. This was startling! Shocking! It didn't seem very attractive to me either. How was I showing up?

And, it was true. I was seeing myself as 'unworthy'. From 'unworthy,' I wondered why people would choose me. I had put the 'reject' stamp on my very own forehead! Do you see the problem here? I was polluting the beautiful Creation I was meant to be. This was a profound wake-up call to the pattern of self-abuse I was perpetuating for myself.

I was a smart woman but seriously tangled inside. I had more negative Beliefs about myself than positive ones. I was in deep pain. My unconscious negative Beliefs, ones that I didn't filter, were adding up to the unhappy quality of my life. Despite all my successes, I was desperate for change. My outward achievements were not enough to negate the inward pain swamp that I was living in.

The Crisis and Challenge phases of my Journey put roadblocks in my Path. It was clear in this highly stressful time that I could not afford to diminish myself with my negative Beliefs any longer. I needed my Strength to carry on. It was do or die.

If I was going to survive, I would have to shift my Beliefs. And the vital choice was apparent. Was I going to see myself as 'unworthy' or 'worthy'? I had to make this critical choice on the Path to becoming the Heroine of my own life.

Now, the *Midwife* had a job to do. To become a Heroine, I had to die to my Belief of unworthiness and be reborn into the Belief of my inherent worthiness. I got this loud and clear: I am Worthy!

Life could not shift until I shifted this Belief.

So, we ask: Why are Beliefs Important to Your Heroine's Journey?

Let me tell you. It's mathematics. If you have more negative Beliefs than positive ones running around, noodling in your head, about yourself — you will stay stuck, or worse.

By contrast, If you have more positive Beliefs than negative Beliefs thriving in your head, you will set yourself up to move forward to a glorious life. It's simple math, and it works!

Here's the magic: There *is* a way to get out of pain and dysfunction … sort your Beliefs and reframe them! "Wow, that sounds big, you say! How do I do that?"

How do you do this? To begin this process, I will ask you to join me in picturing a garden in your head.

We'll be visualizing this garden. This garden has lots of weeds. Picture them, and they grow up in and around the flowers. They are so tangled that the flowers get choked and bear few blossoms. Hey, life is as simple as nature.

Now, relax in a comfortable position. That's it, a cozy chair and a few breaths.

In your mind's eye, visualize that you are in your very own garden. You cross a little bridge into the fertile ground. As you stroll around this plot of nature in abundance, settle on a spot to sit. Take into your mind's eye all that is around you. I'm inviting you to feel into all that is growing and presenting itself in nature's beauty: the sensual blue sky, the buzz of the bees, and the tinkling sound of the nearby stream.

But notice as you return here now, that there are some weeds in your untended garden. They are taking up space and pushing out some magnificence of some of the flowers. You see that the flowers are there but struggling to peek out between the weeds. These weeds are like negative thoughts growing in your mind that strangle your life too.

Picture young flower sprouts on the ground that yearn to display their colors to you. These flowers are fighting with the weeds for water, space, and sunshine. They are struggling to grow in the sunshine and present themselves. The weeds are holding them back.

What does each weed say to you?

"I don't have the strength."
"I don't have what I need."
"I am all alone."
"I can't do this."
"I am not good enough."
"I am not lovable."
"I hope they don't see the real me."

What other negative thoughts are lurking in your weeds? What are they saying to you?

Take a minute and listen carefully. Listen … Keep listening … hear their repetitive messages …

You are the Mistress Gardener. It's up to you to clear the space so that beauty can abound with color bursting forth. Tend to your garden by grabbing each weed and pulling it out by the root. Tell the Belief: "I love you, but you no longer serve me."

Pull the first one: "I love you, but you no longer serve."

Pull the second one, now another.

Keep going. Keep pulling. This is the only way your garden will thrive, Heroine.

Now, notice that the space begins to clear. You can see all the beautiful flowers. There are so many vibrant colors. Beautiful shapes. Soft scents. These flowers are the positive thoughts you give yourself to create beauty in your life.

Listen carefully again to the flowers. What does each flower say about you?

"I am loved."
"I am wise."
"I have Strength and Courage."

"I am Worthy."

"I am fully approved."

"I am valuable."

"I have gifts to share."

"I am capable."

Listen carefully ... keep listening ... deeply receive what they are saying ...

These are the flowers that are blooming your garden. Grow them with your love. Tend to them. . . Give each one water.

One by one, acknowledge each of these flowers. Say to these Beliefs: "I love you, grow and thrive."

"I love you, grow and thrive."

"I love you, grow and thrive."

How beautiful is your garden with these blooms? It is YOUR garden. You are the Mistress Gardener who created it. It depends upon you for its nourishment. Take a moment to delight in the beauty you have created and how your garden nourishes your soul, lights up your spirit, makes your day joyful, and puts you into action.

You can come to your garden anytime. Ahhhh…

Now, reach for your journal and write down what your subconscious mind revealed in the Garden Visualization about your negative and positive Beliefs for yourself.

In your Journal — Pick the most essential Beliefs that have an emotional impact on your life — list up to 12 of each, negative ones and positive ones. Keep your Beliefs compact with potent but minimal words so that they pack a punch.

Be truthful about putting down the negative and positive Beliefs. Have the Courage to consciously hear what your subconscious has been telling you about yourself. This is the first Step in the process of weeding in your mind.

You'll want to do this well because we'll be using this information shortly.

You have life-saving work to do as you identify the Beliefs that have been driving your life and have led you to the results you have gotten so far.

You may have noticed that you have a lot of negative Beliefs. Don't beat yourself up. Instead, replace these negative Beliefs with positive Beliefs. OK, so that may not sound so easy. Help is on the way to learning how to choose Beliefs that work for you effectively.

CHOOSING BELIEFS THAT WORK

Here's the Truth, Sister — if you persist with messages to yourself that tangle and twist you, that make you unworthy and wicked — that's the behavior you will project on others. For goodness sake, Heroine, clean up so you can show up!

What you have created on the inside of you will be what emanates from you. How can you have compassion for another if you don't have compassion for yourself? How can you believe in someone else's goodness if you don't believe in your worthiness? It all starts with you.

Heroines clean up — to show up!

Don't wait until someone comes along and gives you proof that some negative Belief is useless and that you are so much more. You don't need social proof that you are Worthy. You simply are! I know it. And it is time for you to know it, too. Your life hangs in the balance of your Self-Worth. This is fundamentally true!

You are capable and have only so many days on the planet to sing your most blessed song. You can change your Belief with a snap of the finger! You get to choose! You get to rewrite the Story. You get to do just this, as I'll show you.

Here's the turning point where you take action.

This is the creative, hopeful, and self-loving process of actively reframing the Beliefs that handicap you. You transform them into Beliefs that propel you forward.

Now, you have the power to choose.

You are the one who gets to choose how you develop your Beliefs. Here is the exciting part: when you see a negative thought as untrue, it loses its power to shape your life.

Victory!

It's time to give yourself the gift of mental/emotional space to stand firmly in your positive Beliefs. And this is an ongoing process to stay on top of — you love you! This first time will be your major readjusting — and choosing Beliefs is not a 'once and done' — it's an ongoing centurion of being the guard of what goes in, gets held firmly in your mind, and is only to be there when it supports your Heroine quest.

If you are chomping at the bit to get started shifting the old, outdated Beliefs that still take up residence in your thinking, no worries, we are leading into a process that will help you do just this. This will take those personal negative Beliefs that you listed in your journal in the Garden Story and rewrite them with your new, bigger Heroine-Self in mind.

First, though, let's explore where Beliefs come from so we can be more savvy in identifying them. Once we root them out, we can choose to shift them.

Your Beliefs come from two directions.

1. What The World Says About You - I call this Beliefs from Others
2. What You're Saying About Yourself - I call this Beliefs from Yourself.

You get a thought about yourself, and it unconsciously gets interpreted in either a limiting, self-deprecating way — or in a bigger, self-fulfilling way. You have the power to choose how you view both types of Beliefs, the ones the world is delivering, and the ones you hear yourself espouse.

Here come the Beliefs Others hand to you — and what do you have to say about it?

If what the world says about you isn't supportive, you have the power to rewrite it in your own awareness. That's a *Yahoo!*

Here are a couple of outdated Beliefs about Women that our modern Culture has fortunately rewritten. This demonstrates the distance Women have traveled in our lifetime to a fuller expression of ourselves, no longer letting our Culture define us in these limited ways.

A Woman:

1. Doesn't have a Heroine's Journey. She stays home and cries.
2. Is not smart enough to vote.
3. Can't take 'risk' and start her own business.
4. Is not as capable as a man.
5. Is only useful when she is young and pretty.
6. Belongs at home.
7. Has crazy times of the month when she is insane!
8. Doesn't do math!

That last one makes me chuckle — Do you remember when Mattel came out with a Barbie Doll that said, "she couldn't do math?" Mattel was forced to take that version off the market very quickly!! Women would not let that Belief get promoted – Oh, heck NO!

That arcane sentiment about Women and numbers was echoed again when my book came out, 'A Girl Needs Cash.' I offered to write a column for Glamour Magazine, and the response that I got back was that their readers were not interested in articles about 'Money.' (And yet their advertisers are hoping that the readers buy expensive clothes and makeup. With what money?)

I'm glad to live in times when these cultural Beliefs have run out of steam. I'm glad for the Fierce Feminine that opposed these Beliefs. Thank goodness! Reframing these Beliefs collectively has opened up great freedoms for Women. Our lives have been liberated in new ways.

Also, it takes reframing your Beliefs individually to live freely. Now, it is time to do our own individual work. How do you personally take on Beliefs from others?

For instance, is there someone in your life who is the external narrator of your worst self? You can spot them. Clearly, what they say is not objective — or helpful in growing your Best-Self.

They might routinely say something like:

"You are always late and so inconsiderate."
"You talk too much. You are so insecure."

Oh my goodness! We've all encountered this person...Here's the rub. If you let them tell you who you are, they have the power to get you and keep you stuck. Likely, you can't validate what they say about you, and you'll go around in circles trying to make sense of it. This is a waste of your time. Heroines are more cleaver than this!

I love the old adage: "What you think of me is *none* of my business." So, true.

What someone else thinks of you is, for the moment, in a particular situation through the filters that they have in place, through their biases and misperceptions, and the mood that they are in. This isn't good information. It's not objective and unbiased.

For instance, if something not so appealing is said about you, you can frame this information quickly as ... "They don't know the whole of me. My Belief about myself is that I am so much more than what that person can see in me momentarily, and while I forgive them, I am sure that my big value will be seen in time."

Never believe what they say *is* who you are. No one gets to define you, label you, objectify you, or make you just one thing all of the time.

Sidestep those Beliefs that shouldn't land on your Self-Worth. This is a judo move. To tap into your full potential, *you* must sidestep these comments. *You* are the one responsible for what you believe about yourself. This is how you claim your Self-Worth.

This is your most precious asset to guard. Hold on to it tightly and watch out for any thieves who are out to steal it.

At all costs, protect your Self-Worth!

Can I tell you a story about just that? A letter that triggered me to hinder my Self-Worth and what I did to counter it.

Here's a true story about how I learned how crazy-making people try to tell you who and what you are. I twisted and turned, trying to understand this situation, until the light bulb went on for me.

This happened at a very chaotic time when I was in the early stages of divorce. I was vulnerable to negative messages because I didn't have much Self-Worth at the time. I was feeling depressed, defeated, and hopeless. I was wallowing in the muck. I didn't need more to put me under; I needed the Heroine stuff to raise me up. I had to do something. Here's how it went...

I got a letter from the 'soon-to-be-ex-husband'…and that letter was so full of blame and criticism. I was desperately searching in the letter to understand if his recriminations of me were true. If they were, I was willing to change. But what he was saying didn't make sense to me. Somewhere in me, I knew that I wasn't all that bad.

In desperation, I took the letter to my Therapist. I felt like 'I was the problem' and 'how could I fix myself.' She pointed out how much time I was wasting in this exercise and how I was getting totally stuck. She powerfully showed me how to sidestep the truckload of garbage that was being dumped on my head. And confirmed how I surely did not want to be under that garbage pile, accumulate it or carry it with me further. All liberating.

Here's how the conversation went:

Me: I'm just confused by this awful letter. It doesn't make sense to me. I just don't see myself this way and don't know how to digest his criticisms of me.

Her: Don't digest them.

Me: How do I do that? It feels so personal and hurtful. And am I supposed to learn something about myself from this?

Her: Yes, you are. That this letter is not about you. Do you want to see how?

Me: You bet.

Her: OK…here's how we do it. Take the letter and reverse the '*To*' and the '*From*.' Make the letter to the Ex from You. Now read the letter again to me.

Me: Dear 'Ex….blaah, blaah, blaah. From, Joan.'….*Wow!*

Her: Now, does that make more sense to you?

Me: It sure does. He's writing this letter to me, but he's really talking about himself. It makes perfect sense now. He's trying to blame me for who he is. *Yikes!*

Her: That's right. You need to sidestep everything he's saying because it is not about you.

Me: Wow, that's a relief. I feel better about myself already. That was garbage I didn't need to collect.

Her: You are fine as you are. Don't stop your life with his attacks. Just keep moving, and your life will shine.

Here's what I learned. He was projecting onto me what he needed to tell himself about *himself.* What I learned is that angry people are not the ones to offer you a clear perspective about yourself.

All I needed to know was that 'I am Worthy,' and nothing changes that fact. No one else's opinion is going to mess with that Belief — ever again!

Lovely Sister, are there people in your life who plant weeds in your garden? Here's a path forward. Consider these steps:

Beliefs from Others Reframe Steps:

1. If someone is saying something that doesn't feel true about you, you'll know it. Use the practice to pull this weed out of your beautiful garden so it doesn't take root. This takes Strength and Courage.
2. Create distance between you and the Projector. Find a space where you can feel free to choose the Beliefs you wish to cultivate in yourself.
3. If what they are saying has a hint of Truth, remember it is not who you *truly* are. Don't take it on as a Belief. It is just information. If it has any usefulness, simply use it to work on yourself to refine your expression in the world. That's the Journey of life.

Are you vigilant? Or are others planting lots of weeds, and your life becomes really choked? Remember, you can always pull the weeds. This creates the beautiful blossoming garden of the life where you really want to live.

Next, let's ask, what Beliefs are you telling yourself? Beliefs that are coming from within you?

Weeds pop up. You look around, and oops ... there's a new weed in the garden of your mind.

No worries. Each of us plants weeds in our own garden of the mind. When you lose sight of your magnificent Self, the mind can easily make up 'mean girl' stories about yourself. Then, if you hold on to these, they become unsupportive Beliefs about yourself. Like: "I'm screwed, life is really f-ing hard," or "No one loves me." "I don't have what it takes." "I can't do this."

None of this will help you on your Heroine's Journey to your Best-Self.

Instead, your Heroine-Self must actively intervene. When I heard those unsupportive inner messages, here's what I did. I realized I was saying things to myself that were punishing me unfairly. I decided to be a good friend to myself and not say things to myself that a cherished friend wouldn't say to me. This was the beginning.

The singer 'Pink' says it all in her song, 'You're Perfect':

"Change the voices in your head, make them like you instead....

Pretty, pretty, please don't you ever feel that you are less than perfect..."

~Pink, Singer

It's so true. Now, you have to get busy and change the negative thoughts. There are always two sides to a story. You recognize your thought and then shift it to another, better version of the thought.

This process is called 'Reframing'. Here's how it works...

Reframing your Beliefs about yourself is an active process. One that you are conscious of and regularly engage in.

Reframing your Beliefs about yourself is a two-part process. And it's fun!!

The first part is to proactively dig deep and excavate the long-standing negative Beliefs that are the weeds in your garden. Here's an exercise to reframe these long-standing negative Beliefs.

<u>Step One:</u>

First, you actively change your perspective about a message or Belief that you are hearing yourself say repeatedly. Take the old Belief, and then reframe it into a new Belief that you design, one that is supportive.

Here's how I do it. You'll have your own version, but you get the gist. I am choosing five Beliefs that would not support me, then reframing to ones that do support me.

Old Beliefs vs New Beliefs:

"I don't have what it takes." >>> **"I am smart enough to figure anything out that life throws at me."**

"I can't do this." >>> **"One day at a time. I can create a solid plan to gain some ground each day."**

"No one loves me." >>> **"I am lovable, and I am capable of having loving relationships."**

"My life is ruined." >>> **"I am not going to be defined by my fall, but measured by my rise."**

"I'm screwed; life is really f-ing hard" >>> **"My life is perfect as it is at this moment. I trust that I am here for my soul's Journey. I am getting the life lessons that are perfectly designed to help me grow into the human being I desire to be."**

Now my Beliefs are rearranged as I'm Worthy, I'm Lovable, I'm Strong Enough, I Can Figure It Out … Beliefs that motor me along on the Journey. That's the point of it all.

I'll give you a template to help you through this process of rewriting the negative Beliefs into positive ones.

There's also a quick snap technique … it goes like this …

<u>Step 2:</u>

This is a second technique that is a quick fix. You do it immediately, on the spot, to handle a negative Belief that comes up quickly, one that you recognize as non-supportive. It's called 'Cancel, Clear'. You can literally say this out loud — and have some fun because people will wonder, 'What's she doing?'.

It's the 'Cancel, Clear' technique …

This second part of the weeding-out process happens on the fly. What if a negative thought crops up or you say something undermining about yourself? Get on it. Tag that right away as a negative Belief that doesn't support you. Say "Cancel, Clear" (out loud and boldly), and reframe and upgrade the Belief, statement, or action. It looks like this:

"Oh, my thighs are way too fat to go to the beach."

Cancel, Clear!

"I love going to the beach, and I am going to enjoy a day of freedom."

"This guy is so great he cannot possibly love *me*."

Cancel, Clear!

"I am wonderful, and he sees this. That's why he loves me."

"When they get to know me, they'll discover the ugly truth about me."

Cancel, Clear!

"When they get to know me, they will see my inner Heroine."

Isn't it great to now have tools to keep your Beliefs positive and be generous to yourself? This is absolutely, *absolutely* fundamental to growing your Self-Worth and happiness while traveling the Journey.

Now grab your journal again, review those negative Beliefs you listed — cross them out with vigor — and write a new supportive Belief to reframe the old one. *Get on it!*

Once you reframe your Beliefs, they become the fuel for your flight. Now we can get some lift off!…and some help from our Lighthouses …

YOUR LIGHTHOUSE

Wonderful! Here we are at one of my favorite resources. This really supported me — it gave me Strength and Courage and anchored me in the storm. Much like a boat that is well tied to the dock, I drew on this to feel connected and secure.

You will be introduced to your 'Lighthouse', your beacon that shines out in the fog and gives you a point of reference. What is this? Well, it is a term I coined for the supportive voice you can hear in your heart, who reminds you that you have the Strength to carry on. This is the Voice that inspires you to keep moving.

Your Lighthouse serves as your super-conscious. It is the Voice you hear that inspires you and lifts you up into your Best-Self. It is the one who reminds you, "Yes, I can!"

Through creating a lasting relationship with your Lighthouse, you'll always have a beacon for staying on course. Your Lighthouse will reassure you of your ability to navigate out of rough seas to calm waters.

Who is this Lighthouse? What's her role in your life?

Your Lighthouse serves as an inner narrator of your *Best-Self* or a reminder and inspiration of who you truly are. Your Lighthouse has a higher perspective, and is a brilliant shining light that illuminates the bigger picture, makes you laugh when you need it, or just gives some honest truth. You aren't alone when your Lighthouse is with you.

And you can have as many Lighthouses as you choose.

Your Lighthouse may be someone you know: Your best friend, Grandfather, or 5th-grade teacher. Or it may be someone whom you have never met but who serves as a source of inspiration for you. This could be a poet from the 1800s, an astronaut, or Mother Teresa. There are so many to choose from.

I want to share a few of my Lighthouses with you and some of the Wisdom they have imparted to me. These women's voices guide my Journey and remind me that I have the fortitude to carry on. They give me hope when I need it the most.

Eleanor Roosevelt gives me Strength by reminding me:

'A Woman is like a teabag — you don't know her
Strength until you put her in hot water.

~Eleanor Roosevelt

Emily Dickinson gives me Hope by reminding me:

"Dwell in Possibility."

~Emily Dickinson

Marilyn Monroe keeps me committed to my Heroine's Journey by reminding me:

"Everything happens for a reason. Sometimes good things fall apart, so better things can come together."

~Marilyn Monroe

I'm including a list of over 100 quotes from *Women With Strong Beliefs.* You might discover that one of these Women speaks into your heart and becomes your Lighthouse.

I love stories.

Can I tell you this true story that inspires me? It's the story of Ivri's Lighthouse.

Like each of us, Ivri is a Heroine. She is on The Heroine's Journey. And like each of us, she has faced the Steps of Crisis and Challenge. She says that in those dark times, it was her Lighthouse that showed her the way!

Ivri's Lighthouse is her Great-Grandfather (who died before she was born). He was a man who had a great impact on the world and a person she had always admired. She did not know the importance of the legacy he left her for her own Heroine's Journey until later in her life.

Her 'Grandfather,' as the family calls him, started the first commercial airline in the days when the public was afraid to fly, and for a good reason. Eventually, one of his planes crashed, and all aboard lost their lives. As a result of the lawsuits, Grandfather lost everything material in his life. But he was not deterred. He started again. And then another crash. People lost their lives, and Grandfather lost his company, wealth, and assets yet again.

As Ivri relates…"This time, he used the adversity to drive him to find new solutions and a new dream. He realized if commercial aviation was going to be sustainable and ultimately thrive, it was going to need some Financial Stability. So, he took action to found the first aviation insurance company. This allowed the birth of the big airlines, like United and American. Subsequently, my Grandfather built a vast financial fortune."

Ivri was an heiress to her Great Grandfather's big fortune. But nine years ago, her financial advisor stole everything, leaving her with $56 as a single Mom and sole financial support for her young son. It looked really dark.

After some soul searching, she reached out through the ethers to Grandfather for his help and Wisdom. Here is what he guided her to realize:

"If Grandfather could create such impact and success, I must also be able to. I can see him in me. His gift was not the money I inherited. The real gift was the eternal Wisdom and fortitude that it took to create that kind of impact and prosperity. His legacy to me is 'Out of adversity comes opportunity.' Yes, I can create something great."

Life gave Ivri adversity, a Crisis, but like Grandfather, she was determined to turn it into an opportunity. It gave her the wake-up call to shift her life in very meaningful ways. She progressed quickly on her Heroine's Journey. She moved to another city, which allowed her to find a better education for her son. She started her own business, creating a six-figure income her first year, which has grown ever since. She is dedicated to maintaining her Stability so that life's adversities don't *completely* derail her *ever again*. Most importantly, she is doing what she loves with Courage.

Here is how she sums up the gift her Lighthouse gave her:

"As an aviator, Grandfather *literally* taught me how to put my wings on and fly."

Wow!... that's beautiful!

And you can choose your Lighthouse too! One or more that inspire your best, call you to your Strength and Courage and light your way. Having your Lighthouse is a must!!

Now is your moment to reflect on your Lighthouse. You can choose your Lighthouse from the list of Women with Strong Beliefs, as I did, or from someone in your own life, as Ivri did, or from someone in this life or not. Take a moment to do this. It's fun. You might choose one now and more later, as I did also.

Picture your Lighthouse now in your mind's eye. Can you see them clearly? If you are not exactly sure, don't worry about it. Just let your intuition pick someone for now as you enter the following contemplation.

Go with me here again. Let's actively imagine a conversation with your Lighthouse.

Let's have some playtime. Let's ask your Lighthouse for their Wisdom through an active dialogue, much like Ivri did with her Grandfather. She got Wisdom, and let's see if you get some too.

Grab your Journal and a pen once again. I will give you four questions for you to ask your Lighthouse.

Listen carefully to their answers. These questions ask for keys of Wisdom that they have for you, for who you truly are, and the possibilities that lie ahead on your Heroine's Journey.

Now, picture your Lighthouse in front of you in your mind's eye. Welcome your Lighthouse, and thank them for being there with you in support of your True Self.

Begin with the first question:

Lighthouse, who are you, and what shall I call you?

Now that you've connected, ask the second question:

Lighthouse, is there comfort that you can offer me right now?
Listen fully to the answer. Be open and soak in the support.

Now, in the third question, dig a little deeper to ask:

Lighthouse, what Wisdom can you share with me now that will open my heart and my eyes?

This is your time to be vulnerable. Know that your Lighthouse has great Wisdom to share with you. Listen deeply.

You are building Trust with your Lighthouse. Now ask:

Lighthouse, what Steps shall I take next on my Journey?

Thank your Lighthouse for their presence and generous Wisdom. Let them know you will call on them again soon, knowing they are so happy to serve your momentum.

Return again. New Wisdom will offer itself.

I posted the Wisdom from Eleanor Roosevelt, Emily Dickinson, and Marylin Monroe right next to my computer. Days when I needed it, they were there to remind me. Connecting with them, I could feel their Strength and Courage as Heroine women. I didn't feel alone with them there. It hadn't been easy for them either, but they transformed into their notability. They were cheerleading for me!

To get your free Resource 'Women With Strong Beliefs' — just go to: www.HeroinesBook.com/Free-Resources

HEROINE'S PROCLAMATION

Heads up on this one!

There is one Belief that trumps all other Beliefs that you have about yourself.

This Belief arises in an instant! We call this your 'One Defining Moment.' It bursts through in Step #4, your Character Revelation, just when the pressure from the Crisis and Challenge Steps is boiling.

What is your One Defining Moment?

Your One Defining Moment is the moment your Inner Heroine awakens! She says, "I am a Heroine, watch me fly!"

It's the moment you choose to be the Heroine of your own Journey. This is a universal passage of transformation on your Path. It's the point of truly claiming your life. This trump Belief, that you are *Worthy*, subjugates all lingering negative Beliefs. It is so strong that it serves to navigate your decisions and actions from this moment forward. You are forever changed.

Your One Defining Moment is a huge moment in the development of your Heroine's Journey. This is *the* moment when the circumstances of your life feel like you are being thrust through the eye of the needle. It can be painful, startling, and feel like you are screaming into the wind. With this drama, something erupts in you. You are literally squeezed into being. You are compelled to proclaim your Self-Worth, your intrinsic value, and you become convicted to express it.

You decide you will not be a victim or defined by your circumstances or what other people think of you. Yes, you will take control and navigate your Journey. Birth is a painful process, and you made it.

The purpose of any adversity that you have experienced in your life was to get you to *this* moment — *your One Defining Moment*! I would best describe it as a 'F you!' moment. The Universe has piled up so much crap around you that you finally take a stand. It's a Heroine moment. It's the moment you choose to be the Heroine of your own life.

You may be able to hear yourself shouting new bold-woman Heroine Beliefs that speak loudly and clearly to you and forcibly give you motivation and direction for your Journey.

It is a conviction that defies all else and announces, 'Watch me, I can and I will!' This moment can set you on your way to living your purpose. In this moment, you are fully in your body, and the Life-Force energy rises from the ground through the top of your head. You are making a statement about your life and choosing to live it.

This One Defining Moment is a universal passage to growing yourself on your Path. It's the point of claiming your life. Do you recognize it?

You may have just started this Journey, and you are in the process now of claiming your Self-Worth, or you may be further down the Path, and you can look back to see the moment when you took a stand with all of your will and determination and proclaimed that You-Believe-In-You. This Belief is so strong that it guides your decisions and actions from this moment forward.

You hear *your* Heroine's rebel yell. It may sound something like, "I *Can* and I *Will!*" or another version of this release of pent up woman-power. Welcome to life, Heroine! These inner words that arise from the fire in your belly are your Heroine's Proclamation and *your* most powerful Belief.

This new indomitable Belief now gives you the Strength to dedicate yourself to the process of creating your Stability.

Your Heroine's Proclamation — Do You Hear It? Have you felt that Fierce Feminine moment when your will arises like a phoenix out of the ashes? When it is all about you taking a stand. The emotion just bursts forth in you with conviction and resolve – and you put a stake in the ground! You told everyone around you — Do Not Cross – I stand firmly right here, and I will defend my position! Just watch me!

From your One Defining Moment, your 'Heroine's Proclamation' is born!

It's your rebel yell, the specific words that burst forth from your soul. Words that empower who you are now and how you will live. It is the Fierce Feminine rising, the rallying cry that delivers you into utilizing the inherent power within you.

Here's how my Heroine's Proclamation arose. I had a 'Phoenix from the Ashes' moment when everything was burning down around me.

I was just freaking done with trying to be something other than myself, others telling me who I was, trying to make money in ways that did not align with my values, and with people who hurt me. It was all tearing me down — in an instant, I changed that.

I remember so clearly the sense of the old me burning and my Spirit rising up out of the inferno. I heard my own voice inside of me make my Heroine's Proclamation with a conviction that came from the core of me. I heard my own Inner Voice cry:

"I am not going to be defined by my fall, I am going to be measured by my rise." (Watch me!)

Finally, I was free! I was free to be me and relieved of all the illusions I had to be in the past. It was a turning point that shaped all my future decisions and actions. I was fueled by new Courage and Strength. Now, I was firmly on The Heroine's Journey, and I was going to make it through.

The beauty was in the contrast between that terrible moment of life burning down all around me versus the profound proclamation of my Inner Truth. The contrast allowed me to see the full potential of myself. Like the lyrics of Macy Gray's song:

"Deep in my suffering, I found the beauty of me."

~Macy Gray

My Heroine's Proclamation was such a gift because it startled me into accepting the power of who I truly am. This was the bridge I needed to cross, from the pain inside me to a life of joy and happiness. It was the moment I rejected living in suffering and embraced the intrinsic beauty of all of life.

The Path rises to meet you when you stand up and proclaim your Truth.

Visualize Your Heroine's Proclamation

It's time for you to identify your 'One Defining Moment,' that moment of Character Revelation when your Heroine's Proclamation bursts forth from within you.

Whether you have a clear picture of that moment or are still a bit unsure, let's take some time together now to do a guided visualization to explore this together and harness its power for your highest good.

Sit quietly. Relax. Close your eyes for a minute to drop into your inner self. Feel your breath deepen and then release.

You are safe now. I'm here with you as you travel back in time.

Let your mind roll back over the incidents of your life. When you wrote your Heroine's Journey Story in your Journal in Chapter 1, was there a particular incident where you felt victimized and powerless? When did you feel incredible pressure? Was there a moment in your Story when you felt thrust through the eye of the needle?

Relax at this moment. You are surveying your life from a safe place now. Just take a look at the times of the Challenge. The pressure was building. So much was coming so fast, or maybe you felt under the garbage pile. Was there a moment when you felt your blood rise? Where were you? What was going on?

Then, suddenly, there was a moment when you had an internal combustion that blew through the opposition. Your Heroine-Self awoke! You drew a line in the sand … "*Not* me, *No* more!"

What words rose up in your Heroine's Voice from within? What was your victory statement? What announced your Self-Worth and your conviction?

Take your time, no hurry, as you search for this important moment and how you took it on. You can pause here for a moment if you need more time to reflect.

Oh, Heroine, you know the moment of your birth! You have made Your Heroine's Proclamation. Hear *your* roar! This will be your guiding Belief to a great life.

Give yourself love and gratitude that you broke through. Your words are precious. Know who you are. You are a Heroine!

Throw your arms around your shoulders and give yourself a hug. You deserve it!

PS…put your Heroine's Proclamation on your bathroom mirror (with red lipstick or your artistic version drawn out boldly!) — to call to you each morning as you rise and brush your teeth! Cheers!

We've now fully explored Beliefs, which is the very first Cornerstone of building Your Stability. Your chosen Beliefs that are truly supportive of you confirm your power to light your inner ignition, and are the inner scaffolding that supports you as you continue on the Journey. Congratulations! — this is big work for promoting your life.

And there is more support to be had on this wild Journey. Come with me to our next discussion: *Physical*. You are going to see how progressing on your Heroine's Journey does not come about from casual choices for your personal Well-Being.

You will become intentional to gather Life-Force energy for the Journey ahead. This is the second Cornerstone for creating your Stability.

Free Resources

More free resources for you at:
www.HeroinesBook.com/Free-Resources

Here you'll find the wonderful quotes of 'Women With Strong Beliefs' and 'The Four Cornerstones.'

4

Cornerstone Two: Physical

Let's Get Physical

Sourcing Life-Force From The Outside

Sourcing Life-Force From The Inside

Safety First For You

Bolster Your Life-Force

LET'S GET PHYSICAL

*A*re you setting yourself up physically and energetically so you can meet the demands of the Journey? Well, that's a good question to ask.

The Heroine's Journey is a rigorous Path, requiring you to muster good energy to hoist your wings on and fly. When you are Called to the Crusade in Step #5, you are confronted with critical circumstances that awaken your primal instinct for self-preservation.

Here is what you face on this Step of the Journey:

Step 5: Called to The Crusade

Confront new realities

The circumstances are dire. There is no way out but to go through. You are wounded, hurt, and suffering. And still, you decide not to let it take you out. With a primal instinct for self-preservation, you finally take a stand for yourself. You know you must survive, and you use this to invoke your perseverance. Like it or not, now, you must deal with your life as it is. You are being forced into new realities. There are some Tasks you just have to get done now, however unpleasant they are. It's big, and it is scary. You do it anyway. Digging deep, you find the fire in your belly. You get Fierce Feminine. You hoist your wings on and muster up Courage and Strength for a Journey into the wild.

As you embark on your Crusade, you might feel a lag energetically, and you wonder, "Do I have the Strength for this? How can I possibly help myself? This is urgent, how do I pick myself up?"

Your Strength is so important, not only emotionally but physically as well. There are two areas of Physical Strength to cultivate. Now is the time to put your foot on the gas.

These are:

1. Bolstering your energy from the Inside, this is taking care of your physical body.
2. Fostering your energy from the Outside, this is setting up your physical environment to sustain you.

Your personal bodily Strength and the strong physical foundation you create around yourself add up to the amount of '*OOMPH*' you can muster up to forge ahead. The magic is: You gotta power through.

Hey, you can truly fall off the Path if you cannot sustain yourself. I did. I thought I could out-sustain things that were hampering my Life-Force. But I couldn't. I am a Heroine, but I am not a superwoman. I fell off, and I had to pay attention. I had to make some corrections pretty quickly to get through.

Changes ahead on the Journey require energy, flexibility, Strength, and consistency in adapting to new ways of life. This takes bolstering the conditions in your 'Inner' and 'Outer' environment through daily choices to move forward on the Journey with stamina. It's surprising what can bottom out your Life-Force energies, putting you in a critical shortage. I'll talk about that as we go on here.

Your Physical Well-Being is highly important on the Path, so *help* yourself! Rally and strengthen your Life-Force Energy to hoist your wings on.

What is your Life-Force Energy?

This natural and spiritual energy animates you with vitality, Strength, and Courage. It's the force that has you take action and be creative, expressive, and passionate. You are humming when you have Life-Force cursing through your Being. Your unique essence, that dynamic force, runs through you to activate your Being, allowing you to heal, correct, innovate, and persist.

It is your Life-Force that propels you through the entire Heroine's Journey, the kindling that revs your internal spirit, love, and commitments.

Your Life-Force is an activation engine in your body, and your personal environment is the container that holds you safe and sound. Both need to be set up correctly to create your Stability. And remember, this is one of the 4 Cornerstones of creating your Stability.

Recognition of what is going on 'Inside' and 'Outside' of you is critical. Your 'Inner' and 'Outer' conditions and environment add up to the sum total of your Life-Force. A strong Life-Force allows you to spring from the 'muck' and go the distance on the Path to your Best-Self.

This is about practices to energize your Life-Force. Grab onto these. Do kindle the fires within you to ignite your Life-Force.

This requires intention, plans and follow-through, my lovely Sister! Let's talk about how to activate your Being so you can sustain the Journey.

The focus is on caring for yourself. You are your own watch dog, self-loving Being and advocate.

What's going on with you 'internally'? And, what's going on with you 'externally'? What changes do you need to make? You might be surprised as we discuss what is not supporting you; I was!

Hey, I get it — lots of information about health and exercise comes our way, but that is different than what I am covering here. This is about combining all the practices, tools, and adjustments you leverage to increase your consistent Life-Force. It's a bundle.

When life goes through major transitions, what you have is *you*! So, putting your attention on amplifying the energy you generate is key. There is up-leveling to do in your Inner and Outer environment to generate the energy you need.

Truth be told, we must align ourselves with the laws of Nature, or we experience roadblocks: ill health, mental instability, ineffectiveness, frustration, stuckedness and more — something is out of whack here. And these are sending out signals to change.

The Heroine's Journey takes you from survival to thrival. The Heroine thrives. She does this by really considering the Physical aspects of her life, taking action with a game plan, building Life-Force, and Creating Stability.

Let's first address any concerns. As you are reading this, you may be in a state of Crisis, and I want to stop here for a moment to help you. Life may be all wine and roses for you now — but it may be that you've encountered your worst time ever, and what I am going to talk about with you in this Chapter is Triage Care for you.

My Journey took me to rock bottom. I got flipped from the middle of the road into the gutter brutally, and tossed to the gutter on the other side again and again. My Stability rocked like a ship in a violent open ocean. I got through it, and you will too. Everything in this book is about getting you back on course. For me, it wasn't about course correction but about dramatic measures to regain my Life-Force energy and Stability. These were my lessons to be here now with you.

Part of this work is to set up your life so you don't get thrown so far out of whack. But life also throws us surprises. Have you noticed this?

You can use all of the teachings in this Book as Triage Care. Do what you must and make it as easy as possible for yourself. Right now if it's just about getting through the narrows of life's Journey, take heart that the process will move you along.

And, here's my suggestion too. When you make plans to improve your physical environment, both inner and outer, be budget-sensitive, your physical stress will be lessened if you are careful not to add more financial stress.

Right now, you may be going through some pretty immediate physical changes that can be rather taxing. But life won't always be this way. The Journey will lead to new horizons. I can tell you this from experience.

Here's my Story, my Heroine's Journey as I confronted the Physical Cornerstone on this Step of the Journey...

When my Heroine's Journey was upon me, I lost everything and sat at square numero uno. I knew I would stay there painfully in the Challenge Step forever if I didn't heed the call to the Crusade. But there was a big obstacle.

I was clearly in the worst moments of my life, and as a psychosomatic result, my body was also screaming in pain. My whole Being was getting tortured by the brutal circumstances that I was going through. My worst moments were causing upset, stress, fatigue and bodily rebellion.

Now was the time that I needed the best from my physical body. I needed it to help me get out of the dire circumstances that I was in. "Please," I said to her, "don't cause me more grief. I'm up to my max already. What can I do so you'll calm down and work with me instead of against me?"

I could hardly get out of bed in the morning. My head was so foggy that putting two and two together was a struggle. I was engulfed in depression and low on Hope. This was a clear sign that my Life-Force was slipping away. I could feel it. Really, my flame was almost snuffed out.

When the will to claim my life and put one foot in front of the other finally kicked in, I knew I couldn't rise without shoring up my energetic Being. I decided that *all of me* was going to carry on. I couldn't languish and expect that I was going to overcome. There were more tests ahead of me, and they would take energy too. I needed a plan because I felt miserable.

One of the first things I did was deal with my own head. Blaming other people for this pot of boiling water I'd landed in was no good. It drained my energy when I needed to ramp it up. And it worked both ways. It was equally a drain to beat myself up for my situation. I reminded myself, "What is, you make what is." That was real, and starting with 'real' was in order.

I needed to release resistance, accept things as they were, and allow myself to open to what was next. Once my head started to clear, I realized that If I was going to make progress, I needed to pick myself up. *That* was going to be *a lot* of work initially. But that was 'real' too.

Here's what I did. I made a list each day of what I would do to support my Life-Force. And I was sure to do what was on the list so I could be proud that I'd done the day's Tasks.

I went to yoga three times a week. I took supplements for the effects of stress. I did cleanses to clean the sluggishness out of my body. I got more rest than normal. I ate lots of vegetables and life-giving nutrients. I moved into a place where I felt safe and could enjoy the quiet. I listened to music, took walks with my dogs at the beach, went to church, did little things for myself, like flowers, and meditated almost daily to enhance my spiritual energy.

I did *everything it took to bolster my Physical energy* to ensure that my body had the energy and Strength to support me on the Journey.

It took big changes on the Outside and Inside, but I rallied my Life-Force for the Crusade and was victorious!

Now, I'm very conscious of the things that improve (or could potentially harm) my Life-Force energies so that I support myself and am not putting myself in the dire straits where I was before. This is a daily evaluation.

Your Well-Being is your daily evaluation too. My Father told me that I should 'save for a rainy day.' I remember that I told him that I wasn't going to have any rainy days! That was naive of me. And well, the best-laid plans of 'mice and men' do not always work out. Rainy days happen. I was surprised, and I was unprepared when they did happen. He was right, I was wrong (I'll remember to tell him that when we meet in heaven!)

Your Well-Being is paramount on the Journey. You deserve to give yourself what you need so your essence is nurtured and strong and you are prepared for strange and bizarre circumstances. Heroines keep going. Yes, they do!

The practices I'm sharing next are designed to help you gather your energies. And second, they support you to reign in any place in your life where you are being ineffective or physically overtaxed.

Make this time in your life truly designed for your own Well-Being. This is about centering yourself in your own Physical body and your immediate environment to position yourself on The Heroine's Journey. It's 'OOMPH' time!

Yep, a word of caution. This is not about making yourself look better in the outer world; it is about bolstering your inner world so you can make true progress. Let go of any attachment to looking good for others. Your OOMPH — This is the core of what makes you hummmm….

It's all about you feeling good on the inside. A Heroine knows that if she is good on the inside, all the rest of her world will shine!

SOURCING LIFE-FORCE FROM THE OUTSIDE

Changes in your life? Let's see.

Let's talk about your external Physical environment and adjusting your living style to fit your current circumstances. This could mean some changes, depending on what's happening in your life as you view it now.

The overall goal is to make any shifts and upgrades needed to support yourself physically, emotionally, and financially. Your goal is to create Your Stability, even if it means making some temporary or longer changes.

Is it time to make some new Physical choices so that you are more comfortable and your Life-Force is enhanced? It's about keeping your self supported and any stressors to a minimum.

Ask yourself what changes to your Physical environment you need to make to easily progress. Here are a few of the simple ones. Do you need to move, sell a car, shop less and live with the wardrobe you have, get rid of stuff, organize your belongings to optimize your functionality, or something else?

I admit – I've seen myself repetitively doing unsupportive things, like buying more stuff for my house that I don't need so that it's cluttered — and doing this unconsciously. This is a simple example but the point is — when I've called my attention to what I'm doing, I sometimes see that choices are actually handicapping my spirit rather than improving it. That's when I decided it was time for a change!

Where can you benefit from making Physical changes in your immediate environment? There can be so many things that affect your energy from the Outside - where you spend your time, as well as where you live and what you do. Just be open to consider how your Physical surroundings are impacting you. Here are a couple of things to considerate to raise your OOMPH meter:

1. Choosing Places of Freedom:

Generally, you can choose what physical environments you put yourself in. As best you can, choose to go to places that are physically and emotionally supportive for you. And avoid places that draw Life-Force energy away from you.

For example, it is best to avoid places filled with bad memories. If you broke up with your husband at the local diner, don't go there again. Stay away from places or certain events if they cause distress until you are free of the pain. Choose not to waste your energy trying to rectify the bad places of the past at this point. Move on to places where you feel good.

Really protect your sense of what fills you up energetically. Recognize that some places zap you, and others help you to feel free. Restoring your 'feel good' is not only your inalienable right, it's also critical to your progress, sustainability and growing happiness. What puts a smile on your face, makes you laugh, and eases your tensions? — these are your places of freedom — actively seek them.

2. Recharging in Nature:

It's good to be in places where you draw energy.

For example, spending time in Nature can ground, inspire, and bring peace to your spirit and soul. Ahhhhhhh….

You can go to the beach, take a hike, just gaze out the window, or sit on your front porch for this bliss. Focus on the blue sky, the trees as they breathe, and the flowers as they bloom. Remind yourself that Nature has its own process and natural evolution. You are part of Nature. When you merge your Life-Force with the force of Nature, you get supercharged for the Journey.

You'll recognize when you need to create these breaks for yourself and include them in your daily routine. It's just a way to be kind to yourself. Moments to breathe and take in the good things around you, awaken your senses to life's joy.

3. Your Living Space:

Think about the Physical environment that most impacts your life — where you live! Does it truly support you? Can you afford it? Does it make you feel safe? Does the energy feel good to you? This is foundational to how you are setting yourself up for progress.

Often, at the start of The Heroine's Journey, it is typical to experience some pretty major upheaval. You could be called to make significant changes rather quickly. Sometimes, this includes where you reside. As this occurs, maybe you realize you need a new place to live for a variety of reasons:

What can you afford?
Who lives in the space with you?
Who might you need to move away from?
What is the best geographic location related to family or work?

Whatever it is, it means change. Whether you need to move or simply modify your current living choice, the approach is to make some changes — ones that feel more stabilizing for you, where you can be happier and less pressured. You will be preserving your Life-Force energy in the face of these changes you need to make.

It is so important to be flexible along with these changes. You can lessen your suffering if you don't resist. Let's call it! Change can be scary; truthfully, this is an essential part of the process. If you can move through it with ease and surrender, this will be incredibly helpful.

Realistically, you may not have any other choice. Make it as easy as possible on yourself.

Sometimes, you must go *through* changes to get to calmer places. I have tried to go up and around, or over and under — and finally just moved *through* with as much elegance and ease as possible.

Amazingly, these physical changes do lead to a new sense of freedom.

The new situation can add to your greater momentum and feeling good if you allow it. See it as a sign of progress. You are moving forward for right now. The future will bring something else. But right now, do what you need to do.

You will find your way and amp up your Life-Force in the process.

4. Making More of Less:

You probably need less than you think you do. You can't travel easily with a lot of baggage when you are building your Stability. Having less will give you a sense of freedom. It's lighter and easier this way.

As you grow in your success, more 'stuff' will come to you. But in this phase, it is about celebrating '*less*'. Time to get back to basics. To enhance your Life-Force, get rid of what does not serve you or weighs you down. This is part of opening up to your new life.

Here's a sure thing to do. Get rid of or burn those things given to you by people who bring up hurt feelings. These items have 'no good' energy for you, no matter how valuable the item may be. You don't want to trigger yourself into those old memories. If you can't get rid of it — box it up and put it away for a time when you are feeling much stronger. At a later time, you won't get triggered in the same way.

This is important in creating a supportive space for you. It's not supportive to keep things that take you out, make you defensive, or burden you emotionally or physically that are what you are seeing each day.

Keep what adds to your joy. Now, you can welcome in what serves you in your *new* life — what you love, what you can use, what brings you comfort.

Some of my happiest moments were when everything fit into my yellow Chevrolet Camaro car. *Hah! Hah!*

When you travel light, life can be more flexible and malleable. This gives you more energy for the Journey.

Physical environment changes can be so powerful. As you shift your Physical environment, keep in mind that you may 'let go' of a lot of what you currently possess. These changes are not losses. When you release some thing, idea, or person, remember this: Anything that is meant to be in your life will come back around to you. That's the way it works.

Just listen to this story…

I want to tell you a true story so incredible you may find this hard to believe.

When my friend lost everything financially in the Crisis phase of her life, she had to make some very quick and dramatic changes to ensure that she and her 9-year-old son could make it through the narrows together.

As she entered the Challenge phase, her son was the one who taught her a valuable lesson about the sweetness of living with less.

She told the Story that their financial crash on the rocks was so extreme that they had to move out of their big, beautiful dream house into a 300 square-foot rustic one-room cabin with one electrical outlet and no real shower. It was a dramatic change.

Apprehensive about the prospect of living nearly on top of one another, my friend started to get rid of most of the material possessions they owned. All the stuff simply would not fit. She got rid of pretty clothes, fancy kitchen gadgets, beautiful bobbles, and so much of the stuff she had loved.

Finally, she could delay the inevitable no more. She had to ask her precious little boy to clean out his toy-filled room and pare down to only what would fit in his small sleeping loft. He could keep so little.

He began the task in good spirits, filling bag after bag with his most cherished possessions to give to charity. Mom went to get more bags, and as she returned, she saw him putting his favorite rainbow-colored stuffed dragon into a bag. He was actually going to part with the thing he loved most.

Her expression changed to tearful compassion, which got her son's attention. He looked at her with complete peace and said, "It's OK,

Mom. I can give it *all* away. Anything I am truly meant to have will come back to me." Out of the mouths of babes! Her little boy had given her the greatest gift of surrender, faith, and the ability to fully embrace living with less. How was he so young and he knew this wisdom? She pushed back a tear.

A year passed, and they had a grand ol' time living in that one-room cabin, probably the best time of their lives. Mom generated the resources she needed, and they moved out of that tiny space and resumed the life they were more accustomed to living.

A few weeks later, they were in a thrift store in a town over an hour and a half away from home. Hearing her son's laughter, she looked over to find him holding the same rainbow-colored stuffed dragon he had given away the year before. *Incredible!* He was indeed right! Anything you are truly meant to have will come back to you.

They bought the dragon and took him home to a beautiful house filled with plenty. It served as a constant reminder that, yes, you can be happy with less. Sometimes, you are given more. And sometimes even the dragon returns … Lovely!

Let's talk about a 5-Part Process that you can use to optimize your living space — it's about space-centric happiness. Once you have identified the best way for you to live, the fun begins. It doesn't matter how big or small your space is, and you *can* be happy in it.

Here is a simple Process to enhance your Stability, your happiness and ramp up your Life-Force.

5-Part Process to Optimize Your Living Space:

1. Create Good Energy.

Work with your space's energy to feel nurturing and vibrationally clean. Here are some examples:

- Smudge your space with sage
- Air it out regularly
- Bring in some plants
- Play soothing music

- Adopt a loving pet
- Invite only supportive people
- Use feng shui or Vaastu to optimize the energy

Good chi makes for strong Life-Force.

2. Personalize.

Make your space feel like you. Here are some ways to do just this:

- Ensure that there is something beautiful and inspiring around you in each room
- If you are emotionally transitioning, reclaim your space by repainting it with your favorite colors, using new fabrics, or changing the layout
- Adorn your bed with soft and fluffy bedding, and have an extra throw blanket to snuggle under for a nap or reading a book
- Add some naturally scented candles
- Use soft lighting
- Also, bring your personality to your outdoor spaces. Plant a garden, add a swing, make a comfortable space to enjoy your outdoor environment, and recharge
- Be creative, making only those changes you can afford to make

Know that you will flourish when your space is beautiful, comfortable, and affordable.

3. Make It Healthy.

Your space should not only support your emotions and your budget; in your quest to support your Physical Life-Force, your home can also be part of this goal when it is healthy.

- Choose materials, scents, and cleaning products that are natural and healthy

- Remove allergens and toxins like dust or synthetic materials — Try using an air purifier

There is much information online to help you through this process. Use it to create a healthy environment that bolsters your Life-Force energy.

4. Organize.

Here's a big one: Get rid of excess stuff that drags your energy down or takes up your time and OOMPH to maintain. You can easily distract yourself from what must be done on The Heroine's Journey by making up stories about how you need to manage all your physical stuff — not a good ploy.

It is best to get rid of most of it and keep only what truly serves your progress. Organize what you have left so that you can find it easily and utilize it efficiently.

Here's the truth: an uncluttered space facilitates an uncluttered mind and your Life-Force.

5. Inspire.

Here is a tip to propel yourself toward your ultimate vision of your best life.

- Display mementos of your accomplishments and abundance around your space to remind you of who you are
- All circumstances are temporary — Be reminded of the phases of life that felt very aligned and accomplished
- Create an environment that always sends you the message that you are loved, valuable, and have much to contribute
- Create a space that supports who you are becoming with intention — You can do this with many reminders, like posting a quote from your Lighthouse reminding you of your Self-Worth

If you don't have your own space or you are living in someone else's space now, you can scale down the action items in each of the 5 steps. It doesn't always require big gestures. It is about working with the space and the resources you have at the moment. Remember, "Small is beautiful."

Now, grab your Journal again, and make notes to give you opportunities to practice the '**5-Part Process for Optimizing Your Living Space**'.

But first, decide if you need to move. If you do, then come back to this exercise once you have your new space. And, get going if you are in a home that supports your Journey.

Here's an example. Under the heading for each of the 5 part, you will write down 3 things that you commit to doing in the next 4 weeks to optimize your space.

For example, in step #4, called 'Organize,' I would write:

1. Clean out my seasonal closet and donate what I have not worn in more than a year.
2. Organize the garage. Remove and return — via a 3rd party — all of my former husband's personal stuff.
3. Set up an organized office space in the 3rd bedroom so that I can easily attend to my business and personal matters.

Make it easy for yourself. Do what is simple, fits into your available time, and honors your budget.

Enjoy the transformation and observe how this grows your Life-Force energy.

Optimizing your Outer environment is one-half of the Physical component of Creating Your Stability. Next, it's time to consider optimizing the other half, the internal part of your Physical body. Combining these two halves gives you the whole formula for optimizing your OOMPH — Your Life-Force to Create Your Stability.

SOURCING LIFE-FORCE FROM THE INSIDE

Inside and Outside, that's the simplicity of it. The energy of your body and your environment add up to your Life-Force — *your OOMPH, Sister!*

Life is just more fun when you are filled with Life-Force energy, and you know that you are fueled for your flight. When The Heroine's Journey gets revved up, your Stability will depend upon doing all that you can to energize yourself.

Are you ready to up-level how you treat yourself from the inside? Even if you have neglected certain aspects of caring for your Physical body, be gentle with yourself. Start where you are right now, and rest assured that your progress will assist you on your Heroine's Journey.

Have you assessed your inner Well-Being? First, think about your current state of Physical Well-Being. Your body will reveal to you its wisdom if you ask the right questions. You can undergo a more complete assessment by seeing your personal physician or a holistic practitioner.

Once you know the Strength of your Physical Well-Being, get to it. Use some of the tried and true tools I'm offering to you in this Book to tune up your Life-Force energy.

Are you in a state of healing?

If you have received a medical diagnosis, there is an opportunity. Think of it this way: Your circumstances are a powerful part of how your Heroine's Journey has been designed specifically for you. This is perfect for you to discover more of the truth of who you are. The depths of any Journey through health, financial, or relationship issues naturally take us each into the realm of greater self-awareness. I know it's unbelievable, but there is a gift in this for you.

Try this: Imagine how you can reframe your health condition in your thinking so you are not limiting yourself. How can you focus on what creates healing rather than what is ailing?

Here is how the old thought might have rattled around in your head:

"My adrenal glands are very stressed. I am exhausted. I can't do another thing. I have to go lie down right now before I fall down."

You can shift to a new health-affirming thought like this:

"I am honoring my health. I have accomplished all that I need to for today. I am going to lie down and relish rejuvenation as my gift to myself."

Being your best health advocate, including how you think, is important.

Celebrate the Life-Force you have now and continue getting medical — holistic or allopathic — treatment so that you can remove the blockage in your Life-Force and be on your way to your full measure of Life-Force energy.

And, hey! ... I have **7 Simple Superchargers** for you that will ramp up your OOMPH meter and speed up your progress!

Don't we know that there are certain things to do for our Physical body that will propel our Well-Being? And it is sooooo easy to avoid doing them. Our bodies can handle the abuse when we are young, or so we think they can, but things add up over time, and we learn that our finely-tuned bodies are just not indestructible.

Our busy pace can conveniently cause us to avoid thinking about making them a priority, but heads up: *Life-Force energy is everything!* To make sure that you keep the Life-Force 'must dos' top of mind and accessible, here's a list of essentials.

After you get the blessing of your primary health care professional, use our **7 Simple Superchargers** to boost your Physical Well-Being. These practices will supercharge your Life-Force.

The 7 Simple Superchargers:

7 Simple Supercharger #1: **Stress Management**

Stress is part of our lives in the modern world. Additionally, on The Heroine's Journey there are phases that elicit a more significant stress response and require conscientious stress management as you move along. The Journey is not about getting rid of the stressors in your life. Truly, the stresses you feel on this Path serve to transform on your Journey by getting your attention. So, best to welcome them with as much ease as possible, and to ride through them tactfully.

It is key to remember that in times of stress, your body needs extra support to journey onward. Stress is known to rob our OOMPH. It's important to note it as a depletion factor to be carefully watched. The practice below will help you quell the frenetic energy that can burn us out of our Life-Force and disrupt our progress forward.

Can I share my personal practice for dealing with stress effectively with you? It really is my lifeline when I am internally freaking out. I always use this when the 3 am fear monster rears its head.

I call it the **Stress Storm Relief Practice***. Here's how it works:

Get the Alert. Feel the adrenaline move through your body like a lightning storm as a stressful thought gets triggered. Do you notice a change in your breathing? Realize it is an alert to get your attention.

Let It Pass. Science reveals that a feeling only lasts 9 seconds. Just let it pass.

Take the Controls. Realize that this thought can immobilize you, or you can take control. It is there for a reason — to get you to pay attention to something important.

Re-write the Thought. Acknowledge the stressful thought. Re-write the stressful thought to one that allows you to handle the situation gracefully.

Breathe. Breathe into a peaceful state. Inhale for 4 seconds and exhale for 4 seconds. Do this for at least three rounds.

Release the Story. Notice how the original stressful thought was born from an old story that no longer serves you. Let that go. Now, you get to be the author of your own life.

Take Healthy Action. Do something constructive rather than reactive to resolve the situation. The result will likely be better than your old thought would have produced. Consider that you really do have many options — you're not trapped.

Break the Cycle. Learn to identify habitual stress triggers and eliminate them from your life.

The Stress Storm Relief Practice is not a substitute for medical and psycho-logical treatment.

7 Simple Supercharger #2: **Sleep & Rest**

One of the quickest ways to have a more healthy, joyful, inspired, and productive life is *sleep*! The National Institute of Health advises that adults need between 7.5 to 9 hours of sleep per night. No kidding, your body really needs that 8 hours of sleep each night.

Your body is naturally attuned to the circadian rhythms of the earth. To sleep and wake in harmony with this rhythm allows you the most productive rest and is a foundation for Creating Your Stability. Research-ers generally agree that it is best to go to sleep by 10 pm and wake at 6 am. Tune into a healthy sleep pattern you consistently practice to regain control of your Life-Force energies.

Sleep deprivation doesn't just affect your appearance but also wreaks havoc on your body and mental state. It undermines decision-making, work life, relationships, and even our sex lives. It's attributed to weight gain, diabetes, mental disorders, and other serious illnesses. For example, getting only 6 hours of sleep per night is like driving after drinking a six-pack of beer. *Yikes!*…that would have you weaving down the road.

In other words, "You are on the road of life driving drunk!" says Arianna Huffington in her book, 'The Sleep Revolution.'

Arianna Huffington, founder of the Huffington Post, says some-thing funny: "As women, we are literally going to sleep our way to the top." She says this because the quality of our sleep enhances our power and Strength — makes us more effective and smarter.

As a society, we are beginning to acknowledge that sleep deprivation is a symbol of stupidity, not success. This is a good thing!

Parade Magazine and Huffington Post conducted a study of 15,000 people. 95% of the respondents felt they needed more sleep. 60% of the respondents say that they take sleep meds.

If you experience insomnia, you might want to trade in the sleep meds for more natural means to help you relax. Try going to bed earlier, essen-tial oils, theta wave music, mantra repetition, and natural supplements.

True also, that technology can negatively impact your sleep in several ways. If you read on a digital device before bed, the light that emits from the screen can affect the melatonin production in your body and thus overstimulate you before you plan to drift off into sleep. If you have your smartphone next to your bed, the EMFs that are constantly generated from the phone agitate your brain waves. In addition, the beeping, vibrating, and flashing signals jolt your body into alertness each time you get a message. If you want a good rest, put your tech to rest, too.

This goes for your TV as well. Constantly negative news and listening to endless drama before you go to bed is not going to help you sleep. Unplug and calm your mind.

Sleep transforms your life one night at a time. Expanding research continues to determine sleep's benefits, including how sleep maintains our brain functionality and clears toxic waste that gathers between brain cells during the day. In other words, sleep regenerates and relaxes your brain, and makes you more effective. Who doesn't love that?

It's not just sleeping at night that is regenerative; so are daily periods of deep rest. Each day, allocate some time to just be. In a world where multitasking is valued and your success is often measured by how much you do, train yourself to fully rejoice in 'doing nothing' for a short period each day — take a nap, watch the sunset, read, stroll, gaze at Nature, bird watch, enjoy your garden, sing a song, read poetry, knit, pet your cat, sit and watch the world go by. What gives you peaceful pleasure? Indulge!

I find that massage is also a fantastic way to allow my body to move into a state of restful relaxation. Did you know that 1 hour of massage is worth 4 hours of rest? Every now and then, you might give yourself this gift, too. You're worth it.

7 Simple Supercharger #3: Good Nutrition

Food becomes energy in the body, and then energy powers our Life-Force. The more energetic the raw materials you put into your body, the more energy you produce for the Journey. The age-old adage is, "What you put in is what you get out."

While many fad diets are in the media, the answer is never in a diet. The answer is to create a lifelong pattern of nutrition that meets your unique physiological needs. Your holistic practitioner can test you for food allergies, bio-physical processing, and acid/alkaline balance. You should be aware of these things to make optimal food choices.

Some basic nutrition principles can be helpful to all of us in increasing our vitality. Hey Sister, no'body' escapes these universal nutritional truths. So here it is in straight talk:

1. Drink purified water—at least eight glasses per day.
2. Drink a superfood smoothie each morning: consider adding dark leafy greens, berries (rather than high glycemic fruits), chia seeds, goji berries, soaked and blanched almonds, spirulina, food-based vitamin C, raw plant-based protein powder. Add in whatever else feels really good to your body. I also love adding avocado. It's so good for you and makes it creamy.
3. Shop at your local farmer's market, where food is freshly harvested and retains more of its Life-Force vital nutrients.
4. Shop the outer ring of the supermarket where fresh foods are offered. Avoid the middle of the supermarket, where processed and packaged foods are grouped and lack vitality.
5. Eat organic. Pesticides are neurotoxins. They mess not only with your body but with your mind.
6. Enjoy a plant-strong diet. A full array of nutrients, including protein, are offered in the plant world.
7. Read the ingredients label before you buy. There may be surprise additives even though the front label appears to say 'healthy.' Many toxins are hidden in foods. There are more than 17,000 chemicals that the FDA allows food manufacturers to call 'spices' on their labels. This is an illustration of the hidden poisons that can be found in processed foods.
8. Choose wisely. Eat an apple with raw almond butter rather than a bag of baked chips.
9. Avoid refined sugar and white starchy foods such as bread, rice, potatoes, and pasta.

10. Eat less. Give your body a break from working to process so many extra calories. It's OK to feel hungry sometimes.
11. Eat smaller portions often. Keep your blood sugar stable.
12. Search healthy recipes online and delight in discovering new foods and flavors that fully satisfy you. It is never about denying your desires. It's about feeding your whole self.

7 Simple Supercharger #4: **Supplements**

Good food is excellent nutrition; however, with our planetary soils being ever more depleted, food alone may not be enough to get all the nutrients, vitamins, and minerals required for optimal body and brain functioning. Choose natural nutritional supplements to replenish and boost the vitality in your body.

In high-stress situations, your body and your brain's reserves of nutrients are very quickly depleted. This is the time to prioritize supplemental support. If your body and mind are not feeling as vital as you would like, a customized supplement program can jump-start the engines — ramping up your OOPMH.

Your natural healthcare provider can do a full blood test and recommend a supplement regime specifically designed to meet your body's needs.

7 Simple Supercharger #5: **Detoxify**

Our cells store toxins from our environment, food, and stress-released chemicals that our bodies produce. Removing these toxins allows your body to function with greater vitality. It's necessary to detoxify our cells conscientiously. Here are some simple ideas. Please let me remind you to consult your health provider before beginning any new health protocol.

1. Flush your body with water upon awakening. Your body releases toxins as you sleep at night, so it is important to remove them with water in the morning.
2. Zeolite clay is a natural detoxifier. You can add it to your smoothie in the morning.

3. You can choose from many detox programs to amp up your vitality. You can start your research with credible internet sources.

4. Green juice fasting (just the juice, not fiber from green veggies) is an excellent way to send the body into the process of autolysis, where the body kills off unhealthy cells. The process of autolysis begins on the third day. Avoid fruit juices as they cause spikes in blood sugar and feed the candida in your body. You can do much research on the internet for green juice fasting support.

7 Simple Supercharger #6: Exercise & Movement

This is your play time. Remember when you were a kid and loved to dance, skip, twirl, climb, roll, and relish all the ways your body can move? It was an exploration of what your body could do and how fun it could be. Now we hear that we must exercise every day. Your reaction might be, "Ugh. I hate to exercise. It is boring, hard, and regimented. I don't have time to do something I hate."

Let's re-write the exercise paradigm. How can you move your unique body so that it brings you freedom, joy, creativity, balance, awareness, oxygen, blood flow, muscle tone, and Strength? What movement sets your soul on fire: salsa dancing, biking in the hills, ecstatic dance, centering yoga, tai chi, water ballet, jogging, racquet sports, walking on the beach, aerial silk acrobatics, Zumba, rock climbing, pilates or even pole dancing? My favorite is pickleball!

What movement expresses your true nature? Pick one to three that you will explore and move your body. You remember the song from the movie Madagascar: "I like to move it, move it. I like to move it, move it." The point is you gotta like it.

Here are some of the benefits of 'moving it':

Moves chi or prana and increases vitality
Releases endorphins — your happy chemicals
Relieves stress
Clears your head so new ideas arise

Oxygenates and increases blood flow
Builds muscle and creates flexibility
Encourages weight loss
Aids detoxification
Improves sleep
Helps digestion & elimination

Now that you know all the good that exercise can do, don't you just want to put on your leggings and sneakers and work up a sweat? Go for it … Cheers!

7 Simple Supercharger #7: **Meditation**

In the Crisis and Challenge phases of The Heroine's Journey you first need to find a refuge — a place to go to feel OK. This could be on a yoga mat, in a chair, or seated on the floor — in meditation.

This is important because otherwise, to relieve the stress, it could be tempting to turn to food, sex, or seek material pleasures that don't offer you long-term stabilizing benefits. And they can ultimately derail each of us from the Journey. Meditation cultivates a healthy refuge within. It takes you to find your calm, peaceful spot — that self-accepting place of your vast spirit. You can feel flight within when you meditate.

In times when it feels like everything is being ripped away, it can be a knee-jerk response to try to hold on even tighter to the life you have been attached to. The great paradox is that Creating Your Stability is found in surrendering — 'letting go.' It's interesting to note that when you let go of the ground, you can fly in the air.

Meditation is the practice that cultivates the inner surrender response. By meditating, you are cultivating your 'surrender-ability.' Next time you face a crisis or challenge, you know how to go with the flow rather than fighting the situation and getting stuck there.

Meditation can create an amplified brain state that transforms your entire life experience. You will feel more relaxed, internally connected, free, energized, happy, safe, stable, and hopeful with this practice. It can take you out of the chaos of the day and your self-centered ego, and land you into the realm of peace and a larger perspective of being.

It may sound 'out there,' but you can do some form of meditation quickly and easily anytime you need it (except when operating heavy machinery, *ha ha*!).

Practically speaking, meditation research reveals a significant reduction of several psychological indices related to worry, anxiety, and depression when you meditate. In addition, meditation is attributed to improved concentration, slower aging, lower blood pressure, improved cardiovascular health, and improved breathing and oxygenation.

For the progress and success you yearn to cultivate, it's very important to make a regular meditation practice part of your life. Interestingly, a study showed that most of the leaders in Silicon Valley meditate! Wired Magazine said: "In Silicon Valley, Meditation is no fad. It could make your career."

There are many forms of Meditation, all of which provide great benefits. You can easily find a group where you can learn and practice within your hometown. Although the forms vary, meditation can involve:

Breath
Mantra (repetition of a word or sacred sound)
Visualization
Sensation awareness
Stillness or gentle, rhythmic movement

Find what brings you relief, surrender, and peace — and enjoy deeply. Are you already implementing many of the **7 Simple Superchargers**? Are there some that really need your attention? Let's get optimized! Be honest: are you amping up your Life-Force intentionally every day, or are you letting it slide?

Are you rockin' it, Heroine?

SAFETY FIRST FOR YOU!

Now, we are going to shift gears from the warrior who supercharges to the feminine spirit inside of you that absolutely needs your protection.

We'll get grounded in a conversation about protecting you and your Life-Force. This is a vulnerable and eye-opening conversation about ensuring your Safety in all areas of your life.

We will unpack some of the tougher issues involving vulnerability and Self-Worth here.

The Heroine's Journey is ultimately about valuing *your* life in the grandest fashion. There will be tests along the way as you travel this Journey of life, some of which will surprise you and some of which may be dangerous for you. You'll need the tools to honor your *Safety First*.

Protecting your Life-Force and keeping yourself safe is foundational to Creating Stability. Your Journey will be derailed if you aren't absolutely certain that you are securing your Safety.

Even as an intelligent woman, in the past, I so often compromised my Safety - in all sorts of ways: physically, emotionally, and financially. Here I was, seemingly a smart woman, missing this foundational support for my life. What was I thinking? *DA!!!* I got derailed, had to recover, and got this lesson the hard way — Yikes!

I undermined my Safety because I didn't care for myself. First and foremost, my Self-Worth was way undervalued and was the core of my problems. What I learned through painful experiences is that if I am not keeping myself safe and secure, I can't be good for myself and others and do what needs to be done. This is the painful truth: I was a victim and not a Heroine at that time. Boy, that's not the road I wanted to be on — U-Turn time, for sure!

As I have shared my Story, I find that way too many of my smart, strong, beautiful, capable Sisters have also been in jeopardy and diminished their lives for periods of time. This is the lesson of valuing yourself. To be on The Heroine's Journey requires self-acceptance and acknowledgment of Self-Worth. Is it time for you to rethink what you are doing and believing?

This next part addresses some very sensitive topics about being safe as a woman. It is time to lift the veil on some of the 'secrets' we try to keep hidden away so that we can keep up appearances. To become a true Heroine, which is the focus of this study, you must reveal yourself to trusted advocates about what is happening in your life and determine what changes you need to make.

Before you go any further in this Book, make sure you have the appropriate resources available to you for your physical and emotional support. If you are in the care of a mental health practitioner, you may want to let them know that you are undertaking this work and request their added support.

We will start with the easy Safety topics first and then dig deeper. Stay committed to the process. Freedom awaits you.

1. Home Safety

Earlier, we talked about creating a beautiful home that nurtures your Well-Being.

We would be remiss if we did not take this opportunity to reflect upon how safe and secure you are where you live. Do you live in a low-crime neighborhood? Do you need to add additional locks on windows or doors to feel more safe? Would a home security system make you feel more comfortable? Do you need to add lighting by your door or car parking area? Do you need to move to a better neighborhood or even a better State — to feel physically safe?

There's also the aspect of environmental Safety to consider. Do you live in a low-toxin home? Do you use chemical pest control that may be weakening your immune system? Have you switched to organic, bio-degradable cleaning products? Are there high-tension power lines over your home? Are you on a jet path near an airport? You might want to look into the home health system called Building Biology *(Bau Biologie)*. You can do more research on the internet. There are many ways to improve the environmental quality of where you live and support your own Physical Well-Being in the process.

2. Your Physical Safety

Your Physical body is your most precious asset to keep safe.

Young and foolish, right? But the impulses of the mind soon give way to the reality of the body. We learn we are more vulnerable than we think. You must learn to adapt, try, tweak, and pivot to keep your momentum going. Your attitude shifts about what risks you can take and how much you can endure as your body speaks to your brain. If you are wise, you listen.

We experience our vulnerability. And, we get more realistic about what it takes. Truly, protecting our Life-Force is the most critical thing to do. This means being *safe*.

The following discussions will help you explore how you live now and how it may support or undermine your fundamental Physical Safety.

Are you practicing Healthy Sexuality?

Let's start with this one — sexuality because it can play a big part in your foundational Stability. It can rock you and roll you or help you to blossom.

In addition to protecting your body — you also are protecting your Self-Worth, which is tied up in the way you handle your body sexually.

Sexual energy, creative energy, and Life-Force energy are closely intertwined — and combined for OOMPH. These are all parts of the fuel that propels your Journey. How you use your sexuality can either increase or decrease your Life-Force. The questions to ask yourself are:

Do I feel safe?

Is my sexual encounter and partner energizing (Yes) or de-energizing me (No)?

Are my choices contributing to my Self-Worth and Stability?

Am I doing what I believe is the right thing for me in my sexual choices?

Do I feel trapped (No), or am I using my free will (Yes)?

If you answer 'No' to any of these, it's time for a dead 'Stop'. Perhaps it's time to meditate on one or more of these questions. Would you be better off going home alone?...

When you are traveling in the early part of the Heroine's Journey, you may feel lonely or fearful — or just flat out find yourself 'lookin' for love. It can happen when you are vulnerable and self-deflated.

This is not the best state of mind from which to choose a sexual partner. If you let sexual partners in without carefully vetting them, they can derail you from your next Journey Steps. This is because you are in such a fluid state that your own boundaries are shifting. At this phase, the needed focus is on building your own personal Stability first. To do that, you must maintain concentration and conserve your Life-Force energy.

While engaging in sex, there is an energy transfer between the partners. So, you must choose a partner whose energy you resonate harmoniously with. We, as Women, are receptors of energy. Our sexual partner pours their energy into us. Choose wisely. If it's not healthy energy, don't invite them into your vagina!

As Tim McGraw says in his song *Humble and Kind*:

"Know the difference between sleeping with someone and sleeping with someone you love."

~Tim McGraw, Singer

Suppose you are blessed to have a committed sexual partner who can support you through this process, all the better. But if you're currently in or thinking about starting a sexual relationship that requires you to overextend yourself, consider the risk. It may take you off course. The last thing you want to do is to find yourself used and abused in your tender state. *Protect Yourself.*

Sexuality is a sacred part of your Womanhood. And there may be many ways to express your sexuality. It is essential to allow yourself to choose what feels right for you.

When it comes to sex, *you get to choose with whom, when, where, and how*. These are the essential elements of sexual Safety. Make it your practice to consider each of these elements before a sexual encounter carefully.

If even one aspect feels 'off' put your Safety First. '*No*' is a valuable word — a sign of your Self-Worth and power emerging.

We are blessed to live in a culture where we, as Women, can say '*yes*' or '*no*' depending upon our own evaluation. This freedom was hard-won from times when women were owned by men, fathers, or husbands. Truly, and thankfully now — a Heroine recognizes her independence and ability to provide for her precious Safety and security — and that sexuality includes some inherent risks she needs to factor in so that her Journey continues optimally.

How will you make decisions about your sexuality and current sexual encounters to best support you?

Ask yourself this question and be honest with your heartfelt response. You might have some strong Beliefs that come up. Circle back around to the Cornerstone - Beliefs Chapter 3, and re-write any of the Beliefs that may cause you to undermine your sexual Safety.

If you need support, be sure to Heroine-Up and get it now.

Now, here's the next one. What's going on with you with addictions?

Wow, addictions are hard to admit and can be the nemesis of your Journey. These are the compulsive behaviors that can rip you off the Heroine's Path and present immediate dangers.

They can include:

Drugs & Alcohol
Overeating
Sex addiction
Gambling
Media
Shopping

When you go through the Challenge and Crisis phases of the Journey, a temptation is to self-medicate to numb the discomfort. At the very least, even dabbling in these behaviors creates a distraction that will hamper you, my Sister.

Here's one of my favorite sayings that couldn't be more true here:

"There is no cheese down that hole."

~Unknown

There is no reward for you in this self-medication that can promote your happiness or fuel your flight. Let's be honest. I'm here for you.

What are you doing that could thwart you? Are you keeping these behaviors to a minimum and moderating them so you can continue on the Journey? Is there something that may be time to notice and curtail, lest your focus be on this behavior instead of things that are going to move you forward? We all have something in this regard. What's yours?

Make sure your lifestyle choices do not undermine generating your Stability. If you experience addictions, they may require treatment. Get the professional support you need. There is no shame in healing your body/mind. This is an act of Courage on The Heroine's Journey.

OK, truth be told — yep, my addiction (where I've had to reign myself in admitting my vulnerability) — it's shopping!

Here's my Story and how I recognize the grip on me.

I admit it! I have a shopping addiction. I don't use credit cards or spend more than I have. But I blow through cash like a tornado through an Illinois cornfield. When I do, I feel shameful for undermining my long-term Stability with my addictive behavior.

Recently, I had a trip planned to go to a resort with people I wanted to impress. So, of course, I needed a new wardrobe. I made a list of every possible thing I could buy to look sexy and fabulous. If I only planned my life with half the enthusiasm that I had in planning this trip …

So, I head out armed with my list to my very favorite department store. As the door opens automatically in front of me, it beckons me into paradise. My senses are in ecstasy with the mouth-watering colors and sensual feel of expensive fabrics. I yearn to possess them. I imagine how it will make me feel to be adorned with them, how great I'll look in my adventures. I become invincible, and all my problems are solved.

I lose myself in the ecstatic act of shopping. My arms are full of the booty of finery, and I am headed to the Mecca of the cash register when I trip on a stray hanger. Ooppsss....splat!

I come to my senses as I am sprawled out flat on the floor with silk and rhinestones strewn all around me — my real ones this time, not the ones that were mesmerized by the colors and textures and the fantasy world I was creating.

Holy Crap! … I've done it again. I am succumbing to the temptation. No, I must not! I cannot. *I - will - not - buy - another - thing.* I have all of this in my closet like 12 times over. And furthermore, if it is not good enough to be who I am, then no resort wear is going to be able to do the job for me.

So as not to let my humiliation get the best of me, I actually ask for help. The sales girl gets me off the floor and helps me gather random pieces of clothing that no longer entice me. I let her know she could keep them all.

I turned with as much grace as I could and walked out without the habitual rush and release when the debit card was swiped.

What usually fulfills me is getting into my car accompanied by the sound of crinkling shopping bags. But this time, I drive away empty-handed, with my Self-Worth full and glamorous.

Lessening the grip of addiction — well, it adds directly to your Self-Worth, bottom-line. Got that? And we're all about Self-Worth — what feeds, fortifies, and glorifies your Self-Worth!

Hey, Heroine, let me ask you this next question …

Are you experiencing physical abuse? – Now, a step further into the tough issues.

Let's go a step deeper in our conversation into something most of us don't talk about. You cannot progress on The Heroine's Journey while suffering physical abuse. *Period.*

It will keep you in the Crisis phase, with no hope of moving forward until you are free from the abuser. Sister, my heart goes out to you here — because I've been there. It's confusing, heart-breaking, painful. I know abuse all too well. I know the denial, the isolation, and the twisted-torment. I know that I thought that it was my problem, something that I was doing that caused it — it was not.

An abuser's objective is to destabilize you so they can maintain total control. Some abusive behaviors are overt, while others are thinly veiled so the abuser can maintain an image of righteousness. Can you let yourself see the red flags?

Physical abuse takes many forms, including:

Physically isolating you
Controlling your freedom to come & go as you please
Making up stories that diminish you and telling others
Locking you up or out
Cutting off your support from others
Hitting, shoving, or restraining
Objectifying you
Strangulation
Force-feeding or starvation
Sexual domination or violation
Threatening your life or your children
Making you feel physically afraid or unsafe
Stealing
Alcoholic lifestyle
Bipolar behavior
Narcissism
Uncontrollable Anger
Required Obedience
Battering and Constant Criticism
Actively harming your Self-Worth

This is a hard conversation, but let's call it out! *Smart Women* find themselves in abusive situations all the time but don't always know how to identify the abuse before it impacts their lives.

I was one of those smart women who had achieved all the prizes — owned my own successful business and beautiful house, written a best-selling book, traveled the world, earned multiple degrees, and yet … I was living with a dark secret. My husband badly abused me, physically and emotionally, for years and years. I diminished myself to try to minimize the abuse. I tried to work around it. I capitulated. I surmised it was me causing aggravation. I tried to believe it wasn't happening. I resisted accepting this reality. The problem was that this didn't work — none of it.

The time between the abuse incidents got closer and closer together over time. I got more and more into denial. I became more and more wounded and fearful. It didn't get better; it got worse. I felt like a fly wrapped tight by a spider's web. It suffocated me, immobilized me, and sucked the life right out of me. My Self-Worth went to the depths of the ocean. I hung on till I had no Self-Worth left because his attack was so incessant. His alcoholism made life at home miserable. There was narcissism. Screech, my life derailed. Plop, I was in the gutter. This was a big detour for me. I had to recognize that I wasn't the problem, but my life, my hopes and dreams, my energies — were all being compromised — and *I was responsible* for this imposition on my life. I was in a trash compacter, that squeezed me tighter as time went on.

I was the one who had to make the change. It's taken a long, long climb back to recover my Stability, get going again, and get my joy back. I had the right, I learned, to get out of the trash compactor, to protect myself and my Self-Worth, to restore. Restore, revitalize, reinvent — this drama nearly did me in, but my Heroine said: "Oh, No!", not for me — I am here for a reason and it's not to be assaulted, it's for me to claim myself and live fully. It was truly a hard climb out, but that's the only way for a Heroine!

The truth is that *no woman* deserves to live in fear. There is never any justification for abuse. You have not done anything to deserve it. And it will not get better. You can only clear the way forward.

If there is someone in your life who is exhibiting any of these behaviors, you must get free. It is important to have a freedom strategy that protects your Safety, security and Self-Worth.

Here are some ideas:

1. **Tell the Truth.** Truthfully acknowledge to yourself that this behavior is going on and it *is* impairing your life.
2. **Get Support.** Confide in a trustworthy friend, family member, counselor, clergy person, legal professional, or women's abuse agency. You can easily find a local hotline number in your area to call for support.
3. **Separate yourself.** Find a safe location with trusted people who can bear witness and protect you.
4. **Don't go back.** Follow through with permanently removing the abuser from all areas of your life, no matter how hard it may seem at the time.
5. **Rebuild your Self-Worth.** Get counseling to support you as you move your life beyond abuse and blossom into the Heroine that you are. Do not let the event define who you are. You are a magnificent manifestation of Creation, beautiful in every way. Step into this truth and shine. The world needs your brilliant light.

Breaking through into new freedom is what propels you out of crisis and onward in the Journey. It's an opportunity to bring forth your Courage and Strength. It is a wake-up call to becoming your fuller self. You must claim yourself before you can move forward. Don't allow yourself to be abused. This is my wish, Hope, and strong proclamation for you. I got out, moved on, and am a Heroine – this is for you too.

From all of us who have survived physical abuse and broken free, we send you fierce love and Courage for you to break free. We are celebrating you as you become a Heroine.

Are you Experiencing Depression?

Safety for your mental state is Well-Being as well. Honestly, can you be Creating Your Stability when depression is handicapping you?

I was really depressed. I didn't even know what it was or recognize its impact on me. I went to a therapist, and his answer was — 'drugs for the rest of your life.' That wasn't my answer, and I bolted out of his door.

There were circumstances in my own life that I wasn't addressing, things that I needed to pay attention to that were robbing me of joy, and actions that I needed to take. I got it when I felt threatened by someone who wanted to drug me perpetually. NO!! The Heroine arose in me, and I heard myself say, "Whatever it takes, I'm going to address this!". It took some time, but I depended upon my own conviction first – I needed all the where-with-all that I had to face where I was. I endured some pain, but I got into action.

According to Kelly Brogan, MD in her book, 'A Mind of Your Own' — "One in four women in their forties and fifties use psychiatric drugs." She goes on to say — "And if you think that a pill can save, cure, or 'correct' you, you're dead wrong. This about as misguided as a taking an aspirin for a nail stuck in your foot." Further, "The dirtiest little secret of all is that antidepressants are among the most difficult drugs to taper from, more so than alcohol and opiates...characterized by fiercely debilitating physical and psychological reactions."

What she is also saying from her professional-medical-experiential viewpoint is that — to medicate for what is going on in your life may be to overshadow the real reason that needs to be discovered for your distress — and Heroine, this can get you stuck on the Heroine's Path. There is more discovery to do to enable your way forward.

If you experience sadness that lasts more than a few weeks or is seriously impacting your life, it may be depression. It affects your mood, body, energy levels, concentration, and overall outlook on life.

Traumatic events, life changes, loss, financial disruption, abuse, serious illness, substance abuse, and food choices can cause depression. Depression does not mean you are broken. It simply means that your body chemistry is responding to life's challenges in the best way it knows how at the moment.

Depression feels like you want to pull in all your Life-Force energies into a small ball deep inside where you are alone and untouchable. The danger in depression is that you stop valuing your life and being your own proactive advocate. You may tolerate far less than ideal situations, give up, get complacent, or fail to take critical action. You are handicapped and ineffective.

There is a wakeup call in depression for you to take action to manage your Life-Force. This is part of Heroining-Up. The shift is in catalyzing your energy from being latent to being productive. This can involve a process. The key to depression is not banishment but management.

Here are a few helpful ways to safely address depression. We call this the **Blues to Blue Skies Practice***. Here are the steps we suggest:

Blues to Blue Skies Practice*

1. Be aware when depression is arising.
2. Give it temporary space for it to reveal its wisdom. Ask "what is there to be learned"?
3. Give yourself what you need. A day in bed is a blessing. But don't stay there.
4. Share your feelings with a trusted companion or support professional.
5. Optimize your biochemistry: follow optimal nutrition and a customized supplement program.
6. Exercise to release endorphins.
7. Generate Oxytocin — the feel-good hormone — by petting an animal, receiving a hug that lasts at least 7 seconds, laughing, taking a walk, and taking deep breaths.
8. Meditate while listening to uplifting music.
9. Enjoy reading an inspiring book, especially by a real-life Heroine or Hero.
10. Acknowledge what is good. Write in your Journal about all that you have to be grateful for (even if you don't feel so grateful at the moment).

The Blues to Blue Skies Practice is not a substitute for medical and psychological treatment.

Even if you engage pharmaceutical support, you can still benefit from the above practice to optimize your Well-Being.

Most all women experience some form of depression at some point in their lives. There is no need to suffer in silence. The opportunity is to manage your occasional or even chronic depression so that you can reboot your Life-Force and build Stability.

You chose not to be a victim — but a Heroine.

Do you experience Suicidal Ideation?

A natural temporary condition on The Heroine's Journey in the 'Crisis Step' is the condition of losing Hope. Sometimes, loss of Hope brings with it feelings of suicidal ideation.

There is no shame in this — it's your whole body crying for help. The thing is that you need help from others because you're having trouble helping yourself.

When this happens to you, it is probably not a conversation you would likely share with others. We hide in the dark corner of our private thoughts. But yet, so many women have experienced these thoughts at some point in their lives. Suicide claims more lives than car crashes and all other accidents combined, yet we keep it so quiet.

You are not alone; most of us have had these passing thoughts. You must reach out. There is someone to tell.

We need to have this conversation so we can address protecting ourselves – Safety.

Suicide is an 'opt-out' plan. It is 'crashing on the rocks below' rather than choosing to put your wings on and fly. Suicide is the worst option. We need a better plan — and that's The Heroine's Journey. On the Journey when you see new horizons and new opportunities, life takes on new meaning and enjoyment. Your motivation will grow, and you will continue to climb to blue skies.

I'm going to tell you here that I have met so many many women who have expressed to me these feelings and their concern for their lives. I can tell you too that reaching out saved each one of those who expressed this deep concern to me. I can also tell you they have told me that they so so so would not have wanted to have missed the joys, happiness, accomplishments and loving times that followed when they moved on to become the Heroines of their own lives.

And they had to fight through to become the women that I proudly call Heroines today. This is your way too.

It takes reaching out, and finding out that this is not uncommon — when we go through what can be extreme trials and tribulations on the Journey; you are truly not alone here, there is no shame in finding yourself with these feelings, and within your reach are many many women who acknowledge needing to guard themselves with self-preservation. Many do get professional help, and many found groups of women that supported them — this can put a rudder under your ship — and then you get a broader perspective that can balance your thinking. I couldn't have done the hard parts on my Journey alone. Isolation only hampered me.

And with progress these ill-sought feelings do go away. There is more you to come.

There is more life. More joy. More contentment. Circumstances are usually temporary. The Path is to become the Heroine of your own life — so let's get on with laying that all out before you!

We do the work of The Heroine's Journey, but it is also no substitute for medical treatment. If you experience suicidal thoughts, it is imperative to get professional support. You must have qualified guides that can help you navigate this phase for your Safety.

It's out of our commitment to you and your Well-Being that we have created this very personal and revealing work so that we can be an inspiration to you to reach out for love and support wisely. You are a beautiful creation, fully 'approved' when you came roaring down the birth canal, with many gifts and skills — and we support you in Heroining-Up for your Best-Self to reveal itself for you to bring your impact for all of the world to see.

There's The Dark Night of The Soul…

Life is not for the faint of heart, that's for sure. It can take some very devastating dips. At that time, you just have to hold on and keep truckin'…

Part of the process is to go through conditions that plague you as best you can — sometimes not even knowing where to step next. Sometimes, it doesn't look graceful … I've been through this myself, as have Heroine women who have forged their way forward before us.

Hope is vital on this Journey because it represents the light ahead you are navigating toward. When you lose Hope it is as if the light has gone out. This is what St. John of the Cross called 'the dark night of the soul.' You do not know where you are or where you are headed. Nothing makes sense. There is no foothold. The only way out is through. One foot in front of the other. Just keep moving. Move through the darkness.

I love how Winston Churchill sums it up,

> "If you're going through hell, keep going."
>
> ~Winston Churchill

You cannot see the possibilities ahead, but there are possibilities greater than you can imagine in your future. Surrender to the forces of the Universe and have faith. Eventually, you will find the light again.

Somehow, you are lifted off the cliff by Grace - from total darkness into light. This is a natural transformation process from your old, limited self into a new, more expanded version of you. We all go through the darkness in the becoming of Heroines.

Let's consider this in our open and heartfelt conversation here.

There's Value of Life Trauma …

Many of us experience what I call 'Value of Life Trauma.' Something happened in our early development that caused us to believe we were unworthy to be alive.

In my own Story, when I was 32 years old, I was talking with my Mother and a group of her friends as we stood circled around at a cocktail party. I have such a 'frozen' picture of this moment in the lovely, well-appointed living room of my Mother's friend's house. My Mother looked at the woman next to me and said, "If I could have, I would have had an abortion." It was like getting punched hard right in the middle of my gut. My Mother actually said that? I watched the faces of my Mother's friends who were encircling our conversation drop like stones. Had she been drinking too much, did she really not realize what she'd just said? I was her daughter standing right next to her with her friends, witnessing her words. I could feel the sudden air that went out of the space as our chins fell forward. It was a traumatic moment for me.

My Mother's best friend apologized to me for what she'd seen the next day; she was well aware that it had crushed my spirit. I knew that my Mother was being truthful for herself — she just was blind to its impact on me. I could give my Mother grace — but the problem was that I carried this incident forward with me as something that I tucked away into my subconscious. And it had an effect on me that bubbled up in the ways that I came to think about myself later on.

Later, I came to realize that I experienced a not so subtle feeling often — that gave me the message that I was unworthy to be here on this planet. And as it reoccurred, I had an underlying repetitive feeling of desiring a way out.

I had to recognize this imposition and handicap to my Life-Force energy — and be responsible for clearing and changing it too — so that it was no longer a Belief that I harbored.

While I have been on my own Heroine's Journey, I have come to understand something very important. The Journey is truly about claiming and growing your own Self-Worth — blossoming it Big. To do this, it is vital to transform the Value of Life Trauma where you may have harbored feelings of worthlessness, unworthiness, criticisms, and failures — to embrace your unique gifts and be fully alive. This is the life that you get — you came roaring down the birth canal, fully approved from creation — no person or circumstance gets in the way. Nope, it's your life; full, complete and yours to live.

While you are here — nothing is useful to stop you from being fully alive — from fully claiming your Self-Worth. Not even something your Mother or Father or another important person in your life says or does (that temporarily hurts) — it is just not justified in derailing that you are perfectly made and are here to function and blossom to your fullest, vibrant, capable, loving Best-Self!

That's what a Heroine chooses. Remember, it is a choice. You get to power your progress. As I dealt with this, I said to myself often: "I am a child of God." You are a child of Creation. I was delivered from infinite possibility. That's a responsibility. A Heroine is deeply committed to her Self-Worth because she knows it's her birthright. That's non-negotiable. No one can take that away (and a Heroine is very careful not to give away any stake in her Self-Worth) under her watch! She guards it very carefully.

Each one of us has a purpose in being here on this planet. However, feelings of unworthiness can shroud your gifts. The Heroine's Journey is the process you go through to expose, first to yourself and then to the world, your unique purpose for being here.

Even so, your Value of Life Trauma is likely to rear its head on occasion, especially the challenging ones. So here is a practice I recommend to free yourself so that you can embrace the deep value that is your own enlivened soul.

I call this the **Value of Life Practice,** and it goes like this:

The Value of Life Practice*

1. **Notice the Black Cloud**. A thought arises that makes you feel worthless. You might feel a physical heaviness. Do you start telling yourself negative stories? Why am I even here? Nobody wants me.
2. **Re-write the thought.** Ask yourself, "Is this thought absolutely true?" Or is it just an overwhelming feeling? Can you re-write this thought or story to something that shines you in a better light? It doesn't have to be butterflies and rainbows; it just has to contain a ray of Hope.
3. **Recognize you are a contribution.** How do you already share your gifts with others?

4. **Bolster your Self-Worth.** Acknowledge your positive impact on the world.
5. **Stay connected in love.** Reach out to someone who celebrates you so you can feel love.
6. **Claim your freedom.** Put your past behind you. Those old stories are no longer valid. Your Heroine's Journey is the new narrative you are writing.

The Value of Life Practice is not a substitute for medical and psychological treatment.

Yahoo, you made it through this Chapter! You have to talk about and help your Sisters through this too. Claim your Safety first!

This Chapter aims to show you that these challenging topics are essential to address if you are going to Create Your Stability and sustain yourself on The Heroine's Journey.

Even if you are confronting any one of these conditions at this very moment, they do not have dominion over you.

Each time, the challenges bring lessons to inspire your Strength and Courage. Although humbling, as you free yourself from them, you reveal a Path for your future that you may not have otherwise seen. Even though Safety challenges can later be seen as gifts, they show you clearly where you need to draw new boundaries, proclaim the value of your own life, and make radical changes.

Protect your Self-Worth!…, your most valuable treasure…get your Fierce Feminine on it!

PS…take a look around and note the women in your life and how they struggle with, are recognizing, dealing with, and exposing these issues in their lives. Can you be compassionate and reach out? They need you in our circle of Sisterhood. First is your Safety… then others. I did this and had a deep conversation with my Japanese friend, Aya.

Our conversation unveiled her confinement in physical abuse. She told me how if she got home later than her husband's imposed curfew, that he would open the door just a crack and make her get down on her knees in humiliation to bow and apologize to him. I am so proud of her.

She got Heroine. She's a remarkable woman who has written five books and been acclaimed. She removed the interference that was impacting her Self-Worth. She told me that our conversation really helped her thinking. She got divorced, and she was happy to tell me recently about finding someone who has the capability to safely regard her Self-Worth.

Have conversations with women friends that brooch the topics we've discussed in this Chapter, suggest this Book — and further their gifts and joy for them to see the importance of the Fierce Feminine protecting their Self-Worth.

This is the moment to get radically honest with yourself. Are you enhancing your Safety? Are you actively advocating for your Safety? Tell your Journal.

Next, let's look at some tools to support you in Creating Stability throughout your Physical life.

BOLSTER YOUR LIFE-FORCE

Just like in the movie 'The Wizard of Oz' – I love that one! While we all acquired resources of intelligence, heart, and Courage on the Path – Dorothy and her crew were still faced with the Physical dangers of the tornado, being in an unknown land, the wicked witch, the attacking flying monkeys, the poppy fields, and more.

The yellow brick road of life has obstacles. Dorothy, the Tin Man, The Lion, and The Scarecrow — they picked each other up and went on.

This is the story of all of our lives as we navigate the things that jump out and scare us. While the movie showed us a childhood fantasy, it was real life depicted with a message.

Keep going — your Life-Force will take you home. The message of the movie and the wisdom for our own Journey is to keep moving down the yellow brick road with heart, mind, and Courage.

To ensure you keep moving, you'll need a plan, and that's where we are headed.

You've done a lot of exploration about amping up your Life-Force. For your success to be long-lasting and sustainable, have a plan. We're ready to establish a 3-part process for taking Physical action consistently.

Let's get to it …

Let's design your Life-Force Commitment Statement.

Are you going to show up half-assed to your life, or are you going to draw your line in the sand and claim your Life-Force and Create Your Stability? This is what it comes down to. It's a choice and a commitment you make to yourself.

Once you claim your Life-Force, you will be Fierce Feminine in your commitment to it, no matter what circumstances show up in your life. Life-Force is what allows the Phoenix to rise from the ashes, putting your wings on to fly.

Having a Life-Force Commitment Statement is your rally cry and will help you stay the course.

Here is an example of my Life-Force Commitment Statement:

> *My Life-Force is an incredible gift that was Divinely given to me. It strengthens me to be the Fierce Feminine Force that creates my wonderful life. I actively cultivate my Physical energy and attend to my Physical space to ensure it enhances my flow of energy. Each day, I use my Life-Force-enhancing tools so that I have the power to be my Best-Self.*

This Statement is what I tap into when I feel that I am neglecting some Physical aspect of myself or my environment. It reminds me to get moving, even when I have resistance. Cultivating my Life-Force is a conscientious practice that requires attentiveness and dedication.

How would you write your Life-Force Commitment Statement? You can even copy mine! Add it to your Journal.

What specific changes do you need to make now to enhance your Life-Force Energy?

With your Journal and pen in hand, sit in a comfortable place. Grab a cup of tea if that sounds soothing. Here's a funny thing: I even like to put a single rose in a vase in front of me to remind me of the vibrant color, unfolding, and mystery of the rose's beauty — while I plan.

Take some time to document specific changes you will make to remove things currently holding up your Life-Force energies.

For me, it was very apparent when I first did this planning. I quickly identified five things that needed to be removed or greatly curtailed if I was going to honor my Life-Force. These were:

1. *Protect myself from a physically abusive relationship*
2. *Stop staying up too late and being ineffective the next day*
3. *Eliminate sugary foods as the basis of my diet*
4. *Plan to sell my big house that I could no longer afford*
5. *Soothe my anxiety response to the changes and unknown places my life was going*

While some big things were on the list, it gave me a plan to address each one. These were key to me making progress. The divorce had thrown me into a spin, but these five things were a basis for direction. They sent me moving forward. My Life-Force got stronger, and I began reshaping my life.

What's holding you up may be more dramatic or less dramatic than mine. They may take more or less time to blow through. The point is that these things are in *your* way, and releasing them will give you the freedom to build your Life-Force and new life.

Wow! This is a lot — you've covered a lot in this Chapter. It deserves some recapping.

In this Chapter - **Nurture Your Physical Well-Being from the Inside and Outside** - you have learned a number of tools to enhance your Life-Force. They include:

- The 5-Part Process to Optimize Your Living Space
- The 7 Simple Superchargers
- Stress Storm Relief Practice
- Blues to Blue Skies Practice
- The Value of Life Practice

Suggestion … for any of these practices to benefit you, make them accessible when you need them. One or all of them may be just what you need and can come to your aid, soothing your spirit. I suggest posting them somewhere where you have quick access to help yourself.

I had big stuff to deal with when I worked through this process. And I needed guidance to keep me moving. The divorce and more that I was going through at the time required some tactical approaches, so I moved from survival to thrival. I was in the narrows of my life on my Heroine's Journey.

So, I sat down with my Journal, pen, and beautiful blossoming rose and wrote a Physical Action Plan. It was all the things that promoted my Life-Force energies. Where you are in your Heroine's Journey may be more or less of a drama than where I was when I sat down with paper and pen. I was in a world of hurt. And it was the way through.

Here is what **My Physical Action Plan** looked like:

1. Pick a good therapist and go once a week *to* expose my unconscious harboring of Value of Life Trauma and acknowledge the work of owning my own life.
2. Leave my physically abusive husband immediately and file a protective order.
3. Sell my big house and invest the capital for living expenses in the interim.
4. Move into a smaller investment property that I previously used as rental income. Make it feel like home with new bedding and candles.
5. Throw away all the sugary foods from my pantry and do a cleanse week.
6. Take yoga classes at least three times a week at the Breathe Studio.
7. Go to bed by 10 pm every night of the week.
8. Attend the 'Transitions' support group at church on Wednesday evenings with others who were going through big stuff too and learning.

9. Have at least three garage sales to sell excess stuff, including clothes and furniture.
10. Carve out 3 hours per week to go to my happy place — the beach.

Some of the criteria that you may want to consider including in your Physical Action Plan are:

1. Resources
2. Support
3. Time required
4. Safety measures
5. Actions steps that will accomplish the Specific Changes you listed above
6. Deadline by which a task will be completed

Now it's your turn. With your Journal, pen, and more — what's your Physical Action Plan? Give it a place in your Journal.

Then, review it daily. As your brain reads it each day, you'll be moved with progress, and enlightened with options. Ask friends and family to help you with accountability.

And here's the fun part — a checkmark next to the items you complete. If it feels overwhelming to accomplish so much so quickly, make it a game to check things off each week. Your Physical Action Plan should not be an added stressor. It is a way of organizing all the loose stressors into a doable plan so you can feel the freedom of massive accomplishment that recharges your Life-Force.

This is what I did, and it works!!! I know it will work for you, too.

Wow, lets both breathe. That was a lot to get through. The Challenge Step of The Heroine's Journey can be challenging — and it calls you to Heroine-Up!

I want to take a moment and acknowledge you for two beautiful accomplishments.

First, for your Courage in bearing witness to all the "attacking flying monkeys, and the wicked witch, and the poppy fields" that can jump out at you on your Path of life and handling them like a Heroine!

And second, the Strength you show in declaring where you need to protect yourself and bolster your Life-Force energy. You're demonstrating that you are truly on The Heroine's Journey by completing this part of our discussion.

Next, we'll go on to the third Cornerstone to Create Your Stability – People! This one was my Achilles' heel, and it has some very fun parts! Journey Onward!

Free Resources:

And yet again:

Go *now* to —
www.HeroinesBook.com/Free-Resources

You'll find …the 'Safety Self Assessment' and 'The 5 Simple Super Chargers' for you to download and inspire you onward!

5

Cornerstone 3: People

The Importance of People

People Picker Metrics

Drive Carefully

The Sticker System

Circle of Love

THE IMPORTANCE OF YOUR PEOPLE

*W*ho taught you about People? How do you pick them in your life? Their importance? Well, listen in …

Heroine, to put your wings on and fly — here's a *must*: You *must* carefully *choose* the People in your life so that you are in relationships where you are supported and loved.

It's an old myth that *you* can go it alone. The truth is my Sister, hearts that collaborate make more magic happen. As a Heroine, you foster connections that are enriching!

Life is juicier and more productive when you gather the People into your life that lift you up and cheer your flight. How do you do this? That's our discussion in this Chapter, and we will explore ways to align with good souls. When your connections are heartfelt, and you see

People for who they are, even when a Challenge comes up, you'll be surrounded by People who guide, nurture, and promote your Journey.

This was a very significant change that I made along my Path, and I can assure you that it was a change that shifted my life into happiness and joy. Honestly, it transformed life from painful to sensational for me. Most importantly, this shift is fundamental to Create Your Stability. Yep, for *you* too!

On the Heroine's Journey, unexpected People show up to aid your progress and offer help. It can be a surprise when they show up; and a gift they did at just the right moment. You'll want to watch out for this!

Remember Step #6 on The Heroine's Journey, Angels Show Up? Here is how we say it:

Step 6: Angles Show Up

Your support system arrives

Here come the Angels, those who arrive to support you and steady your wings on your back. As your Journey progresses, People you never expected come to help as if a universal energy called them to your aid. You thought you were alone on the Path, but now you welcome their help. You can discern who supports and guides you, and you move away from People who impair you. Your Angels have a new perspective on your Journey. They provide critical support and pieces of the solution. You are ready to receive humbly. You are self-revealing. You accept your humanness. Your Angels are there to encourage your flight and give you confidence. They believe in you. There is Hope.

When these angel People announce themselves in your life, you'll awaken to the realization that there are just some People who show up and help make your life better. On the flip side, those Crises and Challenges in your life serve as a 'heads up' that there will be People who need a 'boot' right out of your life!

Discerning People is a must-have skill!

Here's a story: My Angel Showed Up

Here's my Story about the wake-up call and the importance of picking my People and having connections with loving, supportive humans.

Just after my divorce hit, I was losing my house, my office building, my income, my business, and my sense of Self-Worth. Let's just say it was terrible. It was a total annihilation that was unexpected and extremely painful. I was taking a nose dive into the rocks below, desperate to escape my circumstances. These were the times for loving support.

When I was on my knees and asked for compassion, the first friend I went to promptly informed me, "Your problems are too big; don't count on me." I felt that brutal comment, and I was rocked to my core. My head fogged, and my hearing dulled. I felt the stab in my gut by those who recognized my pain but declined to help. It was awful on top of all that had happened.

The gift was that I got a new lesson. I quickly realized that I had not consciously cultivated People in my life who see me as a human being and are willing to be there for me in the ups — and the downs. I had cultivated People who were happy to use me in the good times and throw me under the bus in the bad times. Yikes! Now, when I needed some help, it felt like there was no one.

But my Heroine's Journey was underway ... and Angels Show Up! Unexpectedly open-hearted People can come to your aid during this Step. And an angel showed up for me.

I didn't know Rob when the tsunami hit. I was at church one Sunday when I saw him walk down the steps. My inner voice nudged me: "You need to know him." I argued with that voice, then finally surrendered and walked toward him. He barely noticed me. I was embarrassed, so I tucked my tail and walked away. "No!"... shrieked my inner voice. "You need to know him now!" it proclaimed again, louder and more forceful this time. "Get going!" ... "Ok, Ok!" I retorted to that persistent voice nagging me.

This time, I took a strategic walk around the coffee buffet table and he actually had to move to get out of my way. This got his attention, and he was beckoned into conversation with me. With a few opening lines, somehow, I quickly learned that he had an Aussie Shepherd dog. Me too. I have a Toy Aussie (the cutest thing in the world), and instantly, we had a connection. My little Jassey was a smaller version of his bigger dog.

The next week, he left me a sign at my office door, 'Wanna play?' it said. I couldn't play. I couldn't get myself out of the fog and even imagine playing because I was wavering, uncertain, and doubting myself.

I mustered up the Courage to share the truth with my new friend. This was the moment that was the turning point in my life. It was hard for me. I shared with Rob, "My life isn't what it looks like from the outside. There are big problems here." That was a vulnerable admission, but I needed to say it.

He saw my lovely house, me at work in my palatial office, and the illusion of 'having it all together' that I had projected. While I had always looked the part of grandeur in the past, in this moment, I took a risk to reveal the real me — my truth. I was hurt and wounded and had no clue how I was going to fix it all. I was in a big mess.

What I instantly loved was that my confession didn't frighten him. He stayed with me, and in fact, it awakened his compassion. He was a good soul and pitched in to help me from that moment on.

Rob showed up regularly and at just the right time. As he came to understand the situation and how paralyzed I was. He stepped in, and he literally gave me a list each day of what to do. It was way too hurtful for me to think down the road. I could just barely take the steps of the day. He assured me that I didn't need to look too far ahead. I just needed to do what was in front of me at the moment. I felt comforted and assured by his presence.

One day, Rob said, "You have to move *now*." That was a real jolt, and I felt myself freeze.

I had owned my house for twenty-five years. I couldn't bear the thought of change. Later, when Rob arrived to help me pack up everything I owned, he found me sitting cross-legged on the living room floor looking through stacks of old pictures. I was in fantasyland, traveling down memory lane. He was living in reality and there to help me get packed. He was the helpful spirit I needed. He literally picked me up off the floor and got me moving. Day by day, he inspired me to take action. Left on my own, I was headed for the rocks in a head-first fall.

I came to know Rob as a true friend. He has a heart. He helped me when I couldn't help myself, and I am forever grateful for that. He showed up for me in my worst moments and was there to steward me to better ones. He's definitely an angel in my life, still to this day. I hope he gets a gold star when he arrives in heaven. Indeed, he'll be celebrated for his goodness.

He was an Angel who arrived when I least expected it and stewarded me on my Journey.

Watch out for your Angels to appear when you least expect them!

Have you presented an image — instead of the real you?

My Story has another nugget of truth to glean from it, too. I shared my confession with you that I projected an illusion of grandeur for years even though I felt impoverished on the inside. This was the system that I grew up in, and many of us have experienced this.

Here's the rub. Our culture (and sometimes our family of origin) teaches us to be valued by our external assets: our bikini body, job title, financial worth, or our children's accomplishments. I was trying to be likable by projecting outward success. When the outward success went away, what was left?

The devastation I had experienced had the potential to make me feel worthless. Seeing myself as 'worthless' was a sure path to the rocks below. I needed support to stay in tune with my *Self-Worth*.

Creating Stability is not about the way things look. If you are playing that game and the focus is on your image, you will end up lonely and drawing the wrong People to you. Like I had to do, you have to get real and get vulnerable. This is how the 'right' People can see and love you. The right People know and reinforce your value.

The real you has to be revealed for the heartfelt connections you need to flourish.

The shift is understanding that the heart connections sustain us and serve you to Create Your Stability. This is the way of The Heroine's Journey. When the going gets tough, you know who your friends truly are.

These People are not judging you. They are supporting you. These are the relationships of true friendship, ones that we will learn new ways of identifying and cultivating in this Chapter. Yay, these are your 'peeps.' These are the People you are attuned to and who resonate with you. With these People, your life will sing!

What is it that makes People so important?

When you Create Your Stability, People are especially important. They either build you up or tear you down. It really is that black and white. That's why it's a vital skill to be able to discern the People in your life and the impact they are making on your life and in your world.

Your Heroine's Path is to honor yourself by actively surrounding yourself with People that will lift you up and help you on your Journey. It may start with a blessing, like one Angel showing up for you in a moment of despair, and then it grows. Your Self-Worth can blossom this way ...

The Heroine is all about growing this emotional impact that radiates outward from her being. She has a sense of her value and wants to be around People who value her. She knows that this forms the circle of energy that engages her to give to others and have others give to her.

We call this your Circle of Love, and you will see how to develop this for yourself as we cover this concept in this Chapter. It's one of my favorite things! And it's so big to do that I am conscious of putting it into practice every day.

First, we are going to have fun with a few key tools and processes to help you improve your *People-Picker*. You'll love this.

PEOPLE-PICKER METRICS

Get set to meet your People! This is going to bloom your happiness, connectedness, and adventure. It is also essential to create Stability.

Let's talk about how you arrive at where you love *all* the People around you. Why shouldn't you? This is your life. You need to feel inspired and energized to bloom to your Best-Self.

Loving the People around you is fundamental to your Stability *and* loving your life. Imagine waking up in the morning knowing that the People in your day will bring you delight and encouragement. These are the People who will take you to new insights, new opportunities, and new ways of seeing yourself. The Heroine walks through life arm in arm with her Peeps. This is the way of The Heroine's Journey.

In this Chapter, I'm going to give you a fun system for ensuring that you pick the right Peeps for your Journey. That's a teaser because you will enjoy this fun, easy, and accessible tool you can use daily. Who taught you to pick people, anyway? This will!

First, though, let's build the foundation for people-picking by talking about what role *you* have been playing in your relationships. Have you been letting whoever shows up come into your life without discernment? Do you have an open-door policy? I did for a long time.

What I learned about myself was that I had a broken People-Picker! Once that changed, my life changed.

Let's take a sharp look at what is bouncing back at you from the People who are populating your life.

There are 3 People Metrics to Discover.

While you are in the Stability phase of your Journey you cannot afford *anyone* who undermines you in *any* way. Please read that again.

That's because, during Stability building, you are learning to energize your mind and your spirit with your sense of Self-Worth. It's up to you to see that no one is messing with your life. While that may be easier said than done, you gotta arrange this gift for yourself in your life.

I'll give you the tools to figure it out along the way, and pretty soon, you'll be saying: "Yes! My freedom flourishes when I feel good about myself. How can I get there faster?"

Here's the deal. Even though some of us were encouraged to be the 'nice girl,' that perspective handicaps us. To best feel good about yourself, you don't have to like everyone or extend yourself to everyone. You can choose to use 'People discernment.' Your Stability includes the freedom to decide who you stand next to or not — you can actively choose.

That is a new concept for some of us!

It can be a bit tricky to actively choose the best People for you. How do you gather useful information and use it to make good People-Picking choices?

I'm glad you asked. I use three quick metrics to assess People when considering bringing them into my life. Make notes so that you can actively use them, too.

1. FACES

The first one, I remember as 'FACES': F-A-C-E-S. It's an acronym for some quick questions I ask myself about the Person I'm meeting. Here's how it goes:

Feedback: Do they have the flexibility to receive *Feedback*?

Attitude: Do they convey a positive *Attitude*?

Connection: Are they available for open-hearted *Connection*?

Energy: Do they radiate good *Energy*?

Skills: Do they offer helpful *Skills*?

It's Feedback, Attitude, Connection, Energy and Skills. If they show these qualities, it's a good indication that these are safe People, and you get to have fun exploring where it goes with them.

2. Red Flags

Here's the second metric. It's to keep your antenna up to see if there are any 'red flags.' You know when they are there. They *will* present themselves. Oops, I've seen and ignored them and gotten myself into trouble! Truth be told, *You* have to be willing to see them. A Heroine advocates for herself, and red flags can't be missed to stay on the Journey.

That red flag is sometimes a small voice you hear inside that is really trying to help you prevent going down the wrong road. It's your protector. It is an awareness, not a judgment. It can steer you in the right direction and save you from trouble. Heads up that you acknowledge them!

Once you are aware of the 'red flags,' you can make a wise choice, which may mean going in the opposite direction! If you heed the 'red flag' now, it means you won't have to wave a 'white flag' later in surrender, admitting to yourself that you made a horrible People-Picker blunder.

3. Stability Test

Now, you can go a little deeper with the third metric. You mentally run the Person you see through the Stability model, the same one you are learning for yourself here in this Book. You want Peeps in your life who also demonstrate Stability in their lives. Here, you note if they have the four Cornerstones of Stability in place. Check out these:

Beliefs: Do they have healthy Beliefs about themselves and the world?

Physical: Do they take care of their Physical Well-Being inwardly and outwardly?

People: Do they have good, supportive People in their lives?

Financial: Are they Financially capable and responsible?

If the Person you are meeting has built Stability, they are safe for you to partner with in business, friendship, or relationship. When you create relationships with Stable People, there is a better chance that they won't bring problems into your life.

This is so important because you don't want your relationships to undermine the Stability you are currently creating for your life. Stable People can even contribute gifts toward *your* Stability. This is a really great thing!

A Story About The 'Questions on One Hand'

One of my Heroine Sisters told me this story about her people - picking
- choice.

"I want to share a story of how, in the past, I *used to* determine who I
brought into my world. Although I find it a bit embarrassing now, I tell
this Story to admit that it didn't work well. This was long before I was
on my Journey of Stability.

I guess you could say that back then, I made choices based on what
I learned as I grew up. In my world, I learned it was all about setting
up appearances and what other People would think about me. I unconsciously created a methodology for choosing the People in my life who
always seemed to land me in a mess.

One of my early significant love relationships, one in which I
committed and invested a lot of my life, didn't work for me at all, yet
I pigeon-holed myself into it. On the outside, it looked so perfect,
but on the inside, I was so unfulfilled. That's because, when I got to
the heart of it, he was probably gay. Fundamentally, this caused me
to go in the wrong direction. I'd missed acknowledging that when I
chose him.

So, how did she get into this dilemma? Well, it went like this she said:

I asked all the questions on the one hand:

> Does he have a good job? Is he well-educated? Is he good-looking?
> Does he have good parents? Is he successful? I asked the right ques-
> tions from My head about all of the *external* things.

But I missed all the questions on the other hand:

> Does he love ME? Does he listen to ME? Does he speak kindly about
> me to others? Does he support me in my best interest? Does he fulfill
> what I need?
>
> I forgot to ask the internal questions from my heart about how
> he makes me feel. These are the ones that are juicy and life-giving."

She was right — the questions on both hands are *equally* important to create Stability. She fell on one side of the scale, and was only asking the outward questions. She needed to balance that scale by asking the questions, on the other hand, real questions about 'how-am-I-feeling-internally?'…essential!

She went on to say: "I grew terribly unhappy because I had my head in the sand, ignoring what I needed in a relationship. Then life forced me to ask the questions, on the other hand. Now, I realized I was missing the things that would fulfill my heart. I ended up leaving that relationship and moving on."

Her Story is about a man in her life. The same questions apply to a business partner or anyone that you plan to depend upon and create positive results with, for the short-term or long-term.

Once she practiced asking the questions on both hands, her Heroine's Journey grew bigger and better with juicy, yummy People who warmed up her life!

Making sure you ask the questions on both hands is well self worth it!!

DRIVE CAREFULLY

Now, on The Heroine's Journey, you are called to value yourself and consciously choose the People you let into your life. You may have been letting everybody into your life in the past, but now you are being selective for good reason.

This may be a significant shift in your consciousness. Congratulations if it is! This will greatly affect the quality of your Journey each Step of the way.

Let's consider some pretty deep subconscious programming that often has us bringing the wrong People into our lives. Once we are aware of and address it, it's possible to clear the slate for healthy and rewarding relationships.

Here's a delicate question. When you are pondering a relationship, have you noticed that you are considering what that other Person can do and be for you? But do you also consider what you expect to do and be for them? Fast forward, when a relationship is set up only according to what *they* can do for you, that's when the partnership can end badly.

Two deeply seated unconscious drives often control the destiny of our relationships and their effect on our Self-Worth and Stability. We are going to unveil them in this Chapter: the 'Projection Drive' and the 'Bandwagon Drive.' Once we bring them fully into our awareness, we have the ability to steer clear of this programming consciously.

The Heroine is on the road to her ultimate destination on the Journey, her own True Wealth and True Self. She is careful not to get derailed by driving in the wrong direction. She has the map and follows it to get where she is going while navigating roadblocks. And let's face it, my Sisters, the wrong relationship dynamics can certainly create a hazard on the road. It is up to us to navigate our own way.

Hang with me, and let your awesome self consider how this works.

Have you noticed what happens when your head is in control?

If you are a person who wants to do well, then chances are that you've created a vision in your mind for what doing well looks like. We create a picture of a future the way *we* see it, with the notion that it will be designed to keep us safe and comfortable. Until you are awake, you go about trying to execute that vision with your head taking the driver's seat. This is where the problem arises.

We have reason to protect the vision that we've created. Then, we invite others to come into *our* picture. With this type of head-thinking, rather than heart-being, you will become susceptible to the types of People that fit your vision but not your highest good. These People fit the criteria for how life should look, but they may not commit to the truest parts of *you*.

The first Caution Sign: the 'Projection Drive'.

It's true — you, me, we are all trying to get what we need and want as part of engineering our worlds. This often includes not thinking of what we need to give. This is called the Projection Drive. We have a strong unconscious impulse to project our wants and needs onto someone else, hoping they will fulfill them.

When we do this, we fall into the pothole of seeing other People in a light other than who they truly are. Why? Because we want our own wishes and needs to be fulfilled quickly. This becomes 'blinders' to really seeing someone else.

You can feel this projection problem. It's when the Energy is not going around in a give-and-take way. You get frustrated because sometimes you want something from someone else, but they are not giving it. When there is not a good heart connection, they may even withhold.

How do we unconsciously run over others with our Projection Drive? It might include putting pressure on someone to bend them to your wants. Trying to cajole them into the way *you* think things should be. You might find yourself getting angry, using that Energy to get what you want. Guilt and blame are also rotten approaches to use. Have you found yourself in these kinds of situations or been the target of this? I know I have.

When Projection occurs, one Person wants a short-term outcome that meets an immediate need. The classic one is: "I need to be married because I should be by this age, and you're the one that fits the bill." It causes us to jump in too fast to meet an impending need. In this fashion, you can be going for too much too soon without determining who the other Person truly is. The drive is steering you in the wrong direction.

When you are projecting, you don't ask the necessary questions because, ironically, you don't really want to know. You don't want to see clearly. You just want them to be what you need. The Projection Drive is an unspoken agreement not to live the truth. This becomes a detour on the Path that gets you hopelessly lost.

The bottom line for our conversation here is to start asking the right questions and be willing to hear the answers honestly. Take a moment to notice when what you are trying to project may not work for someone else. Conversely, the vision or life design someone is trying to project onto you may not work for you. When you are aware, you can steer clear!

The second Caution Sign: The 'Bandwagon Drive'.

There is a flip side to Projection, which is jumping onto the Bandwagon. Both types of drives are ways, in the short term, to opt out of managing *your own life*. And, oops ... eventually, they mess with your sanity and become hazards on your Path. True true!

The Bandwagon Drive is when you gleefully jump into someone else's life in an effort to quickly solve your wants and needs (problems and issues). Or someone else is willing to jump onto the Bandwagon of your vision and is hoping you meet their needs (problems and issues). It's an attempt to magically change the reality of what needs to be handled. It's hoping that another will get you to your destination.

Either way, this means looking for someone else to take over the challenges of making your own life work out well. It is like turning off your own inner GPS and hoping to simply follow the traffic. Well, the traffic isn't going to get you to a better place. You must know your unique destination and navigate with attention. Truth be told: no one else gets us to our own joy, prosperity and freedom — it's an inside job!

Owning Up To Avoid the Hazard Signs.

I call Projection and Bandwagon '*Drives*' because they can be so unconscious that they run our lives covertly and subtly without us even seeing the warning signs. Or we see the signs, but we think if we just speed up, we can outrun the natural laws that govern the progress of our Journey.

But driving headlong into 'Projection' or 'Bandwagon' will not solve your problem. Later down the road, the partnership gets plagued with resentment. Being unconsciously driven never promotes collaboration.

Succumbing to the Projection or the Bandwagon Drive is not the way of the Heroine. We're supposed to navigate our own lives and our partnerships using our own internal GPS. Being towed or towing another along simply burns up too much fuel, and we cannot lift into flight.

If you are finding yourself in this situation now, you may have to make some changes. It's time to untangle yourself. This is where your freedom lies. Really consider what choices to make for your progress.

Eventually, your True Self will long for real expression, and your Heroine's Journey will unfold for you to blossom. Remember, you are going towards your own personal joy, prosperity and freedom — which you personally craft and propel.

You wake up to the Journey when you realize that you are responsible for all that has happened in your life and all that will happen. It's your life, and your choices are what sets it in motion. You are not the victim of your relationships; you are responsible for them because you ultimately had a role in choosing them.

The hard knock truth is that, as an adult, if you draw or tolerate unsupportive, abusive, or irresponsible People into your life, you are as responsible for the outcome as they are. Did you get that?

You get to own it. This is both the fun and the work of life; it's in your hands. No one is going to take you out of handling your life, and you are not there to take anyone out of doing their life. Dropping the Projection and Bandwagon Drives brings you back to a full focus on your life and how to make progress.

After some really hard knocks with People in my life, I took this new approach. I started to own it. I found that this was far easier than getting myself out of yet another messy relationship that steered me way off course. I began to see that partnership is important in life, both personally and professionally, if I want to enjoy the road ahead, and I began to clean up my act!

Now that you are in the driver's seat, wouldn't you like to see how to choose your travel companions better? Would you like to see People more clearly and join forces with those who can help you soar? That's just what a Heroine does.

A Heroine asks the questions.

There is a skill to this. The skill is to lean into the Courage and the Strength to ask the questions that will reveal the information you need on a timely basis. With good information, you can decide what kinds of People to invite into your life that will support your Stability. This is rev up your People-Picker!

Someone gave me a greeting card many years ago that substantially changed my life. I quickly had it framed, and it has been hanging over my desk for the last 20 years to remind me of this big insight.

It was a quote that re-framed how I looked at things. It took my attention off of desperately seeking answers and onto the art and beauty of the questions themselves. Here's how it reads:

"And the point is to live everything. Live the questions now … Be patient toward all that is unresolved in your heart. Try to love the questions themselves …"

~ Renier Maria Rilke

Story of asking the hard questions.

I used to be afraid to ask the hard questions. It had to do with being a child and finding it difficult to ask for what I needed. When the child in me just wants to be 'loved' – I clam up and just go along, not wanting to make any waves.

This tactic got me into trouble. Sometimes, there are just hard questions that need to be asked, but I only got that lesson after experiencing pain.

Twenty years ago, I saw a strange and appealing man go to the bar, and I intuitively knew that he was an alcoholic. I also noticed that he was cute and seemed successful, and I was looking for a cute, successful guy to marry. I ignored my intuition — and projected on him that maybe he was the one. I just wanted to be loved. It was easy to ignore the 'red flag.' I wanted to be on his Bandwagon.

I didn't have the Courage to ask him the hard question straight up, "Do you drink to get drunk?" I married him without ever asking this question that would clearly impact my life. I lived to regret keeping my mouth politely shut. I experienced many painful circumstances with a partner who drank excessively and who became physically and emotionally abusive when he drank. I knew that there were questions that I needed to have asked, but I had avoided them for fear of getting the answers and then having to responsibly deal with them. It would have given me 'red flags' probably — and then that would have messed with my plans in the moment. However, that would have been some short=term pain that I endured, instead of the long-term grievous misery that I engaged in — YIKES!!!

Fast forward past that relationship, and I dated again. This time, I mustered Courage and compassion to squarely ask what I needed to know. "Do you have more than three drinks a week or use mood-altering drugs?" I was honoring myself. I was discerning who was coming into my life and recognizing what they were bringing with them. I got the information that I needed and a green light to proceed, protected by full disclosure. This way my Heroine could carry on being a Heroine — and not get thrown rudely into 'victim'. Much better!

When I used to want all the right answers that fit my head's vision, I never asked the questions. Now that I love the questions, I am willing to ask them. I know it's more important to use my voice to gather the information I need rather than keeping quiet to be liked. No matter what the answers are, I use the information for my highest good. The heart gets taken care of in the process.

I've released Projections and jumped off the Bandwagon. This allows me to navigate relationships that are heart-felt and have longevity and Stability — the Heroine way.

Now, I've surrendered control.

Be willing to give up your head-vision for the moment and get present to what you are actually seeing in another person and how that truly affects you. This can be a painful experience. It bursts your illusions about how you have tried to keep life together in a tidy package.

Now, on The Heroine's Journey, there is a new me. I am respectful of my own inner being. I can let the outer world be as it is, whatever the answers are. I trust that my Journey is going to bring me the right things at the right time. If the answers aren't the right fit for my Journey, I can let go of trying to fit that Person into my life. I don't need to be in control of what's delivered to me. I consciously choose not to project on them or jump on their Bandwagon. It's up to me, and I just get to choose what is truly supportive of my Journey.

THE STICKER SYSTEM

Now I'll reveal my Sticker System, a fun system for identifying safe and loving People that you resonate with. You will see how playful this is and how rewarding it will be to tune up your relationships and People-Picking abilities.

It's really worked for me!..and it's so fun to tell you!

In fact, it's something I've used to shift my thinking dramatically. I invented it because I needed it! And I am sharing it now because you need it, too.

People are the fuel for your flight, and they can raise you up or keep you grounded. No time to waste muddling with People who make your Journey difficult when you have other options. With these skills, you'll be soaring high!

First, let's review what we've learned so far in this Chapter. We've talked about first quickly assessing People according to The 3 People Metrics. Remember them?

1. FACES
2. Red Flags
3. Stability

The tools we just reviewed help you tune into a person's presence. Now, we are going to go a step further with my Sticker System.

It's time to make a clear choice. Which People do you want to embrace in your life? And who needs to be sent packing?!

Let me introduce the Sticker System to you.

The Sticker System is a quick and easy tool for applying the information you have sensed and gathered about a person and then deciding how to move forward with them or not. It is a "truth-telling" that will help you to identify and remember who is readily available for you and who is a distraction.

Play with me here. This is how the Sticker System works.

I walk around with an imaginary pallet of multi-colored stickers in my back pocket. You know, the round colored dots that you can peel off and stick on. The kind you get at the office store.

As I stand in front of a person, I tune into them. After a few moments of interaction, when I get a beat of the quality of our meeting, I decide which imaginary colored sticker to put on their forehead, figuratively. This indicates to me how safe and positive they are for me. This humors me as effectively my People-Picker goes to work and sorts out the quality of People for my life.

And it makes me feel like the power of choice is fully in my hands.

Here's the meaning of the Sticker Colors:

Here's what the colors on my pallet of stickers mean:

Green - means Good Energy. Happy to be here. I see positive things happening in the relationship.

Yellow - Energy is just a little off. Not quite sure why. Good things could still be here for collaboration.

Orange - I've seen you do something stupid at least twice. I'm not feeling safe. Time to Beware.

Let me stop and hold right here!

Red - House is burning. Gotta go. This would require guns, lawyers, or money to sort out a mess that this could cause.

And here's how to relate to the Sticker Colors.

Here's the fun — how you access the colors:

Green — These are your true advocates. They see you for who you are and celebrate the very best in you. They reflect your brilliance and encourage you to live to your highest potential. Keep these People close. If you forget who you are, trust them to remind you.

Yellow — These People can be good resources. They may have a skill or a talent that adds to what you are doing. They appear trustworthy, and you feel a connection with them. You've had an opportunity to see that they are good team players, but you don't necessarily share a vision or deep soul connection with them.

Orange — These People don't help you thrive. You cannot count on them to have your back. Be careful about disclosing information about yourself or your situation. Some of these People might be part of your life in structural ways (like family, employer, or teacher). You'll need to find ways to protect yourself. Limit time, attention, and involvement; they can hurt you inadvertently.

Red — Must get rid of them completely and immediately. They can potentially resort to harmful behaviors. There is no way for you to solve this problem safely. STOP TALKING. You do not respond to texts, emails, or attempts to reach you. You just simply go the other way if they appear, without any contact.

How is it that you know a person's true color?

How do you know? Good question. This is an art form; it's your ability to get nimble with feeling someone's presence and knowing what color they are for you. It's your best guess at the moment. Giving them a color gives you a starting point. And interestingly enough, your first guess is usually a good one, I find.

The colors in the Sticker System fall onto two sides of the fence. Green and Yellow People are essentially People that you can deal with, while Orange and Red People are ones that you cannot deal with because of how they operate with you.

Here's how you sense them:

1. *Green & Yellow People* — They care what you think. When you give them Feedback, it lands, and they will consider what

you have to say. They generally smile. Even in times of trouble, they lean in to understand the situation and are open to resolution. The truth lands on them.

2. ***Red & Orange People*** — Here's the biggest problem: the problem is never theirs! When you give them Feedback, they will defend their ego. They generally frown because they don't want to hear it. They blame, push away, and reject. They are not flexible in understanding your point of view. The truth does not land on them — they reject it.

How the colors give you a Heads Up

After you sticker someone, you immediately know how to relate to them. You don't have to go through the stories in your head to defend your understanding of them. That decision has already been made. This makes navigating relationships far simpler. It saves your energy for flight.

With that said, if a person goes through a growth transformation, there is always room to change their 'sticker color status' after they prove their positive influence. Remember, though; generally, your first intuition will be a good one, and don't give them a second chance too quickly until you can really account for a change in their actions, attitude and behavior.

In the meantime, the process is to consistently treat People according to the color sticker you have given them. You know who they are, and you handle them accordingly.

'Green & Yellow People' are the only ones you can *afford* in your life when you're building Stability because they are the '*good energy*' People. They are safe, and you can disclose your real self to them. It is important to know that this is the only group of People you can go to for support and resources on your Journey. Your People-Picker needs to pick these People.

By contrast, it is important to know that 'Red & Orange People' will drain your Life-Force energy, and when building Stability, you cannot afford for this to happen. They will derail your plans and dreams. These are People who create drama/crisises that suck your energy. We all know these People and regret engaging with them when we look back on how it turned out badly. Don't be surprised when you have identified someone as a 'Red' in your life that things go amuck — or worst yet they bulldoze your life down. No kidding, the Heroine is watchful to protect her Well-Being, because there are 'Reds' out there!

This is a Red Flag Warning for Orange & Reds

"I love this system" you say, "and I see how it works...but wait! How can I practically apply this when I have an 'Orange' or a 'Red' person in my family, my boss at work, or in my church group?" That's a very good question because you are directly faced with these People, and you'll need some tactical help.

There are two distinctions to be made here. There is a difference between 'Orange People' and 'Red People', and this requires further understanding. While an 'Orange person' will cause you pain, they do it as a byproduct of their behavior. In other words, they don't intentionally intend to hurt you, but they do hurt you as a result of who they are and their actions, such as an alcoholic, bipolar conditions, rage, and more. Because you are standing close to them and unprotected, you get the wide swath of abusive behavior that flows out from them. It is not their direct intention to cause you pain. Nevertheless, they do.

'Red People', on the other hand, intend to hurt you. Make no mistake, they can even wish for your demise. They want to disparage you in many ways and actively thwart your progress and cut you down. They will want to hurt your reputation, make you miserable, demean and diminish you, harm your health, steal your money, punish you for how rotten you are, and physically hurt you. These People actually get an energy jolt out of causing you pain, like a spider that wraps its prey tightly to squeeze the life out of it. It is clearly their full intention to devastate you.

So how do you handle having an 'Orange' or a 'Red' person in your life, that maybe you are bound to in some way and preserve yourself? Honestly, there is a high likelihood that these relationships will fall apart. You are not taken care of in both 'Orange & Red' people situations. Remember, to thrive, you must first survive.

I was married to one of these People, a 'Red person.' I experienced alcoholism, physical abuse, mental battering, blame and ridicule, missing money, infidelity, and much more. I wasn't even surviving. As I struggled, relented and gave in to his behaviors, I wasn't familiar with the 'Red' sticker concept — and I spent years in pain and losing my Self-Worth.

Initially, I thought that I could *fix* it. But I couldn't. This Person intended to hurt me. The only question was how long would I struggle through life tolerating the most abject 'Red' behavior? Why was I doing this? Crazy!!

The marriage did break apart, and I finally stickered him with a 'Red Sticker.' In fact, in a rather short time, I was saying to myself that his girlfriend was my 'new best friend' because she had taken him away along with his problems!

One day, I was sitting outside the hairdresser's, and he walked out of the building next door. He came over to try to talk to me. Immediately, I said loudly to myself, "Red Sticker," and denied all contact with him immediately. I had learned the hard way that there was nothing good to come of it. Red Sticker is 'Red Sticker'. I didn't need to debate any form of conversing with him in my mind again. That horse was already out of the barn.

It's necessary to get 'Orange & Red' People at a safe distance from you. The first thing that you do is recognize the conditions of their ongoing behavior by the sticker color that you gave them. You have identified them. Then there is no 'making up stories' that they are something other than what you have determined — you know it. You know an 'Orange and a Red', and they both cause you grief.

Once Stickered, you know the truth, and you live by it! This is the way of the Heroine.

Here's a practice once you have identified 'Oranges and Reds':

- Get as much distance as possible from them physically;
- Know that you know what color they truly are, and don't sugarcoat it;

- Stop talking; they are not willing to accept their part in the problem;
- Protect the vulnerable parts of you, be careful what they know about you;
- Be respectful, but be very aware of the boundaries that you have constructed with them;
- Plan ways that you will thrive apart from them;
- Hold on tightly to your own Self-Worth.

It is very important to know who you are dealing with, and the Sticker System is your tool for doing this. It will wake you up to the quality of relationships that you have with others. It will enlighten you as to where you need to protect yourself, and where you are nurtured. It will keep you from being disappointed because a 'Red' will repeatedly act like a 'Red'. It's true. Soooo, true.

How you deal with an 'Orange or a Red' in your life is ultimately to manage your way away from them. You send them blessings as you distance yourself because you know they are in their own pain with their ill-designed means of behaving. Their life is not rosy and happy, or they wouldn't be treating you this way. They have work to do on themselves before they make good travel companions. Bless them that they find their way too, and take your leave.

And thank your People-Picker that you no longer hang where it's unsupportive of your Journey to Best-Self! You are looking to make your time joyful, fulfilling and happy — and enhance your Life-Force energy with your People associations. This takes discerning who you open the doors to in your life.

This Story is about Herb Barness, a great 'Green' in my life – Mentor, Teacher, Friend.

Years ago, when I was in my 30s, I would join my friend Herb in Philadelphia at the corner table in the restaurant of the Warwick Hotel on Rittenhouse Square. If you were there at the time and happened to walk by, you would no doubt be stopped in your tracks by the man with the bright copper hair.

He was more than a 'friend' in my life; he was stickered 'Green' and one of my life's most wonderful mentors. He would invite me to join him for the whole day, and I would be rapt with attention. I remember saying to him, "Herb, I learn so much just sitting at your knee and listening." He appreciated my thirst to be a student and invited me to join him where I could learn something new and grow my skills when there were good opportunities.

He conducted all-day-long meetings at that restaurant table. One after another, business People would come to see Herb about various things. Herb was politically influential and a stellar businessman and negotiator. I met various People at Herb's 'knee', including US Presidents, Senators, deal makers, major league sports team owners, and other personalities. I dubbed him my 'Jewish Father' as he favorably educated me.

One day, after a long line of visitors, I said to him, "Herb, I just don't understand this! That man who was just here was terrible. His face was frowning, and he said that you were the meanest man. That's impossible; you are the most generous and thoughtful man I know. How is it possible that he could say such a thing?"

Herb paused and looked at me with those teaching eyes that said to me, "now you better listen very carefully here because what I'm about to tell you is so profound, and I will *only* say it once."

I leaned in. I knew there would be a gift of wisdom I didn't want to miss. I didn't know that what he was about to unveil that day would be one of the most important lessons of my life.

Herb said, "That's right. You know me as nice because that is what you are. *I am whatever they are.*"

Whew! That was big!! What Herb revealed to me was that he treated me as a 'Green.' And the man who had accused Herb of meanness was a 'Red', so Herb treated him that way. Herb had the insight not to try to be a 'Green' to a 'Red.'

Herb had quickly identified that man with a 'Red' sticker. He realized that there was no way to satisfy him. He wasn't wasting another minute in 'Red' energy. Herb simply *stopped talking*. As the man continued on with his temper tantrum until his time was up, Herb didn't try to solve his problem or fix their connection. So, the man accused Herb of being mean. Figures!

This man did not want to learn how to be a better human, he wasn't teachable. But I was. So Herb simply modeled for me how to recognize a 'Red' as a 'Red' and move on without feeling guilty or pulled into his drama. Until you learn how to do this, somewhere in your brain, you may be 'wondering what's wrong with me'. Once you know 'He's a Red,' you can completely let go of the notion that it is about you.

Herb had clarity with People. That's because he valued his own Self-Worth. He didn't try to put on 'Green glasses' when looking at a 'Red' person. A 'Red' is a 'Red'!…is a 'Red'…and done!..done done. And here's what I got: People respected Herb because he treated People according to the color of *their* behavior rather than wasting his time in projections (he identified them, treated them accordingly, and didn't try to change them or get diminished personally in the process of interacting with them).

Truly, that was one of the most brilliant days of my life. In fact, the lesson was so valuable that I have since worked continuously to develop this skill he taught me. Still do.

I practice acknowledging who People are genuinely being and then handling them accordingly as a 'Green,' a 'Yellow,' an 'Orange,' or a 'Red.' Herb lives on with me, even though he is no longer living because he showed up as a super 'Green' in my life and left me his legacy. Thank you, Herb!!

I got such good teaching!

You can't change a 'Red' into a 'Green' by being a 'Green' yourself. Here is your option: You can get burned by a 'Red' a couple of times until you are really ready to cover their whole face with 'Red' stickers as a reminder to yourself!! Or, you can put the 'Red sticker' on the first time you burn and forever avoid the fire.

Let go of the guilt. It is perfectly ok to treat someone as 'Red.' When you reflect on someone and the color they are being, this eliminates mixed messages. This allows them to reflect on who they are and possibly choose a better way to show up with you and others in their lives. And if you are being a 'Red,' hopefully, getting some of your own medicine back will convince you otherwise. Because 'Reds' don't make for a better planet.

Once you get the Sticker System working for you, you'll have the skill Herb taught me, and you'll happily choose 'Green' People to inhabit your world.

Just be truthful with yourself about who in your life is contributing positive emotions and support to your Stability, who makes your heart flutter, and who wants you to prosper.

This period of time is for stripping away those People who aren't supporting you on your Heroine's Journey and making space for those who are great for you to come into your life. You do this by practicing the Sticker System each and every day.

If you do not have any 'Green' People in your life at the moment, just know that you are on The Heroine's Journey, including Step #6, where Angels Show Up.

It's about using the Sticker System to Thrive

As for you, The Sticker System will keep you moving forward on The Heroine's Journey. You are on the Path to happiness and joy, and who you take along on this Journey matters!

You want to travel light with as little baggage as possible, and this means having a People-Picker to choose those who support, nourish, replenish, and grow your mind and your spirit.

When you use the Sticker System, you'll know who these People are and actively look to welcome them.

Now it's time to apply the Sticker System. This is where you sort the People in your life. It's a little bit like organizing your closet. Isn't it so much easier when you go into your closet, and it is orderly, and you know what fits? The Sticker System can help you feel the same satisfaction about the People in your life. You know, the ones that fit and make you feel good!

Grab your Journal again and a cup of tea — and go to work stickering! Get clear on who's to stay and who's for you to make your move away from. Now your People-Picker is working! Hoorah!! Happy day!

CREATING YOUR CIRCLE OF LOVE

Yay! Happy to be here in this discussion. This is an essential foundational element for you to Create Your Stability – Your Circle of Love!

Now that you've identified the 'Green' People in your life, it's time to gather up these warm and fuzzy 'super Green' People into your Circle of Love. Here's the good news — even if you didn't grow up in a loving family of origin, you can create one now!

These are your Lighthouses, advocates, and heartfelt BFF's. Doesn't it give you a good feeling just to think about these People? This Circle is your support base as you encounter the successes and challenges on your Heroine's Journey.

Identifying this Circle of Love and knowing they are firmly in your world is key to creating your Stability. A loving Circle reminds you of your wholeness and value. This is the place where you rest comfortably being yourself. These are the People you turn to when life gets challenging, and these are the People who you reach out to love generously in return.

How is it that your Circle of Love Works?

Here's the way of the Circle: A Circle of Love is 8 to 10 People who love and support you unconditionally with whom you have consciously cultivated a vulnerable and strengthening reciprocal relationship. Your Circle of Love People are there to lend a hand, give you a balanced outside perspective, contribute skills and knowledge, send positive energy and love, and hold you accountable. They increase your Life-Force. You can share your vulnerability and ask for help. They truly care about you. When life gets rocky, you won't feel like you are navigating alone. Your Circle of Love offers Heroine-level and Hero-level support for your Stability.

Your Circle of Love may be comprised of People you have known for a long time or People who have entered into your life relatively recently. With each Person in your Circle of Love, you have a knowing that there is a purposeful connection that will be important to your Journey.

Who is in your Circle of Love?

When you are nominating your favorite People to be in your Circle of Love, you'll ask yourself: Are you loved? Are you supported? Do you join together to create more than you could create alone? Do you feel their caring for you, and do they feel yours? Are you filled up with Self-Worth in their presence?

Only 'Green' People can be in your Circle of Love when you are building Stability. 'Green' People are like green vegetables; they make you healthy and strong. They can lift you up and champion you to your Best-Self and always have your back. You have a purpose and each one of these People is going to play a part with you in the fabrication of your life. You're onto something here. If you are open to the possibility, then you will be shown the more specific roles they are there to play with you.

No one person is your everything. Together your Circle makes up a supportive, responsive, and courageous group of People who inspire you. Doesn't this sound deliciously remarkable?

Your Circle of Love may only begin with a few People, but over time, with intention, you will consciously build it. The Universe may secretly be conspiring to build your Circle of Love right now. Angels can show up rather quietly sometimes. Listen carefully to the inner voice that tells you when you need to know someone, or it's time to connect. When you hear this call, it's readying you to reach out and join up with their energy and gifts.

You may wonder why 'Yellow' People can't be in your Circle of Love. They have been stickered 'Yellow' because either the energy is a little off between you and them, or you do not feel a deep soul connection. Your

Circle of Love is about surrounding yourself only with the *best* positive energy that uplifts your being at your very core.

Circle of Love Story

Here's what Jane emailed to me when I asked her what had happened after she learned The Sticker System and put it right to work in her life…

"In the past I let anyone, and everyone!, in – I wanted to be loved soooooo badly. My gates were wide open, and 'Red' and 'Orange' People flocked in and took up space around me.

Then, I just wasn't happy. My daily life was problematic, and it had way too much drama in it. This was because I had unconsciously populated my life with People that radiated out through a network generated by 'Red & Orange' People – bringing me more misery. The Person I was married to was 'Red' all along. It spanned out and caused trouble in my life. Garbage in, garbage out, so I learned.

Once I applied the Sticker System, I stopped letting everyone in. I had to do some weeding out and starting over. Now, I carefully choose who is in my company and certainly in my Circle of Love. My connections with 'Green' People radiates out. Now, there are more good things happening and I feel energized about my life. I'm happy and this is helping me make great progress.

Now, with 'Green' People in my Circle of Love, I make positive new connections, and miraculous opportunities appear serendipitously. 'Greens' are more generous, come up with creative ideas to share, want to know what you need and if they can be of service, and have good pieces to add to my puzzle of life. This makes life more fun, spontaneous, and fruitful."

You've heard the old adage, "Like attracts like." Well, Green attracts Green. Birds of a feather fly together…

Here's what your Circle of Love contributes:

Gotta love that Circle of Love. Your Circle of Love has a big purpose. They are Angels on your Journey. And, here is how they contribute.

They:

- Help you feel safe and connected
- Allow you to be the real you, vulnerable, more expansive in your truth
- Open doors for new options you might not be considering
- Lend a hand
- See things that you might be missing
- Laugh and play with you
- Hold you to your Best-Self
- Are kind and generous
- Hold you in love no matter how rough life is getting
- Want you to feel good about yourself
- And other yummy things!

Can you feel how life blossoms with these People surrounding you? Isn't life richer, fuller, and more enticing with this energy? How quickly can you overcome trials and tribulations with this support? Can you see how your Circle of Love Peeps are a priceless facet of your True Wealth?

I didn't have this understanding when I was in the Crisis Step of the Journey, and then I created my Circle of Love. And today not only do I have a better sense of myself, I am in the flow of love energy daily. I am constantly reminded of my Heroine-Self this way. This is truly the best!

Recognizing each gift and nurturing each Person is key

You will see that each Person in your Circle of Love has been brought into your life for a reason. It is truly rewarding to identify the gift each Person holds for you. Acknowledge it — Appreciate it — Celebrate it. You are supposed to receive this support to grow into your Best-Self. Being able to connect with each member of your Circle with specific gratitude in your heart amplifies the progress you make along the Path.

Your Circle of Love is all about reciprocity — give and take. They are there for you, and in return, you hold the same space for them. It is a Circle. Energy moves continuously round and round.

At different stages in your Journey, some of your Circle of Love Peeps may hold you more than you hold them. Remember, it is a Circle. What comes around goes around. In the end, all People are nurtured. Just be open to letting this happen.

Here are some suggestions to nurture your Circle of Love:

- Reach out to them regularly to cultivate heart-connections
- Know what's going on in their lives, and pay attention to Crisis and Challenge times
- Be vigilant about telling them the truth about how you feel. Be vulnerable and honest
- Be willing to ask for help
- Acknowledge and thank them for the gifts they continue to bring into your life
- Ask them what you can do for them
- Show up when you are called with your support and love

Your Circle of Love continues to spin, evolve, and grow eternally. Some People stay for the long term. Some People stay for as long as necessary to bring you a big gift. And some People stay in your Circle, even after they die, and you still feel their influence shaping your life. These People leave a legacy that warms your heart and lets you know they made a meaningful impact on your life. They helped you progress, you are better for knowing them, and you treasure your opportunity to have known them in this lifetime.

Here's how it goes, Heroine!

Creating and sustaining your Circle of Love can be synthesized into a very simple process. Here it is:

1. Identify - 'Green' Peeps and enumerate the gifts they have for you;
2. Nominate - Welcome them into your Circle of Love and tell them why you value them;
3. Engage - be vulnerable, reach out, ask for help, and give of yourself.

Get your Journal, that cup of tea, and more — and cheer up your life with your Circle of Love! Put them into your Journal with notes about how you will prize them.

While we've gone through a number of tools in this Chapter – it's all about love, where you get it, and where you give it. Love will make your Journey a beautiful rewarding experience of life.

When you are centered in loving relationships, you more easily release anxiety and get rid of turmoil and drama. You are centered, can think more clearly, and have the freedom to move along your Journey. People picking is essential.

This is fundamental to creating your Stability, for sure!!

Now, let's talk about the fourth Cornerstone: Financial. A Heroine's gotta know her stuff, and this is fuel for her flight to the joy, prosperity, and freedom she desires for her life.

Free Resources

Isn't the Sticker System fun?…I use it regularly…

You can download a 'Description of The Sticker System' and put it up on your bulletin board to refer to as you need it.

Go *now* to —
www.HeroinesBook.com/Free-Resources

6

Cornerstone Four: Financial

Urgency for Money Mastery

Money In, Money Out

Your Money Thinking

Three Money Numbers

Financial Stability Formula

URGENCY FOR MONEY MASTERY

oney, Money, Money is our topic here!

And how it is working for you in your life.

In a Book about the Heroine's Journey to True Wealth, you might be tempted to think that money is the most important topic here — however, not so in the feminine Journey. Most women don't view money as a way to keep score — like our male counterparts. We have a different (a Heroine's view) of Money.

If we have gotten this far along the Path, now, we realize that 'Money' (while it is an essential element) is only one of the Cornerstones to Create Your Stability, preparing for our Journey onward to True Wealth and ultimately to our Best-Selves.

This is the reframe we want to give 'Money' so that women can see it as supportive in our lives — and not just a power tool as our male-centric

culture has deemed it. On the Path of the Heroine, 'Money' has a different concept and context for women — and we'll explore it here in this
Chapter.

So, is Money all that important? You bet it is, Heroine!

So, how do we define Money?

Money is energy. It is a means of exchange that helps you acquire the
earthly resources that you need for the Journey for yourself, and to contribute to others. It's not about 'shiny object' purchases (although that
can be fun) — it's about sustainability, fuel in your tank for the Journey
forward.

Most of the resources that support your needs in the modern world
cost Money, yours or someone else's. You cannot pretend that Money
doesn't exist or that you are above it. There is no need to put your head
in the sand. We've got you on this one. A Heroine knows that she is
capable of gathering all the resources along the way that she requires,
including Money.

Our discussion about Money lands us clearly here … and it goes like
this …

Step 7: Gathering Your Provisions

Acquire fuel for your flight

You will need fuel for the flight. To get off the ground, you must
prepare for the Journey ahead. You draw in Life-Force energy and
all the resources you require to sustain yourself on the Journey. Your
inner Heroine realizes that she must generate plenty to thrive. It
is her birthright to live in abundance. You cannot go on without.
You clearly communicate to the Universe what will sustain you for
the long road ahead. The Heroine is responsible for acquiring what
she needs. Get resourceful to gather resources. From a place of Self-
Worth, she asks herself what gifts and talents she can use to produce

bounty. There is effort in the hunt, yet some supplies may hide in plain sight. There is plenty; go and harvest. You will have ample fuel for the flight if you carefully use only as much as you gather.

I wish for you to progress on your Journey and ultimately live fully in joy, prosperity and freedom. Even if you get a few Steps ahead on the Heroine's Journey without first building your Financial Stability, there will be yet another Crisis or Challenge that will force you to circle back and deal with your lack of a solid financial foundation. Have you experienced this? I know I have. Life just works this way.

So let's get a handle on Financial Stability now so you have the resources for your momentum on the road ahead.

So, how do we define Financial Stability?

*Financial Stability is about making Money in alignment with your **True Self**, gathering what you need, **living within your Means**, keeping your money safe, and being a woman who can support herself **independently throughout her lifetime**. There's a lot to consider here.*

Come play with me in the realm of Money energy.

There's no compromise.

Here's the truth: until you create your life on a financially stable basis — you will always be forced to compromise yourself — sometimes in ways that undermine your values and sense of who you truly are — because you are at the mercy of needing to acquire Money fast.

This is how it plays out, and it's not pretty.

Not a good plan. If you are not stable financially, you will have fearful thoughts of lack about how to keep yourself afloat. These thoughts cause worry, stress and keeping you up at night; and worse. They can literally take you down the wrong way to doing things that aren't in sink with your own personal integrity. We all know this dilemma. When you are derailed — this literally takes you off your Heroine's Path.

Careening along — you may even notice prostituting yourself as you trade '*YOU*' to acquire Money. Oh, No! Prostitution is not what you want, Sister! Not in any form or fashion, because a Heroine knows her Self-Worth and she's here to deliver it.

Notice when you are forced to compromise like this — that Money is your motivator. Whereas a Heroine is motivated to create the life that she truly wants to live. Her life is precious. A Heroine is motivated to create her joy, prosperity and freedom — even if that means reigning in spending or ramping up productivity (or both) to balance herself financially.

Did you read that? It's true. Yikes, a Heroine has to have 'financial legs' — meaning that she has to mobilize her life to be financially stable.

And, if you've got it handled financially — Cheers! — good for you! You have that Cornerstone of your Stability secured.

I had these 3am-panic-moments. I had it handled financially — and then I didn't.

It was when my life fell apart in the Crisis and Challenge Steps of my Journey. I suddenly found myself needing to generate cash quickly and I truly prostituted myself to just get a 'job', and trade 'me' for Money. I went to work as a low-level big box store employee — that chewed up my time and my life, for a very tiny paycheck. I had to bide my time, and play 'smaller' than the true me and my gifts, talents and skills that I possess.

Remember, I had owned a very successful financial business with the accolade of being the first woman-owned investment banking firm in the US to underwrite municipal bonds in the tens of millions of dollars range. That work challenged me, fired up my brain power, inspired me and I brought my unique talents and capabilities to bear to foster this work — my Best-Self.

I felt my life purpose burning in me but I couldn't get to it because I had to 'pay the bills'. This happens.

I needed to make this 'job' a stepping stone and Heroine-Up, with all of my Heroine skills.

I didn't stay there for long — it was just enough time to let me know that I had to muster my Courage and Strength, flap my wings furiously, and be off to new horizons. This experience was a great motivator. It pushed me to show up Fierce Feminine. I had a life to create regardless of the pitfalls I had encountered and the circumstances at the time. My vision was on what I could become to live a life I could love. That life can be different for each of us — it doesn't mean needing to be a rockstar. It means getting your 'financial legs' on so that you can live the life you choose, and one where you have peace of mind!

Hey, even these adverse financial circumstances can be a great teacher. They contrast who you truly want to be and what you must do to become your Best-Self. When you are uncomfortable, it's a great opportunity to be inspired toward making decisions, plans and actions necessary to create your Financial Stability and protect your Well-Being.

Here are the facts: Life will wake you up! To get along — you must have knowledge about Money and power over your own Money's flow. This is true whether you are single, married, broke, gifted with generating money, or deeply entrenched in a career. You must know how Money is working in your life — that's 'getting your financial legs on'!

Let's get going on this juicy subject! It's time, Sisters, to wrap your wings around this one!

How does money serve you?

In our daily lives, Money serves us in a multitude of ways.

Money fuels your flight. It:

meets your basic expenses

meets the needs of dependents (children or parents)

gives peace of mind to know that you can acquire what you need

helps protect you from the inside (like hiring holistic practitioners and affording high-nutrient foods)

helps protect you from the outside (living in a safe place or hiring other professionals to protect your interests) let's you support your favorite causes (animals for me!)

provides Freedom - enables you to express your unique life Path, contributions, and adventures

And more!…it's a good thing to be resourced!

For women, our cultural perspective has confused us about the true nature of Money. That's because Money is described in male terms with male languaging most often, and we have to fit into an understanding that doesn't match with our feminine nature.

In our more masculine-oriented economy, Money is about exerting power and control. This can be a turnoff for many women, causing us to reject the full blossoming of Money into our lives unwisely. That's a strategy for heading for the rocks below. A Heroine is on an upward course of flight, and Money is a resource on our Journey!

Let's reframe Money from our Heroine's point of view. Let's stake an empowered claim to having Money in our lives.

Here's what a Heroine says about Money:

> "***Money*** *is a beautiful form of* ***energy*** *that facilitates me to ground my* ***Stability*** *so that I can ultimately fly. A* ***consistent flow*** *of Money is a generous gift to my life. With it, I can acquire the provisions I need for the Journey ahead. It allows me to* ***fund myself*** *to live into* ***my purpose*** *and make my contribution. Money is a* ***vital aspect*** *of my True Wealth."*

A proper relationship with Money is the groundwork for living a full and meaningful life. Traveling the Heroine's Journey includes incorporating the right Money thinking and the right Money actions. This is getting your wings on to fly!

Whether you're worried, "I have no Money right now, what do I do?" Or you are pondering, "I have plenty of Money, but I don't quite know how it works." — this Chapter will give you the tools you need to build your Financial Stability. Financial is the fourth Cornerstone of Creating your Stability, and the gateway to your joy, prosperity and freedom. Let's Journey onward!

It's ok to think about Money and how it works in your life.

Creating your Financial Stability is quite tactical. I will share some basic tools every woman should have in her pink tool belt. You can use them to ensure you have what you need, when and where you need it. This is good stuff! My mind, spirit and peaceful Journey are much improved with my good Money sense. Yours will be, too.

We'll cover this:

> Get your Money revved up for you to serve your current needs;
>
> Regard your Money and set up your future for the prosperity to fuel your flight;
>
> Become the Mistress of your Money so that it serves you and not you serving it!

The bottom line, getting your Money matters in hand is shaping you up for your travel on the Path of the Heroine. As long as you are scrambling to address your Money needs, you won't have the mental or energetic freedom to step into all the opportunities, joy, and fullness that life can bring to you.

I wish for you to blossom into your full potential so that your gifts can shine out brightly, your spirit can soar, and you can show up in service to the world. It's your birthright — I say!! Cheers!!

It's up to you!

You have to build your own Financial Well-Being. Sorry to say – Heroine, that you can't bypass this Step on the Journey and leap into 'living the dream' as Hollywood cinema and TV commercials would have you believe.

Getting into your 'Financial Wellness Zone' is usually not an overnight process. And it depends on where you are starting from. This Wellness Zone strategy is a clear plan and consistent action — it takes

Heroining Up. When you are in your Financial Wellness Zone — it adds to your OOMPH!

Here's cutting to the chase — The key to your Wellness Zone of Financial Stability is to know your numbers and to live within your Means. Did you let that resonate? Ponder that. It's at the heart of it, your heart of Well-Being.

After accomplishing 'know your numbers and live within your Means' — then you'll be ready to graduate to expanding your Means!

This is the Path of The Heroine's Journey here and now!

Later, as you continue in the Heroine's Coursework, the Steps on the Journey will show you how a Heroine who has become the Mistress of her Money gets purposeful and profitable — this is where you 'Light Up Your Expression', Step #11 — Your Dreams Fly Higher Than Your Fears! Sound good? It's where money gets fun and abundant — because your focus is off of yourself and onto the useful impact of using your unique gifts and talents to light up the lives of other's. Stay tuned!

For each Step of the Path, you must be in the right relationship with Money — and master that Step. Just like having supportive Beliefs, a strong Physical Life-Force and loving People —creating your Money foundation is essential to creating Your Stability. Yikes, it's the fourth Cornerstone!

Here are some National Statistics on Women and Money – to kinda wake you up!

First, let's consider this, and it's not such a pretty picture … the national statistics for a woman's financial future are pretty bleak. Let's learn where we don't want to be so we have a heads-up…

As much as 90% of women will be solely responsible for their finances at some point in their lives due to being single, divorced, or widowed. (National Center for Women and Retirement Research).

There's even a term for it—bag lady syndrome—and it's particularly touchy for baby boomer women, who feel the pressure of impending retirement.

According to the Institute for Women's Policy Research (IWPR), 66 percent of women aged 45 to 59, and 52 percent over 60 worry about not having enough money to retire on.

- In 2020, the poverty rate for women was 12.9%.
- Women also have less financial confidence and greater fears. In a recent TODAY.com survey, 20 percent of our viewers said their biggest fear was having too much debt, and 19 percent felt it was outliving their money.
- According to the Federal Reserve's Report on the Economic Well-Being of U.S. Households in 2020, around 37% of adults said they would have difficulty covering an unexpected expense of $400 with cash or its equivalent that they could pay off in a month.
- Fewer than 1 in 10 women age 50–64 are very confident that they will have enough money to live comfortably throughout their retirement years. (AARP 'Women Ages 50-64 Are Financially Stressed, AARP Study Finds)
- But "gray divorces" — among people over 50 — doubled between 1990 and 2010, even as divorces declined in younger cohorts, said I-Fen Lin, a sociologist at Bowling Green State University in Ohio. (New York Times 'Why Older Women Face a Greater Financial Hardship Than Older Men')

Hey, Heroine, this is not you! What is your plan for rising above these national statistics? You have flights to take and horizons to reach. Adventure awaits you!

Now is a good time.

The statistics show that women often ignore the issue of Money and let themselves become vulnerable in the process. For us, so many other things are going on in life. Then, *Hello*…eventually, something gets your attention. Money is often not crucial to a woman until it crosses with a life event (events like the Crisis and Challenge Steps on The Journey).

Maybe you made a life transition, suffered a financial loss, have a new need, or are experiencing a life change. When life appears in Crisis and Challenge times, Money is right there in the fray of things. Bam, Money becomes essential!

Now, you finally realize it's time to pay attention to it. No more head in the sand, you vow. You need cash flow!

This is the amazing part. While I've known so many women who have been parted from their money or have experienced being empty-handed, there's hope. For many, this was the start of their Heroine's Journey. The financial need ended up being a gift of self-discovery. And, when you discover yourself and live your purpose, that's the fuel for becoming more affluent than ever.

This turns it all into a blessing!

Money is a call to action.

Money is a motivator. Sometimes, it's a '*kick in the pants to get going.*' You are meant to take your talents into the world in exchange for Money. The world needs your talents.

My creative partner and BFF says, "I didn't have any skills until I lost all my money. Then, I said, damn, better go get some in a hurry! I'm proud to be where I am today and wouldn't return to before!" She experienced the need to become more resourceful and capable to step up her cashflow — and many aspects of herself grew in the process.

When you're standing on top of the cliff, and you see the blue sky above and the crashing sea on the rocks below — you need to fly … to feed your child, pay your bills, build your business, and so much more. Money may motivate you to get up, kick the dirt off your feet, leap forward, and start flapping. Heroines do this.

If you had all the Money you needed in the world, you might just be tempted to sit on the couch, eat bonbons, and never explore the heights of who you are. Who would want that? Not a Heroine, that's for sure!

Money teases you out, Sister. It reminds you to russell up your energy and create something. It asks you to magnify your gifts to enhance others, so you get paid for this. You need money, and the world needs your talents and creative input. It's really a perfect system if you approach it with the heart of a Heroine.

Women are a catalyst for change.

Is it the chicken or the egg? Do you develop Financial Stability to give your gifts out into the world, or do you give your gifts in return for Money to establish your Financial Stability? It's done in tandem. They feed on each other. The more you increase your Financial Well-Being and the expression of your gifts, the further along the Path you will be.

We know from the national statistics for women that most women have not created Financial Stability. Then by association, we can determine that most are not magnifying their gifts. This makes me sad! More than ever, we need Women's Courage, Strength and spirit to come alive. We'll have whole new businesses and enterprises when Women lead from their feminine Path and create economic prosperity from their talents and gifts — now's the time!

It's been my life mission to see women blossom financially. My goal is to teach you how Money works and how to work with your Money. I've had you in mind all along as I've thought so long and hard about how we engage Money and grow to our Best-Selves.

Come play full out with me, it's a Path I've been leading women on for over 30 years, and I'm delighted for us to share this conversation in a way that will be uplifting and inspiring for you!

MONEY IN, MONEY OUT

I wish for you that: *'You and Money are friends' and that Money supports you to new heights in your life as you soar into blue skies ahead!!*

I can tell you that this is territory I have traveled personally on my Journey. My Journey and Money have had their ups and downs. I haven't done it perfectly, but the lessons I have learned and my many years of professional knowledge bring together wisdom and insight to serve you.

I just kind of stumbled and bumbled — because who teaches you about Money anyway? I got degrees from schooling, collected a paycheck, went shopping, paid my rent, and then started over the next month. Sound familiar? I was on my own to figure it out. But when I graduated from Business School (where they don't teach you anything about personal financial stuff!) – I had this recurring question that swam around in my head.

It was: "Who has Money, how did they get it, and what do they do with it?" That was an excellent start because it made me curious about Money. Curious is good. It made me see Money as a flow of energy — and not something that I either did or didn't have at the moment. This put me in a relationship with Money.

And that's it. You have a relationship with Money, too. You are off on the right foot when you see it that way. And believe me, you will be partnering with it your whole life! So, best to get into a working relationship right from the start!

Money is really pretty simple.

Surprisingly, you don't need much more than grade school math. The experts have tried to make it more complicated so you'll depend upon them. Don't be fooled, Heroine! Never do that.

Stay in touch with your Money, steward it, and ultimately grow it! You should always be the one who cares more deeply about your Money than anyone else. It impacts your life and your plans — and I'm here to tell you that if you have Money in your checking account when you are in your 70s, you won't need a face lift because you'll be smiling broadly.

This is how you have a relationship with Money.

In this Chapter, you will learn how Money comes and goes from your coffers. Once you establish this, you have a context to witness the ebb and flow of Money in your life and to set the course actively. This sets Money in motion for your life.

Do you know how Money comes to you?

There are three main ways that Money comes to you.

You can:

> Marry it
> Inherit it
> Earn it

That's it. Well, you could steal it or win it in the lottery — but neither of those works well as a solid plan, so we'll eliminate those two!

We are left with: Marry it, Inherit it, or Earn it. You get to choose, but first, consider the following . . .

What are the prospects of marrying for Money?

It's certainly possible to marry for money. My Mother said, "It's just as easy to fall in love with a rich man as a poor man!" By contrast, my Father used to say, "Never marry for money; it's cheaper to borrow it!" You decide which Belief gets to influence you.

There's still a significant consideration. Even if you marry someone with Money, it only counts toward your Stability if you can access your own Money in the partnership. Just getting married isn't the answer. The Money could walk away, and it does many times for women during divorce or if your partner mismanages it as you look the other way.

This can and does happen. Your Stability requires your active relationship with Money.

What are the prospects for inheriting money?

You may be in a position to inherit Money. Large wealth transfers are going on now as the next generation receives the accumulated sums from their parents. But there is a consideration here, too.

The issue with inheriting Money is that if you don't know how to handle it and protect it, it will leave you very quickly. Just inheriting Money isn't the answer. Like marriage, inheriting Money also takes your active participation and development of Money skills.

And, the prospects for earning Money?

Most of us fall into the 'Earn it' category of the way Money populates our checking accounts. It's not the most likely scenario that you will marry or inherit the Money that will carry you through the active parts of your life, sustain your lifestyle, and set up your future.

The Crisis and Challenge stages of the Heroine's Journey often include Money issues, with impending questions about regrouping and generating cash. It's a test for how you will navigate. Frequently, these tests reveal new skills, gifts, talents, and ways of seeing yourself that you wouldn't have seen without the gift of Money drama. Ultimately, these challenges awaken and bolster your ability to earn Money.

Generating your own Money brings dominion over your Financial Stability, the satisfaction of accomplishment and the sense of knowing the value of a dollar — which are all good things.

Many of us start without a nest egg, which is a stash of cash that will forever keep you tidy and flush. It's the more likely scenario. And, if you need cash now, you'll have to employ one of the three ways of how money comes to you.

You could seek to marry it, but marriage for Money alone is prostitution. (Sorry to be blunt, Heroines, but that's the truth.) And truly, how many good rich spouse candidates are available anyway?

You could seek to inherit it quickly. But that would require death, and we never wish that on anybody.

So what's left? You gotta earn it!

Remember that Billie Holiday song that goes like this? It is a biblical idea that she celebrated through song.

"Empty pockets don't ever make the grade. Mama may have. Papa may have. But God bless the child that's got its own."

Maria's Story sheds light on 'Money In.'

I want to share the story of an extraordinary woman named Maria, who I had the opportunity to coach. Maria is a gold-hearted woman who truly dedicated herself to the healing of others through a long career in nursing.

By age 50, Maria had been thoughtful about setting aside Money in her investment account so that later in her life, she could leave nursing and live off of the investment income to pay for her lifestyle.

However, things were changing in nursing and Maria decided to leave her life-long career. She made a decision that appeared to be a good choice for her emotional and physical health, but her loss of income left her at risk. This can happen if you change jobs, lose a job, or other disruptions happen, and suddenly, your cash flow is disrupted.

Maria left nursing quickly without establishing inroads into what her second career would be. As a single woman, she still needed monthly income to pay her mortgage and living expenses. And, then she had an unexpected repair for her car.

To sustain herself, Maria started taking Money out of the principal of her investment account each month, thinking this would only be a temporary fix. She didn't have a solid plan for creating income, and the months turned into years, as they do.

Oops … and then she dwindled her investment funds way down. The Financial Stability she had worked to create all those years in nursing was now dangerously compromised. Her nest egg was depleted.

Stress and anxiety were making her aware that this couldn't go on much longer. Her lack of a strategy for Money coming into her checking account sent her straight for the rocks below, and she told me when we first met.

Maria was at the end of her rope. So much so that not only was her Financial Stability compromised, but so was her physical and emotional stability — because they can go hand in hand. She even compromised herself in a relationship to try to grasp onto someone else to solve her financial issues. She told me that this stress was now far worse than nursing stress had ever been. She was in a pickle!

U-Turn, I began our coaching by helping her see that she needed to change the trajectory of her Financial Stability. She was headed for the rocks below. She needed to pull up. She needed to make some new and tough decisions about her incoming cash flow. She could no longer afford to live on her nest egg. It was time to make sure Money was coming in sustainably.

My suggestion to Maria was that she get a job. This would produce an immediate source of cash flow while she developed a solid plan for creating a new stable form of cash flow that would fulfill her life purpose. She thought that it was time to use her gifts to produce income.

She didn't like my suggestion, though. She felt that going back to work as an employee limited her freedom. Instead, she wanted to start her own business from scratch, with no prior experience, as her solution.

While getting to the point of serving with your gifts is a great place to be, this was a hazardous prospect for Maria. Because businesses don't usually generate immediate cash flow, and most require start-up costs and sweat equity time. Right now, Maria needed to make sure that Money was coming in so that she could turn her flight Path upward.

We talked, and she could see a game plan. If she was serious about creating cash flow and also creating a business, there were some important things to consider:

Here is my advice that I hope is helpful for you as well.

- Start your own business when you have solid proof of its viability.
- Keep your day job as you develop your business in tandem until you prove your earning ability with your new business.
- If you are thinking about earning Money through selling your services, ensure you have a roster of potential clients willing to pay you for it.
- Leave that day job behind once your business generates enough to cover your needs.
- Think of your Financial Stability first to pave your way.

Maria needed cash flow immediately. She was hoping that starting her own business was the answer. But she realized that while a business could be a fabulous long-term solution, it was not the immediate cash-flow vehicle she desperately needed right now.

So, yes, she did indeed go get a job. It gave her exactly what she needed to regroup and reorient to a new plan.

The moral of this story is not how to create your own business. That comes later in the Heroine's Journey. Step 12: Thriving in Life is about living your Expression.

The nugget of knowledge here is about recognizing the immediate need to have Money coming in positive cash flow. This is what ensures your Financial Stability so that you have the stamina to sustain the Journey.

The 'Money Out' Dilemma: Don't Let Money Dwindle

Your first and foremost job is to maintain your Stability. If you have a lump sum of cash through divorce, sale of real estate, legal settlements, insurance claim, savings, sale of a business, inheritance, retirement plan, etc., pay attention here! It will always be in danger of dwindling. *Heads up* on this one!

Here's what can happen: Either you peter it away by spending it, or someone else comes along and tries to take it from you. This is a lesson that I, and many other women, have learned the hard way.

If you let your Money dwindle, you will be weakening your Stability instead of strengthening it. This is not meant to be a glass-half-empty conversation. It is intended to wake you up to the fact that your Financial Stability is a responsibility. You must *keep your principal.* Keep your nest egg. It's so easy to see it dwindle — money quickly runs through our fingers.

The rich count every penny! — that's why they are rich — it's heightened awareness!

Lien's Story sheds light on 'Don't Spend it.'

Here's another story about my friend Lien, who got a large sum of money when she divorced - nearly a million dollars — and a monthly alimony.

However, even with this cash flow, she has been spending a lot. She has been indulging in fine clothes, travel, and the high life — the way she is accustomed to living, spending without regard for having the

Money last. She also financially supports her daughter's family by paying the monthly mortgage on a house that is more than they can afford. She dotes on her grandchildren with clothes, travel, and gifts. Her's is spending, spending, spending — big bucks.

She is living well beyond her Means. Her monthly alimony does not cover the excessive lifestyle she perpetuates and the unsustainable generosity she bestows. So, she has been heavily dipping into her coffers.

One day, when I was visiting Lien at her home, she opened her mail and was shocked to see her brokerage statement. Her account balance was down $75,000. Lien gulped and then said: "Well, I guess they just lose money sometimes." It shocked me how willing she was to part with her Money.

This wasn't ok with me. I saw that this was Money that she needed for her long-term Well-Being. I raised this with her, and we talked about it. She admitted it was not ok to be shorted this Money. She didn't know what to do about it other than just accept it.

Now the million dollars was down to about $300,000. We looked at her brokerage statements and could see also that she had not been making a steady return on her investments.

Then Lien shared with me her real impending problem. Her ex-husband would stop paying her alimony in just about one year. She would no longer have this cash-flow, and her investments certainly were not generating the kind of monthly income she would need. She was seriously worried. It was her wake-up call, and she got middle-of-the-night panics.

Rightly so. When we calculated Lien's income and considered her future expenses, we could see that she had about 2 ½ years before she would run out of money altogether. She is 70 years old and probably needs another 20 years of income.

Where will the Money come from for her to live and pay her monthly expenses and rent? This is a question that we all need to consider. As we live our daily lives and consider our spending patterns, how must we take care of ourselves and consider our life span and the Money we will need? You don't want to run out of Money before you run out of life!

Here's what to know: whether you have a boat load or a little nest egg, hold on to your lump sum of Money! Never invade any principle.

How can you keep it safe?

Whatever Money has come to you has been bestowed upon you for the purpose of your conscious distribution to promote the greater good for you and others. So, keeping your Money safe from loss and theft is important. One aspect of your relationship with Money is as a protector. The 'Money In' should not go out in nefarious ways.

Heads up on this one! Please be aware when you have gained Money in your personal account, you must protect it. There will be those who are greedy and want what you have. This can happen through theft, lawsuits, bad business deals, etc. It has certainly happened to me. You can be in peril if you aren't smart about protective Money strategies.

Consider how you keep your Money safe. If you are married, did you execute a prenuptial agreement if necessary? Do you create written documentation on all business agreements and personal loans? Have you been lured into a bad business deal or charmed into a false investment? Have you left yourself open to costly legal battles?

Ask yourself, "Do I feel I am knowledgeable about my finances to protect my Money from those 'Orange or Red' people who act out of integrity?" They are out there, I can tell you!

Now, do what you must to ensure your Money's safety. Do some research and get good counsel about how you can be proactive to protect your Money. Your Stability depends on it.

There are 5 Kinds of Money that you need in your lifetime.

Here are the five kinds of Money you need. All 5 of these kinds of Money are generated when you successfully travel the Heroine's Journey.

These are:

1. Walking Money: So you have the freedom to walk away from bad situations
2. Spending Money: To take care of your bills, needs and wants

3. Working Money: To actively invest in yourself, your skills, and your business
4. Sustainability Money: To passively invest to support you long into your future
5. Giving Away Money: More than your needs that you actively gift to meet the needs of others

We're here now talking about Create Your Stability — and the good news is that our focus at this stage of the Journey is for you to develop your 'Walking Money' and 'Spending Money.'

These two kinds of Money will establish your Financial Stability. We'll move on to the following three kinds of money further down the Path in later Steps of the Heroine's Journey to True Wealth.

Here in this Book, we're getting tactical about how to create Walking Money and Spending Money. Stability is about getting your 'financial legs' on first to have the endurance for the entire Journey of Money happiness!

Do you have a Money perspective?

I love what Ben Franklin had to say about the strategy of Money. See if his perspective helps you, too! I love his quote, which says so much (I've had it on my bulletin board for many decades) — you, too:

There are two ways of being happy.
We may either diminish our wants or
augment our means — either will do —
the result is the same, and it is for each
(wo)man to decide for himself (herself),
and do that, which happens to be the easiest.
If you are either sick or poor, however
hard it may be to diminish your wants,
it will be harder to augment your means.

If you are active and prosperous or
young and in good health, it may be easier
for you to augment your means than to
diminish your wants.

But if you are wise, you will do both at
the same time, young or old, rich or
poor, sick, or well, and if you are very
wise, you will do both in such a way as
to augment the general happiness of society.

Yeah, Ben Franklin, not much has changed since your time!
You'll be wise, too, if you gain this perspective on Money.
The two sides of the Financial Stability coin are how Money comes
to you and how you steward it for the Journey. (Yes, pun intended).

YOUR MONEY THINKING

Remember, my mission here is that you and Money are friends! It's that
you create from your heart's desire to share your gifts and that Money
flows to you to have life-long prosperity. Let's get this going!

Honestly, call me *geeky* — I love this stuff! And I love how you can
blossom into your most brilliant life when you build your financial
foundation. I'll be with you all the way.

And you'll have to add your work, time, energy, and determination.
Got that? And, that starts with how you are thinking about Money –
what is the conversation going on in your head about your relationship
with Money? You might be surprised to find out how this is affecting
your prosperity.

How you *think* about Money plays a big part in how Money *shows
up* in your life. This isn't surprising — it's the law of nature.

Here's the bottom line on your conversations about Money in your
own head: If you have more negative thoughts and Beliefs about Money
than positive Beliefs — *money* will simply leave you. It's that simple,
really. If you have more positive ways that you think and believe about

Money, than negative ones, you will *invite Money* into your life. A much better plan!

Let's put this into application.

Are you inviting Money to come your way? Do you give yourself permission to generate more Money than you personally need? Believe it or not, the financial results you are experiencing today have everything to do with how you think about Money.

Isn't that good news? Even if your Money thinking so far has ended you up in a precarious place, the good news is that you can change your Money thinking and, ultimately, your Money circumstances.

The first step is to pay attention to and consider your conversations with yourself about Money. What vibration are you creating when you think about Money?

Let's look more closely at what you are saying to yourself and others about Money. Let's start with Myths that can hang us up.

Let's explore these Myths that no longer work.

Hey, Heroine, there are some looming cultural Myths about Money that we have all succumbed to at some point or another. They are clearly no longer working for our creation of abundance! These Myths subconsciously ill-inform our thoughts about Money, causing the negative thoughts to be fed. If we are going to improve our conversation with ourselves about Money, we need to debunk these Myths right now!

Let's just take a moment to bring them to light so you don't get caught in any of them anymore. Until you release them fully, they'll slow down your progress.

#1 Myth is 'The White Knight Myth ...

Are you hoping a partner will magically show up someday to take care of your financial future? It's a superficially comforting concept that we were taught through stories like Cinderella and other fairy tales about the man being our Hero.

A white knight can take many forms — a spouse, lover, broker, business partner, employer, or advisor. The essence is that the White Knight is someone (man or woman) whom you give your financial power to, hoping that they will just take care of Money matters so you don't have to.

Because Money has been shrouded in such mystique, teachings about it are either limited or overly complicated. It has been a taboo subject that lives in the shadows. Most of us secretly want someone else to sweep us off our financial feet and carry us off into riches.

Truth be told, there are fewer and fewer partners who want to or are planning to take care of the financial security of a woman for her life-time.

The White Knight is a totally outdated concept. Our world has changed dramatically in the last 30 years. Heroines, we no longer need a White Knight. As women, we have been *liberated*!

We have the right to own property and businesses, offer our creative energies abundantly to the marketplace, and be paid for them. We have entered the workforce in masses, and a few of us have risen to lead some of the most influential enterprises on the planet.

But a latent and nagging thought form runs in our minds, especially in periods of insecurity. Many of us have deep programming that says that only a man can solve our issue of financial security, a rich man. And he is trotting up on a white horse any day now.

I know that with as much attention as I have given to this issue, the White Knight still looms into my head because I am a product of our culture, the media, and even my Mother's teaching by example.

I watched my Mother play out this Myth with my Father. Even though she demonstrated the tenacity and guts to establish her own Financial Stability and entrepreneurial empire, she stayed in an emotionally unhealthy relationship because she did not feel she could manage the day-to-day responsibilities of life without him. She dubbed my father her White Knight, and she betrayed her own happiness for her cultural belief in security. While many have made advances from this thinking in my Mother's generation, our culture still reinforces the economic prominence of a man.

We'll be diving deeper into why many women may still be at the mercy of the White Knight Myth later in the Heroine's Journey to True Wealth teachings. For now, let's just put this stake in the ground — Don't count on the White Knight showing up to rescue you from a financial mess or lack of planning for your future. You'll be sitting in your own mess if you do this!

Your Financial Stability is up to you. We are Heroines now, and that includes manifesting and managing our own Money. It's time to climb up onto your own white horse and ride with the wind in your hair!

#2 Myth is 'The Big Bundle Myth' ...

Somewhere along the line, you might have bought into the Myth that you need to have a large sum of money to invest and grow your money actively. Not true. This is erroneous thinking.

Not only has Wall Street perpetuated this Big Bundle Myth, but it is one that we self-generate in our own thinking to avoid the subject of creating our own Financial Well-Being. Maybe you're thinking I'm too young or old to generate a big bundle of cash. If you have experienced the Crisis and Challenge stages of the Journey, you most likely know the pressure to create cash flow and that it doesn't happen all at once.

Truth Be Told, wherever you are, it is an act of Courage, Strength, and alignment for you and me, Heroines, to build Financial Stability, starting from little to bigger.

If you make the game too big, you won't play it! So drop the Big Bundle Myth as an excuse and start creating your Financial Stability like your Journey depends upon it. It does!

#3 Myth is 'The Credit Card Myth' ...

Here is a big myth that has been sold to us: *lock, stock, and barrel*: It's ok to spend money you don't have right now — just put the purchase on a credit card.

Do you think that 'cash' is what is printed in the box marked 'available' on your credit card statement? That's not cash; it's your potential for further debt. Yikes!...wrong direction thinking!

Credit cards are the Draculas of the financial world that drain money out of our lives at an alarming rate.

When you see a credit card — think cheeseburger! A credit card is like a cheeseburger: It's full of fat (interest) and, clogs your arteries and makes you feel sluggish (debt), and it's not real nutrition (it's Plastic!). Don't drink the cool-aid. In the short run, it can solve your binge-shopping instinct — but in the long run, it will be detrimental to your financial health.

And like fast-food burgers, credit cards are slickly marketed. They are marketed on college campuses to unsuspecting youth. And, as soon as women entered the workforce in large numbers, banks launched massive campaigns to target those wonderful new consumers. They offered credit cards with pretty pictures and low-interest rates on the front end.

With credit cards in hand, women took shopping to new and glorious heights. Credit card companies taught us lessons about spending, such as 'if something isn't new, it isn't good.' Consumer revolving debt, which is mostly credit card balances, grew $2.3 billion in 2016 to $981 billion, according to the Federal Reserve's G.19 consumer credit report. Cardholders took on $43.4 billion in new credit card debt in 2016 and continued to $856 Billion by the end of 2021 (according to The Federal Reserve Bank of New York).

And check this out…according to a February 7, 2024 article in USA Today: …total credit card debt reached record high:

'Credit card debt, the amount owed by all Americans on their credit cards, rose to a record $1.13 trillion at the end of last year, the Federal Reserve Bank of New York reported Tuesday.'

About 49% of cardholders were carrying over debt in November 2023, according to a Bankrate study. That's up from 39% in 2021 and 47% in July 2023. This is called 'persistent debt' where they are charged more in interest and fees each year than they pay toward the principal, the bureau said.

Card balances increased by about $50 billion, or 4.6%, in the fourth quarter of 2023. Credit card delinquencies, the amount of time in which cardholders fall behind in making payments, also increased. The percentage of card delinquencies 90 days or more rose to 6.4% from 4% in the fourth quarter of 2022.

Wow! ... My hope for you is that you are not part of this club! Run from the debt culture!

Do you look at those ridiculous interest rates of 25-30% per annum on credit card offers and laugh? That's absurd. And, buying into this debt path means you are setting yourself up to be trapped for your whole life. That's what they want. You don't want to be a victim ... Be smarter and a Heroine!

Truth be told, it is possible to live without a credit card. Believe me, it is! Many of us have done fine by never carrying a credit card. We pay as we go using our cash or a debit card.

#4 Myth is 'The Social Security/Pension Myth' ...

It would be nice to think that Social Security or an employer pension will take care of you after your years of working and earning. Wake up, Heroine! That's not going to happen. First, there is much discussion on *whether the Social Security model will* survive through the next decade. Secondly, there has been more than one company that has gone bankrupt, and pensions evaporate, and there is almost no more of that mode of lifetime income around anymore.

Social Security or a pension is not going to save you.

All throughout your earning years, you have the opportunity to build your Financial Well-Being for yourself. If you're wondering how to do this — stay on the Heroine's Journey, and we'll be detailing how to establish long-term financial security through the scope of the Heroine's Journey to True Wealth.

#5 Myth is 'The Tax Myth' ...

When you plan to stop working at your career job, don't make the mistake of thinking that your tax rate will be lower. It won't.

Truth be told, if you intend to keep the same lifestyle and are receiving Money from investments or an investment plan — your tax rate will be the same whether you are working or not. The Money in retirement accounts (IRAs, 401Ks etc) only grew tax-free, but it is fully taxable at your ordinary income tax rate when you withdraw this Money from IRAs and other plans.

The only way that your tax rate will drop is if you receive substantially less Money and reduce your way of living.

#6 Myth is 'The Femininity Myth' ...

"I'm blonde!" It's something I say in jest to a man when it comes to understanding my car's engine or how to fix a clogged sink. While this humor works on mechanics and plumbers, it doesn't work for me or you when creating Financial Stability. This is an area where I simply cannot afford to be 'blonde.'

I'm a Heroine at creating my own wealth. It's plain and simple. I earn Money, put Money aside from my lifestyle, and build assets that can pay me cash down the road. That's it in a nutshell!

This Femininity Myth handicaps women and says that there is something too complicated or unfeminine about being the stewards of our financial lives. This simply isn't true — and don't fall for it for a minute! And you won't because you're a Heroine.

It's easy to see where the Femininity Myth comes from. If you had a Mother who didn't demonstrate her financial ability, or you watched TV back in the days of 'I Love Lucy', or if you unfortunately got one of those Barbie Dolls that said, "I don't do math" (they really existed) — then it's easy to see where this thinking comes from.

Truth be told, this thinking is as outdated as "Girls don't play sports." Of course, we do, and we're good at them! Sports have made us stronger, more courageous, and more prepared for performance in the rest of our lives. This is also true about our capacity for Money — to manifest it and to grow it!

Watch out because women are about to be new leaders and make dramatic changes in the marketplace. We are forging the Path for our own Financial Stability, and we are doing it while remaining feminine, loving, and compassionate.

#7 is the 'Don't Talk About it Myth' ...

When did you last go out to lunch with your girlfriend and talk about manifesting and managing your Money? I know you talk about the latest styles, the deepest parts of your intimate relationship, your family issues, your latest travel adventures — but what about your Money and how you successfully navigate the course to Financial Stability?

We've been raised in a society that believes polite conversation should never include religion, politics, or Money. When Money comes up, do you change the subject because you are uncomfortable opening up (and perhaps admitting that you are starting from scratch)?

Truth be told, when you talk about the taboo stuff, it thrives in the *light*. Sex got better when we brought it into the open and discussed it truthfully — the same is true for Money. Here's an idea. How about cultivating a female friend to be your Financial Accountability partner? Then we will really *bust* the 'Don't Talk About It Myth.' It hasn't done us any good. It only gets in our way when there is so much to be learned from one another.

#8 Myth is 'My Career Is My Financial Life Myth' ...

Here's another misconception. It is that our careers are our financial life. Yes, manifesting Money through a career is one part of the equation. You can work your whole career and earn handsomely, but if you spend what you have made, there is little left for Financial Stability. We see the stories of the sports stars and aging actresses that have blown through their Money.

When they want to leave their profession, they have nothing tucked away and are literally out of luck. They had opportunities all along the way, and they blew it. If you get to the end of your career and you have no Money, you crapped out. As discussed earlier, you need five kinds of money for each dollar you earn in your working years. One of those kinds is Money that you develop to meet your life-time considerations.

And there are different, new, and essential learnings for investing and growing Money. Earning it is one set of thinking; building assets is a whole other set of thinking.

There is a second part to this Money equation. It is about securing, growing, and managing your Money, including asset building. You can earn Money through a career, but intelligent use of your Money is vital to your Financial Stability, including having it work for you.

What's holding up your Money thinking — getting beyond the Myths?

Take the time to look at these Myths carefully. Which ones cloud *your* Money thinking? Make peace with the fact that they don't serve you. Financial Stability is going to require that you toss them out and make space for the Truths that *will* support you.

Grab your Journal and a pen and make some notes. Which Myths have some hold over you, which ones need to go from your thinking, and what new thinking can best serve you?

What are the Money Personas that get you stuck?

Two forms of Money Personas will derail your Journey.

Here they are: Those who think they are the 'haves' and those who think they are the 'have-nots.' Neither of these personas works, and here's why.

The 'haves' live under the false pretense of having plenty of Money. The problem is that they may not have created the right relationship with Money so that it becomes part of their Stability. Here's an example. Even if a woman is married to a wealthy spouse or has inherited a fortune, she must have her own access to funds that belong to her and know how to manage and grow those funds. This is often not the case.

By contrast, the 'have nots' have a different problem. The 'have-nots' live under the false pretense that Money doesn't befriend them. This is a woman who is wondering how she will meet her current expenses. She needs to generate Money now, quickly, and smartly. And here's the rub: this woman often believes that Money is hard to acquire, so she lives in a perpetual cycle of lack.

The Heroine thinks differently. Here's how the Heroine creates Financial Stability!

She thinks clearly about Money.

She knows how Money works.

She has access to her own funds.

She creates a constant flow of cash into her checking account that more than meets her needs.

She creates her Stability by knowing her numbers, generating what she requires, and living within her Means.

She makes Money work for her, growing assets and investments.

This is your formula for Money and happiness in your life!

So, who taught you about Money?

I want to share with you my own story about the Heroine who taught me about Money.

I was lucky. I had a Mother who was my guide. She wasn't afraid to talk about Money, how much she had in her account, what she was doing with it, and how she planned for it to grow. She saw herself as a woman who deserved to have plenty of it because she was confident in her services to earn it.

She saw growing her wealth as a good thing. And each year she consistently profited from her efforts and added to her assets. She also didn't let my Father's intimidation of her financial gain deter her progress. She understood that she created Financial Stability in her life consistently.

I saw that my Mother had more positive Beliefs about Money than negative ones. There were other things that I might have liked to have changed about my Mother, but what she taught me about how to make friends with Money and how to manifest it and manage it were blessings that fell on me! Thanks, Mom!

My dear friend and collaborator, Ivri, learned something different. Her mother taught her a very different way of thinking about Money. Ivri came from an affluent family that lived off of trust funds. Her mom's line was, "Our money grows on a tree in the backyard."

You can imagine that has not served her well as an adult. Her task has been to identify the deeply seated false Beliefs about Money that this story created for her. She had to let that go and become tactical with Money to make her Financial Stability. This was the change of direction that she took on her Heroine's Journey.

And then there's my client, Tanya. Her father was successful in his own right. But, he taught his daughter that she didn't ever need to concern herself with such matters as Money. She would marry a successful man who would take care of everything.

And she did! The problem was he left and took most of the fortune with him. What she did acquire, she had no idea how to manage, and she was soon out of funds. This is the unfortunate statistical reality for so many women.

It's important to consider: who taught you about Money? Was it a parent, a teacher, or your first job? And what did they teach you? Is what you learned useful in your relationship with Money today?

So much of our Money thinking is the subconscious programming we received in our early life.

Get your Journal and a pen out to dig deep and explore who you got your Money lessons from. And ask if those lessons are contributing to your Financial Stability. It's important to uncover your thinking and see what your thinking is producing.

What are you saying to yourself about Money?

If you feel your financial life may be in jeopardy that's a good indication that some of your thinking around Money may need to change. You need to fortify your Financial Cornerstone to buck up your Stability and transform into your Heroine-Self. A Heroine sets herself up for abundance.

Take a minute here to think about how you relate to Money. Do you have positive conversations with yourself about Money that draws Money to you? Are you good-natured about Money? Are you and Money friends? Are you grateful for all that it does for you? Do you respect how it shows up to support your interests? Regard it as a gift that is bestowed upon you for your careful use? Do you say thank you when Money lands in your checking account?

Or do you have negative conversations with yourself about Money? Is Money scarce in your life? Do you often fight with Money? Feel that it has abandoned you? Call it names when it disappoints you? Are you angry that it makes your life more troublesome or difficult? Resent that it doesn't befriend you more readily? Hoard it for only your pleasure? Or, ignore it like it's some insignificant irritant in your existence? Do you think Money is a bad thing? Do you think it's greedy to have it? Or do you feel less than if you don't have it?

Bottom line: Do you want to invite Money into your life with positive conversations or repel it with negative ones? Are you even consciously aware of the conversation you are currently having with yourself about Money?

Recently, I met Janet in a seminar I taught. She confessed that she was having a very negative conversation with Money in her head. Here is the dilemma she talked about. She said that it is easier to be poor than to step up and earn more Money. Her thinking was that earning more money would propel her into a new economic class, and she was concerned she would have to be more responsible with more Money. And, she subconsciously wanted to avoid responsibility.

She acknowledged that this was a shocking insight she had not verbalized before. Together, we realized the truth that the poverty she was experiencing was far more of a burden than managing her Money ever would be. She also realized she was putting a lid on expressing her own skills and talents because of her limited Money thinking.

When she saw these truths, she began formulating her actions to be more productive, expressive, and financially stable. She liberated her Money thinking.

There are many more stories about women and their Money thinking. Here are just a couple of them now.

Jennie, who put everything on hold but her career —

> "I have an MBA from Harvard and still don't know how to do my financial life. I have earned a lot and have lots of jewelry but no cash or financial security."

Sarah, who was the family bookkeeper —

> " I took care of the finances in my marriage, yet I was surprised to learn that there is a vast difference between the bookkeeping I did and planning to grow our cash for the future."

Jamie, who thought she could earn her way out —

> "I thought that if I just made more Money, I could earn my way out of the problem. I worked on this almost to the point of killing myself! I didn't get that having cash was a matter of temperament, not income."

Ruth, who just received an inheritance —

> "I've recently inherited more Money than I ever dreamed of having. It is such a change for me - I am scared that I have a lot to learn, and I'm afraid that I could make a mistake and blow it."

Maria, who'd gotten caught in a femininity myth —

> "I'm just beginning to see that I hold myself back because I'm afraid to make more Money or have more investments than my partner. Because then I might not be loved — how can a partner take care of me if I can take care of myself?"

Isn't it time to liberate your Money thinking?

Do you want to have a positive relationship with Money? Would it be stunning never again to have the thoughts:

> "Why isn't Money working for me?"
> "Growing Money is hard."
> "I don't know how to get out of my financial predicament."

Such thoughts are like hitting the replay button for the Crisis and Challenge phases of your Journey again and again. It is simply self-sabotage.

How *do* we liberate our Money thinking? We re-frame the conversations we repeatedly have with Money. Shifting negative Money conversations to positive ones allows you and me to begin the process of reprogramming the subconscious mind and, therefore, change our Money behaviors.

What does a re-framed Money conversation sound like? When I shift into talking positively about Money in my own head, here are the adjustments in the thoughts that I make:

Negative Thought: Money takes a lot of effort to generate.

Reframed Thought: I generate Money with ease by doing what I love.

Negative Thought: Excess Money = greed.

Reframed Thought: Excess Money = options.

Negative Thought: Excess Money = responsibility.

Reframed Thought: Excess Money = the ability to make a difference in a cause I believe in.

With your Journal, explore your conversations about Money, both positive and negative. Then, you will re-frame the negative thoughts to supportive ones so you can remove the blockages to Financial Stability.

Money madness is real.

Even after we have done the enlightened work of shifting our conscious conversation with Money, there is something crazy that sometimes bubbles up from our subconscious at 3 a.m. I call it 'Money Madness'. I've woken up so many times in the middle of the night thinking about Money, and the 'OMG, how am I going to handle this?!' question plagues me.

Let's call it out. It is fear.

Can you relate to this?

Laying in bed, I picture the dilemma that feels like an angry dog chasing me. This dog is the one thing that could wreck everything in my life. Numbers spin around my head while I wonder if I'll survive the problem or be eaten alive! When fear is gnashing its teeth at me, I summon my Courage and stare it straight in the face. I take this time to listen and seek an answer. Clearly, something is trying to get my attention and speak to me now. Maybe it's wisdom, the Universe, trying to convey new information.

Here's what I've learned. Remaining in fear doesn't help me in times of Money Madness. It's important to recognize this and actively take a new path. It's essential to upgrade from fear to discernment. What's the difference between fear and discernment?

Here it is — *options*! ... OPTIONS!

From a place of discernment, you can see that there are always plenty of options!

What's your 'Money Madness'? What financial concerns are driving you crazy?

Are there scenarios that play over and over in your thinking that wake you up at 3 am?

See that this Money Madness is a call from within to align yourself. Here's a prescription for treating Money Madness.

Money Madness Prescription

1. **Listen with your heart.** Listen to the story you are telling yourself with empathy. Notice that this narrative *predicts* failure and has very *limited* options.

2. **Reframe the story.** Take the time to retell the story according to the facts. Have an active conversation with yourself, and remind yourself that you and Money are friends.

3. **Recognize the gifts.** Yes, there is a gift present in the situation, no matter how difficult it seems right now. You will uncover it. Know that the Universe is conspiring for your good. It always is!

4. **Know what you need.** Review your numbers. Be honest about what is required at this moment. Keep the picture realistic, and don't overburden yourself by creating an inflated picture of lack.

5. **Get off the crazy train.** Remember the **Stress Storm Relief Practice** that we did in Chapter 4 herein - Cornerstone: Physical? Use it now to get centered and let go of fear. Remember that keeping yourself calm is your best path to being open and creative.

6. **Generate options with discernment.** Ask yourself, "*What good options do I have?*" This is the critical turning point in your thinking to go from limitation to liberation. Focusing on your *options* opens up possibilities that couldn't come to you while you were in fear.

7. **Get tactical.** Choose one or two of the good options and create a plan to implement them.

8. **Take action on your plan.** Money Madness is really a motivator. Break your action plan into steps and execute. Yes, you can take action at 3 am! Some of your best ideas can come to life in the middle of the night.

Hey, Heroine, please don't let Money Madness ground your flight. Use the Money Madness Prescription to get into the right thinking so you can travel onward.

Believe this: Money Madness is opening you up to being more resourceful in your life.

While this might seem odd to you, this kind of Money Madness panic catalyzes you to take new action. And everything in your life conspires to take you to your fullest potential on your Heroine's Journey. It's all a big adventure.

Money Madness reminds you not just to put your head in the sand. You must continue moving forward. See this attention-grabber as your friend. It's a reminder that you have an active role in your financial life.

Copy the Money Madness Prescription and keep it by your bedside. It's even better than a warm glass of milk at 3 am.

Remember, if you have more positive thoughts than negative ones, you will attract Money into your life. So, get clear and purposeful about your conversations with yourself.

Yes, there are a tremendous number of options in your glorious future. It won't be realized by waiting for the White Knight to arrive or wishing that a flying carpet will magically appear to lift you above your worldly concerns. You have to live the truths you've discovered.

You are on the Path to building your Financial Stability. No matter your circumstances, you're in a position to fix whatever hasn't been working and improve whatever has. Creating your Financial Stability is within your reach.

The real joy comes from knowing that you've decided to fly and that you've begun to understand the power of Money and your power to welcome Money into your life.

YOUR THREE MONEY NUMBERS

Now that you know what you're saying to yourself about Money, the next step is to know *your* numbers. How much money do you need to fund your life?

Breathe here, it may seem like a big task, but I'm here to show you how to figure out Your 3 Money Numbers: what I call 'Dignity Money,' 'Lifestyle Money,' and 'Dream Money.' This firmly establishes us in Step #7 of the Heroine's Journey, Gather Your Provisions.

Think way back in Step #3, The Challenge. In this Step, you may have been in a precarious financial position that required you to quickly know how much you need to live at bare bones — your Dignity Money. Dignity Money is rock bottom sustaining yourself Money.

You'll be ready for the next Money number as things look up. We'll calculate the income necessary to support your lifestyle — your Lifestyle Money. Lifestyle Money lets you live in the middle of the road.

These are the precursors to calculating the number that is flowing to you for your wildest dreams — your Dream Money.

Without knowing your numbers, you can't have a plan. The key is to know your numbers and live within your Means. Dignity Money and Lifestyle Money establish your Financial Stability. But don't stop there. Big dreams are included in the Heroine's Journey, so we also envision our Dream Money number.

Let's jump into Your 3 Money Numbers now …

What is Dignity Money?

The first number to establish is what I call 'Dignity Money.' It is the amount of Money you need monthly to ensure that your basic needs are met. This minimal, luxury-free amount covers your most pared-down expenses. In other words, this amount of Money is your bare minimum so that you are not left bereft as a 'bag lady.'

You can figure out how much Dignity Money you'll need by determining the smallest amount that it will cost you to live each month. You might think you need things that you don't really need. This is bare bones.

Here are some things to consider trimming the fat on below:

Internet (go to a coffee shop or library)
cable (add an antenna to your roof)
personal property riders on your insurance plan
home and yard services
club memberships
dry cleaning
entertainment
eating out
media subscriptions
new clothes
hair salon
continuing education
veterinarian services
travel
also, consider switching to public transportation

Here's how you add up your Dignity Money. In your Journal, add up what you absolutely *need* to spend each month for:

basic food
transportation
taxes
down-sized housing
telephone
utilities
insurance

Don't include any frills. Here, we're establishing just the basics. Be sure to post your Dignity Money number in your Journal.

Your Dignity Money calculation should be well thought out and accurately calculated, but it doesn't have to be down to the penny. It might be $1,000 a month or $5,000 a month. Each person's sum will be different.

In any event, your Dignity Money number is the amount of cash that comes into your checking account each month to sustain your life. By knowing your Dignity Money and living within those Means, you won't ever need to have anxiety about the basics.

If you already generate Dignity Money, then you can feel at ease. Knowing that you meet this threshold should give you a good feeling and relieve whatever stressful flutters you may have had before you knew this number.

On the other hand, you may currently be in some of the most challenging parts of the Heroine's Journey. Knowing what your Dignity Money number is will help you focus on making ends meet. You may have to slash and burn many of your expenses. Consider downsizing your home, putting the kids in public school, buying a used car, eating in your own kitchen, shopping at Target (rather than Needless Markup), canceling the spa treatments, and planning staycations at home. It's doable.

The caution here is don't rely on your credit card to make up any budgetary gap. At this stage of tightening your belt, the worst thing you can do is add debt because that makes the climb to Financial Stability that much steeper.

I know I was used to being casual and liberal with my Money when I was running my brokerage business. My Heroine's Journey was initiated by divorce and subsequent effects on my business and savings — and suddenly, I had to take a really hard look at what it took for me to live and where that money was coming from each month. It also foreshadowed for me what it takes to think through future retirement with the understanding of the ratio of Money that needs to come in and go out monthly. I had to get back to basics. It was painful, no doubt about it, but that was the start of it to get my feet on the ground. Dignity Money is an important number to know.

While this was a scary and uncertain time in my life, I tried not to beat myself up. I got very tactical about how to manage myself from the inside to direct my life situation on the outside. A big change had occurred. I was no longer living in the affluence that I had once enjoyed. It was a critical time to adjust to the reality of my Dignity number.

I quickly contacted my accountant friend and ran my calculations by her. With numbers in hand, we planned how I could rearrange my life and survive this new and temporary Dignity Money reality.

The Dignity Money stage is full of lessons that are gifts in disguise. It forces you to look deeply at what matters most, what you need most, and how to simplify your life to live with less. It can be very liberating if you maintain a positive conversation with Money while you are living within your Dignity Money number.

As you upgrade your Money thinking and put these gifts into practice, you'll have the fuel for the Journey! The Journey can take you out of the Dignity Money stage and into the Lifestyle Money reality.

What is LifeStyle Money?

Are you keeping up to speed in your Journal? Now, you'll record the second Money Number.

The second Money Number to calculate for yourself is what I call 'Lifestyle Money.' This is the amount of cash you desire to come into your checking account each month to support the lifestyle you want to live. It not only covers your bills, but there is some money to enjoy the frills, and there is excess to invest in building your long-term assets.

Here, you take proactive action from a new and empowered place and live your desired lifestyle sustainably according to your Lifestyle Money number.

In Lifestyle Money, this is no time to get lax though. In the Heroine's Journey, it's predictable that along comes Step #8, 'Wind Currents that Test You.' Remember that? Another Challenge is likely to come your way that tests your Financial Stability. And this may challenge you several more times. You can weather the temporary storms if you've been diligent in Lifestyle Money.

To get control of your Lifestyle Money, you need to know where your cash goes each month so you can see your spending pattern.

Now, using your Journal, start with the basic expenses you listed in Dignity Money and add to them all the ways you spend your Money. Use your bank statements and cash payments (and credit card statements if necessary) to track where your Money really goes. Be as honest and realistic as possible.

If this is new to you, it will be very enlightening. You may be amazed at how much you spend in one category or more as you are tooling along in life, not being conscious of your Money's departure from your checking account. Oops ... "I didn't know that I spent so much money at the grocery store, you might be saying!"

Once you generate your Lifestyle Money Number, you have moved out of the lack and restricted area of Dignity Money and into comfort and relative abundance. This can feel really good.

However, sometimes, it can falsely lure you into looseness in spending. Our psychology tells us we are done with living behind the iron bars of Dignity Money. To a certain degree, we have been set free. But the temptation is to go wild sometimes, thinking we are well past Dignity Money living. This Money mania can throw us off course very quickly and the old ghosts of Money worries begin to haunt us again.

I've had trouble managing myself in this way. Here's the problem that I recognize. I'm a 'shiny object' kind of girl. I'm too quick to part with my cash when I see something and like it. I like the 'girl stuff' — shoes, clothes, pretty things and lots of pots for my garden. And I had to get real with myself to stay on track with my Financial Stability.

Here's what actress and comedian Sophie Tucker has to say: that stirred my thinking, galvanized my action, and led me to write my first book, *A Girl Needs Cash*. She says:

From birth to age 18, a girl needs good parents.
From 18 to 35, she needs good looks.
From 35 to 55, she needs a good personality.
And from 55 on, a girl needs cash.

And I say, don't wait until you are 55. A woman in this era needs her own cash her whole life long. Life goes along quickly, and soon, you'll be happy to have a bundle tucked away.

Are you generating more than you need to meet your Lifestyle Money number? Or are you like most women who live at the cusp of their Lifestyle Money and spend their entire paycheck each month?

Most women invest more money in their clothes closets and makeup drawers than in their savings accounts. What's wrong with this picture? It isn't sustainable! If you are tripping over this elephant under the rug, it's time to come clean and live within your Means.

As you figure out your number for Lifestyle Money, you can create a strategy to generate the right amount and develop a spending plan to have a comfortable lifestyle without overextending your checking account.

Congrats if you are a woman with income beyond what you require for your basic expenses and lifestyle, and you even have an asset-building plan (which we will teach you and encourage you to do later in the Heroine's Journey to True Wealth studies).

As you manage your Lifestyle Money and actively pursue being a woman with cash, it calms your internal Money Madness so you can focus on the next Steps of the Heroine's Journey.

What is 'Dream Money'?

On The Heroine's Journey, most of us get to the Lifestyle Money stage, but too few of us have the tools and tenacity to go to the next stage of 'Dream Money.'

Yippee! In Dream Money, you have far more cash coming into your checking account monthly than you need for yourself. You no longer have debt/credit card balances — this is a thing of the past. And your life is not beholden to accumulating bills. The only debt you have is 'good' debt — mortgages that free up more of your cash to invest elsewhere.

In Dream Money, your lifestyle is secure. And here's the fun part. You feel free to open up to higher visions. Dream Money is where you activate your thinking for that beach house or something else that brings juice and joy to your material life. Maybe for you, it's buying your Mother a house, gifting a big sum to your favorite Animal Rescue organization, or going off to live in Paris for six months. Let your imagination soar in all that is possible.

In your Journal, list some ways that inspire you in Dream Money. Play for a time here! What ways would this Money work for you to bring you and others joy? What dreams do you have when Money is overflowing in your checking account?

Here's what one of my Lighthouses, Eleanor Roosevelt, has to say about this:

"The future belongs to those who believe in the beauty of their dreams."

~ Eleanor Roosevelt

On The Heroine's Journey, the penultimate is when you are living your gifts — when you have leveraged yourself into Dream Money and are a contributor to the greater good. The full scope of The Heroine's Journey to True Wealth leads you through this Journey.

But for now, go calculate Your 3 Money Numbers. Keep them in your Journal. These numbers will show you how much you need coming into your monthly checkbook to cover you from avoiding bag-lady status to funding your bigger Heroine-Self.

And, then review your objectives so your unconscious mind can work on your prosperity!

FINANCIAL STABILITY FORMULA

Now is when the rubber meets the road. The Journey you are on requires your Courage, Strength and yep, you guessed it – ACTION!!

No matter where you are on your Heroine's Journey, the goal is living well. What does 'living well' look like?

Living well *is aligning your* *financial life* *so that your* *Self-Worth* *flourishes and your* *purpose* *can blossom. It's your tactical approach to having a* *good feeling* *about Money in the pit of your stomach, relieving stress, and making your* *Stability* *a top priority in your life.*

Got this? I want this for you!

So many of us have gone through the really rough times that characterize The Heroine's Journey. I certainly have! At those times, feeling down about ourselves and worried about the future is easy. Is this true? Sometimes, your financial life can feel like you're in a boiling pot and you are scrambling to get out of the soup.

Whether you are in the pot or on fire to create financial abundance, there is a plan for you to align yourself with the power of Money. We call it the 'Financial Stability Formula.'

No matter how much Money you have, the way forward is to align with the Financial Stability Formula. You can always bolster your Financial Well-Being. This Formula is here for you to dig deep and make some major tactical upgrades. Follow the Formula to leverage your partnership with Money. It serves as your roots as you stretch your wings. For now, just put one foot in front of the other and follow the Formula. It works!

My big dream is for you and all my Heroine Sisters to prosper — joy, prosperity and freedom.

Now, let's get tactical!

What is the Financial Stability Formula?

It's time to get tactical — the numbers *do* matter. Right now, acknowledge what is not working and fix it! Cha-ching!

You might wander around in the ethers too much if you're a 'Creative' like me. You'll have to adjust your mental meanderings to focus and produce results to complete these Steps of the Journey. You may have to turn on other brain parts to work with the numbers. You can do this, and the 'Financial Stability Formula' will guide you.

Are you ready to grab the reins and charge forward? Keep making notes in your Journal!

There are ten steps in this super-doable **Financial Stability Formula**. I'll first list them for you and then fully explain each one.

Financial Stability Formula:

1. Live Within Your Means

2. Know Your Money Power
3. Create Your Monthly Spending Plan
4. Snap the Spending Chain
5. Say Phooey to Credit Cards
6. Sell Stuff
7. Don't Invade Your Savings
8. Safely Store Your Documents
9. Get Accountability Support
10. Live Like 'Money isn't your whole life.'

You have the power to make radical and necessary changes in your life. Don't get stressed. Get tactical. Dig in, and please don't skip any of these integers in the Formula. They will help you create your financial freedom. Align yourself to these principles so you can live well. Here, they are described in their full glory.

The Financial Stability Formula #1: Live Within Your Means

OK, no getting around this! Here's the truth: *drum roll, please! You've got to live within your Means to stay on The Heroine's Journey.* No exceptions.

If you don't, you will be hassled with Money anxiety that slows down your progress. Your best choice is to commit to a lifestyle where you live within your *Means* so that you have the resources to sustain your Journey fully.

A Heroine embraces this part of her life to move forward and eliminate any confusion and chaos that Money drama causes. She understands that the Journey begins with *living within her Means*, and then, as she blossoms she travels onward to *expanding* her Means.

Living within your Means may sound like a big task. When you look at how people are spending money around you and listen to the coaxing of advertising, you might falsely assume that other people have more financial freedom than you do. It isn't so. Did you know that more than half of Americans live well beyond their Means, spending more than they make monthly? This is causing the anxiety, frustration, and greed-driven society we live in.

Fifty-seven percent of Americans cannot access $1000 in an emergency (according to Bankrate as reported on CNBC). Half of Americans spend more than they earn every year (according to Huffington Post).

As a Heroine, this is your opportunity to take the Path less traveled — acknowledging your reality, counting your cash, and spending only what you have available to support your living expenses before any indulgences. This is the bravery and Courage of a Heroine.

If living within your Means feels restrictive rather than expansive and creative, reframing that thought is very important.

Here's how I see it: Living within my Means holds me accountable. Limited funds help me focus my energy and attention on what I am truly up to in my bigger life plan. When I use my Money purposefully rather than frivolously, I feel in alignment with my larger goals. This is me keeping my commitment to myself. I am a Heroine this way!

And Heroine, that does feel good — even better than the rush of an impulse buy.

The key to living within your Means is to know your numbers. You already know your 3 Money Numbers: Dignity Money, Lifestyle Money, and Dream Money. Now the question is, which number are you able to live in alignment with to maintain Financial Stability?

This will help you; now, you will rate the context of how you live financially. We will use a subjective rating scale called 'The Financial Means Scale,' and it works like this: You will rank your cash capacity right now and it's ability to steward your life.

Here's Financial Means Scale:

1 to 3 — is living in Dignity Money
5 to 7 — is living in Lifestyle Money
9 to 10 — is living in Dream Money

Here is how it breaks down:

1. *means:* You have nothing in your checking account and no assets. Don't lament; it means you are in a place of total potential.

2. *means:* You come up short each month and scramble to make ends meet.
3. *means:* You are just over the wire without room for extras.
4. *means:* You have mastered Dignity Money and are on the cusp of Lifestyle Money.
5. *means:* You have a dollar to spare at the end of the month, and you can indulge in small pleasures, but Money Madness still arises, and there is still more you need to do to create your Financial Stability.
6. *means:* You are generating more cash than you need each month comfortably, and have options for this additional cash.
7. *means:* You are living your desired lifestyle and have money to save. You are progressively establishing your Financial Stability.
8. *means:* You have mastered Lifestyle Money and are on the cusp of Dream Money.
9. *means:* You live abundantly with extra to share. Money is no longer a limitation. You have taken care of your lifestyle and have more Money to use to enable others ...
10. *means:* You can fund your wildest dreams and effect good change in the world with your Money.

By identifying exactly where you fall in this spectrum, you'll get a reality check of what your financial Means actually are.

The information you will gain from the "The Financial Means Scale" can help you be more financially conscious while you answer the following important questions.

- Are you attempting to live higher on the scale, but truthfully, this undermines your Financial Stability?
- Or, Are you living a privileged life before you can afford to do so?
- If you dropped your lifestyle down a point or two would that help to improve your Financial Stability?
- Right now, with your commitments, would it be wise to be more discerning about how Money is leaving your checking account?

Unless you are born with a 'silver spoon,' then there are times to cop to living within your Means. Money is here to teach us all. It's a great teacher, as it ebbs and flows in all of our lives, mine too!

Money ebbed in my life when I underwent so much change on the Path of my Journey. I'd lived 'large,' and then...poof, it was necessary to live 'small.' My happiness depended upon my quick recovery to living a more restrained life, at least temporarily.

I was lucky, and I grew up in the Midwest in the cornfields, where people practiced simplicity and living without the brands, labels and extras. I knew rich people who didn't even have a radio in their car! While it sounds crazy, it's doable. And I had the skills to go back to live simply. To manage the financial change in my life, I had to downsize, and there was not an option. And best to make this a new chapter in life that can be inventive and imaginative. Here's how I started.

First, I reviewed my Dignity Money number because that's where I was. Then, I considered my cash flow at that time to see if I could meet my Dignity expenses. Luckily, I could. But, I had to curtail a few more things, like limiting grocery shopping, doing my own nails and grooming my puppies, no clothes shopping, paying attention to the gas I used and more.

As life got simpler, I got more appreciative of the things that I did have. I had people who supported me, reason to believe in my gifts, and time to stop and see the beauty around me. All was not lost. I have happy memories from that time.

It meant that I ate out less, passed on entertainment tickets, and kept a close eye on utility costs. I didn't do it perfectly, but it got me through.

True, it required me to make some changes. I really focused on living within my Means. I proved to myself that I could. Sure, there were times when I got off course, like an item or two from Target, and this impacted my monthly balance. I recognized it and recommitted to the bigger picture I had for myself: *to live happily within my Means.*

It wouldn't have done any good to beat myself up when I got off course. I needed to be my own best friend, as these were very challenging times. I just gently got back on course. And, you know what? My cash flow grew, and I later had room to expand.

What I learned was to stay within my Means and to work on expanding my Means. Even as I've moved on, this strategy still applies each and every day.

Live within your Means with grace.

Realize if you are or are not living within your Means currently. Either way, right now, commit to this way of life. Allow your consciousness to deliver the message kindly when you have gone off course and correct your course.

Financial Stability Formula #2: Know Your Money Power

Your Money Power is comprised of your cash flow and valuable assets. These are the two things to consider when you need to assess and leverage your resources.

How much comes into your checking account each month? Where does it come from? How dependable are the sources? These questions are essential to know your monthly cash flow. When living within your Means, you take care of all your expenses from this cash flow.

Does your income come from a job, rental, business, alimony, social security, investment, or perhaps some combination? Grab your Journal now — and list all of your sources of income. List each revenue source and add up your monthly income.

In addition to your cash flow, do you have valuable assets that could be converted to cash if you needed to quickly access cash — like real estate, business interests, gold jewelry, antique furniture, and Internet properties?

Grab your Journal again and list all of the 'Valuable Assets' that you have and their cash value. Now, total the cash value of these assets. Don't worry about doing this perfectly – just estimate the value. For instance, if you have a diamond ring from a marriage or other valuable jewelry — just choose a number. You could have it appraised later. The same is true for other assets. This is just for you to ballpark your assets' value.

Now add your yearly cash flow plus your assets to get your Money Power.

This isn't surprising if you don't have any assets because you may not have thought about building assets in the past. But we're going to change that later on in the continuing work of The Heroine's Journey to True Wealth because asset growth is the way of the Heroine.

The best way to live in your Money Power is to know your cash flow and where your worth is stored. A Heroine knows her Financial Power!!!

Financial Stability Formula #3: Create Your Monthly Spending Plan

This is a must — have your Monthly Spending Plan in place. What is a monthly spending plan? It is simply a written way of tracking your expenses and ensuring they are within your monthly income. It's about the relationship and attention you give to your money and the intimacy you develop with how it works for you.

If this sounds daunting, hang in. I am going to help you create your Monthly Spending Plan right here. We are going to get it done elegantly so you can live in your Financial Wellness Zone.

There are many benefits to living according to your Monthly Spending Plan. Here are some of them:

Benefits:

> Brings you into partnership with your Money
> Puts you smack in the middle of reality instead of an emotional story
> Requires you take your head out of the sand
> Supports you to live within your Means
> Gives you the power of knowledge about your numbers
> Helps you live according to your priorities
> Helps you make plans and come up with good options
> Keeps you from straying from the safe spending path
> Gives you Stability

I want to tell you how it works.

Starting from the first of the month, you will calculate the numbers for your *projected* financial activity for the entire month. This includes:

1. Monthly Projected Income
2. Current Monthly Expenses
3. Trimmed Monthly Expenses - this is a process we will do together to identify where you can reduce your spending this month (if necessary)
4. And then the bottom line, which is your Projected Net cash flow, which is the difference between your projected expenses and projected monthly income

You will review your Monthly Spending Plan at the end of the month and track your *actual* financial activity. You will record your:

1. *Actual* Income Earned that month
2. *Actual* Monthly Expenses paid out
3. And your actual bottom line - Your Net cash flow, which is the difference between *actual* expenses and *actual* monthly income, to discover if you successfully lived within your Means.

You'll repeat this exercise each month. Make it a healthy habit, and you'll have many happy returns.

Notice that part of the Monthly Spending Plan is trimming your expenses. Be thoughtful about this process. Ask yourself, what can I eliminate or reduce to minimize my expenses? Remember we talked about some of these ideas when we discussed Dignity Money?

You could cut your cable TV and put an antenna on your roof for free service. Maybe it's a gym membership you haven't been using or no clothes shopping for the next six months until you get your Financial Stability in place.

A good place to start is to ask yourself what you are spending Money for that really doesn't bring you joy. Or, if your situation is more serious, what can you simply live without until you move out of the current cash crunch? What is it that you can lessen, eliminate, live without, or postpone to manage through this time?

Financial Stability Formula #4: Snapping The Spending Chain

Do you need the latest trends, fashions, and labels? Are you a victim of the spending chain? Or is cash in your checking account more important than any bauble, bangle, or trinket?

Here's an unfortunate reality for many of us. As women, we're programmed by our culture and our desire to please, to look really 'hot' when we go out on a dinner date. So we may spend frivolously to look the part. It may work to polish the outside but it doesn't work for the inside. Financial Stability is way sexier — it puts a smile on our pretty faces and a skip in our step, making us more attractive than any makeup or sexy heels. So, true Heroine!

I love the greeting card that states this simple truth: 'If I had a dollar for all of the clothes, jewelry, hairstyles, and cosmetics I've gone through in pursuit of the right man….I'd be so rich I wouldn't need him.' Ha, Hah!!

Are your dollars invested in stuff you bought when it would be better off in your savings account? Is your cash thin and your coffers orphaned because you part with your cash too easily?

Does it sometimes feel like money pours through your hands like water? This has been painfully true for many working women, who spend money on clothes, accessories, and grooming because they must always look good. There are also the added maintenance costs — dry cleaning, laundry, and salon bills - to keep clothes, hair, and nails looking good. The maintenance can slice a big chunk from a paycheck.

Women spend money on other things as well, like vacations, cars, and entertainment. Some drop big bundles on furniture, high-tech kitchen appliances, and sports equipment, or overpriced health clubs and personal trainers. Many others fix up their homes or spend Money on their children, spouses, and partners. And then, some women have no idea how Money spills from their wallets — it simply disappears by the end of the month, and they feel anxious and guilty that their cash is gone.

There are so many ways that our culture teaches us, through advertising, to spend money. And there are very few ways that our culture teaches us to hold on to our cash. We are all bombarded nearly every second with some Money-spending strategy. If we are not very conscious about this waterfall of ways by which we can be parted from our cash, it will surely leave us quickly.

There is a 'small child' within me that says "But I want it!" That 'small child' can be very demanding. There is a rush and a zeal to handing over your debit card and walking away with the prize the child so deeply yearned for. But who's in control here? Is this really going to help you build your Financial Stability?

Once it really came home to me that my Financial Stability was more important and I was willing to Fierce Feminine defend it, I could communicate to that 'small child' within and help her see that the adult in me has a better plan.

Snapping the spending chain can be as easy as snapping your fingers. Done!

Consider snapping Things like:

> More shoes and handbags
> Fancy foods
> Dog and Cat Stuff
> Cosmetics
> Facials
> Personal Trainers
> Excessive vacations
> Entertainment
> Less driving to save on gas
> There are a multitude of ways!

And here's a little trick that will really help you snap the spending chain. For one month, do an experiment. Pay cash — you know, the paper money kind — for everything you purchase.

There is a different psychological impact when you hand over your hard earned cash to the cashier rather than swiping a plastic card. Feel the cash in your hand. You will feel the sting of impulse buys so much more clearly, and you'll be more directly connected to the value of your dollar. It will help you form better spending habits, with your better relationship with Money.

A Heroine needs cash for her Journey, and she needs to snap the spending chain on items that depreciate as soon as they are purchased. Cash is required as fuel for your Journey. Keep as much as you can!!!

Financial Stability Formula #5: Say Phooey to Credit Cards

Here's my best advice about Money: You have to pay cash!

"Why, you say? Isn't a credit card ok?" No! My lovely Heroine! It works like a great paradox. When you can actually use a credit card and not get yourself into trouble — that is when you actually don't need a credit card because you have cash! When you run your life on a 'cash only' basis, you'll better understand what you value, live within your Means, and have less anxiety.

Years ago, I found a toy that shocked me. Wow, so obvious that it inappropriately conditioned young female financial behavior. We all had them, Barbie. This version was Credit Card Barbie! Yep, she's for real. And she can set in motion accepting a lifetime of debt as something attractive. *Yikes!*

The point is advertising conditions us that it is feminine and fun to be in debt. Heroine, we all know that debt is no fun! Don't be duped. Live credit card free. We'd all say 'Boo' If there was a 'Smoking Barbie' that was retailed to increase *that* habit. We say 'no' to programming.

Let's look at the debacle of credit cards as a way of life. Here are the facts: The number of middle and upper-income women struggling with credit card debt has risen faster than the number of lower-income women struggling with credit card debt (Women Debt and Resources).

This shows that women who should be able to live within their Means are using credit cards to live well above their Means. I often wonder if that designer handbag hanging on the shoulder of a woman passing by was purchased on a credit card. It can end up costing two, three, and four times more, as this one-time purchase wastes ongoing resources with excessive interest charges. This is a vicious cycle. And is there any money in her wallet, in that expensive handbag, I wonder?

It requires too much energy to carry around in your head the amounts of money you owe, especially if you have 2 or 3 outstanding balances, which you shift from one card to another. This is a crazy way to complicate life.

Some people have more racked up on their credit card balances than they earn in one or even two year's time. Credit cards have been a primary factor in the alarming increase in personal bankruptcies. Shouldn't there be a warning label on the card like there is on a pack of cigarettes?

Here's the bottom line: Cut up your cards and pay cash! And, cash includes using your Debit Card. That's ok. Only spend balances in your checkbook.

A substitute for a credit card is a debit card with a Visa logo. It allows you to buy an airline ticket or rent a hotel room, but money is immediately debited from your account. With a debit card, you only spend the cash in your checking account and not more. This is a method of living within your Means.

If you have a big balance on your credit card, cut your card up now and create a plan to pay back the balance over time. Revisit your Monthly Spending Plan and make a commitment to pay a regular amount toward your Credit Card each month to reduce the balance continually.

Filing bankruptcy to avoid credit card debt will undermine your ability to have Financial Stability for at least seven years, as you'll have a black mark on your credit. Try not to make big messes any bigger. Take responsibility to clean it up.

The way to live is credit-card-free. If you've been doing this, keep it up. If you haven't been living credit card-free, now's the time to change your strategy. For a Heroine, Financial Freedom is living your daily life on a cash basis. It's so much easier!

Financial Stability Formula #6: Sell Stuff

At some time in your Journey you may look in your wallet and discover that there's not much cash there. Then you check your bank balance online, and it's looking very thin too. This can happen before you build your Financial Stability because when you are unstable, an unpredictable event can really rock your world and leave you cash poor.

If you are in a pinch or a serious bind, as can happen — then you ask, "How can I raise cash fast?" A good and immediate solution is to sell stuff. What can you sell to ease your financial worries? It may be gold jewelry, a second home, clothes, shoes, or handbags. Maybe you have stuff that just sits on shelves in your closet, garage, or basement.

Once you know what to sell, where do you sell it? There are many options for unloading your stuff — a garage sale, consignment shop, and pawn shop, to name a few. Some other friends of mine regularly take their salable items to the local flea market at the Community College. There are also many ways to sell on the internet on sites like Tradesy and Ebay.

You may have some big items that you're ready to sell. These can be offered on CraigsList, where you can sell a car, a boat, or other recreational toys to pair down your lifestyle. My friend had antique furniture that she readily sold via CraigsList to pick up some fast cash. This enabled her to get rid of her storage unit which was an additional monthly fee.

Hopefully, you can sell sufficient stuff to provide some quick short-term funds while making other plans to generate cash for the longer term.

You can accomplish two things simultaneously: raise cash and clear out the clutter. How much cash can you generate by selling your extra stuff?

Financial Stability Formula #7: Don't Invade Your Savings

Whoa! Stop!... Don't invade your savings! If you're thinking, "I could spend some of my savings now to stop the bleeding and replace it later,"....stop right there. That plan will get you deeper into the hole. And one of my favorite sayings is 'There's no cheese down that hole'!

Turn around and go back.

Use your savings only if you have enough to manage your current lifestyle for the rest of your life. But even then, never invade principle; live off of the principal's income.

Here's the deal: never invade your savings, dwindling the principle. If you need cash, time for plan B. Go raise it or earn it. This may mean you need to find a job or search for other creative income to assist your cash flow, like selling your art online, renting out a room in your house, doing short-term projects for friends and acquaintances, and finding odd jobs on Craigslist. You are as young and as able as you are ever going to be right now. Now is the time to get ahead of your cash needs as an alternative to depleting your resources.

Warning: dipping into your savings is the easy way out. But you'll be paying for it over the long term because you are actually invading your Financial Stability.

Think like a Heroine and keep advancing your Financial Well-Being.

Financial Stability Formula #8: Safely Store Your Documents

There is an important component to Financial Stability that involves tractability and organization. It will help your Money thinking and facilitate your Stability to have all your important financial and personal documents together and safely stored in one place.

Often, we have all of this paperwork spread out in various locations and not readily available when needed or when someone you trust needs to find it on your behalf. Part of your Financial Stability is to be organized so that you have immediate access to this information that is so important to your life.

You may need these documents quickly, especially when your Path crosses the Crisis and Challenge Steps on your Journey. I know that when I went through a divorce, I scrambled and sorted through all my files to assemble these documents and access this information. It's best not to do it when you are in a panic.

Have you done this for yourself yet? Is there a safe place where you have assembled all of your important documents? These would include your Will or Living Trust, Insurance documents, bank records, taxes, internet passwords, mortgage information, investment accounts, etc.

Now's the time to get your records in order! Put all the documents in a fireproof safe or file cabinet where someone trusted has access.

And there is one more little tip while you are in this process. Put a laminated card in your wallet of who to contact in case of emergency, someone who knows how these documents can be accessed.

This will give you peace of mind! Ahhhh . . . .

Financial Stability Formula #9: Get Accountability Support

I was proud to say that 'I did it on my own' for much of my life. I was that warrior princess who headed out on The Heroine's Journey to take on the challenges with my guts and grit. But then the circumstances became more than I could handle by myself.

Then it happened, the part of The Journey where the 'Angles' showed up — and I breathed a big sigh of relief that I was no longer on the Journey alone. I was so much better served by the wisdom that others brought that was sometimes bigger than mine.

I learned to look around and see who was divinely guided to me and how these people could make things easier and more successful in my life. It took showing humility to accept the contributions that they were happy to make. My Heroine's Journey gathered speed and happy times when I began partnering!

The first type of partner is the Accountability Partner.

Can a friend or business partner help you be financially accountable? Is there someone you are also willing to hold to this standard of commitment? Could you have an upfront conversation with this person and share how you would like to do this for each other?

Are you willing to talk about where your Money comes from, where it goes, and how you think about how you handle Money? Where can you cultivate this type of relationship with a Financial Accountability Partner?

I have a female financial accountability partner! I'm loving it! It's a new addition to my life. It's a relationship that I've coveted as I've watched some of my favorite male friends accomplish this for themselves. They showed me teamwork, and partnering to support each other.

Ours is a female friendship that is transparent about the taboo subject of Money and where ours is coming from and going. We've developed great trust and intimacy around Money and our Money thinking. I wouldn't make a significant financial move without discussing it with her first.

When we talk about Money together, I have to expose my crazy thinking, which sometimes shows up as White Knight Syndrome, Shiny Object Syndrome, resistance to snapping the spending chain or being temporarily caught in fear or paralysis. I get to put it all on the table, and we laugh about it, knowing that crazy thinking doesn't work. Getting out of the crazy way of thinking allows me to take the right actions.

We call on each other to formulate plans that are in alignment with our values and our commitment to Stability. It's not about checking in for permission to go shopping. When I explain to her what I am doing financially, I ask for feedback about whether this is the 'right' move for me. And she does the same with me.

I've learned that it's amazing and invaluable how we've both grown in our good sense around Money as we've been committed to being transparent about what we are doing financially. Together, we support each other by carefully measuring anything that would potentially mess with the prized condition of being Financially Stable.

I hope that you cultivate a Financial Accountability Partner too. You'll have to reach out to create this relationship actively to make this happen. Here is an opportunity to choose from among those in your Circle of Love who have bright 'Green' stickers.

Once you find them, talk with them about your commitment to helping them achieve Financial Stability and your expectation that they hold you accountable as well. Then, you may want to make a list of your crazy Money thinking and specific Money decisions that you need to make to bolster your Stability.

Transparently share these things with your Accountability Partner in a regular dialogue. Acknowledge their successes and yours as you progress.

Now you and your Partner are on the Journey together!

Another type of partnering: an Accountant

OK, January of the new year rolls around, and it heralds another tax year. One type of Accountability Support that I highly recommend is a good accountant. This can make the January transition easier when you know that you will be up to speed on getting your taxes filed on time.

It's also an assurance that you'll be taking advantage of all the tax deductions available to you. Remember, Uncle Sam does not write you a thank you note if you overpay him. You won't receive a nice card from him that says, 'Becky, it was so thoughtful of you this year to send me an extra bonus amount in your tax payment, and I appreciate your kindness.' Nope!

Did you know there are $1.3 Billion in refunds that are not claimed each year? Claim yours! The IRS announced that it's sitting in its coffers, and encourages taxpayers to come get it.

Here's what my Mother taught me: Report all of your income and take every deduction that you possibly can. She was an intelligent business-woman who loved to engineer her profitability and filed her taxes on time.

Make sure to ask your Accountant to be an Accountability Partner with you. Instruct them to lay the pressure on you to file your taxes on time and not give you endless extensions. Completing up-to-date tax records provides you with the information available when you need to take out a loan or make other business plans.

Make sure your financial matters are in order. Partnering with a good accountant will get you fast-tracked to taking charge of your Money and taxes.

The Ultimate Partner is YOU: Self-Care

There is self-care when it comes to nurturing yourself, like meditating or getting enough sleep. When it comes to managing the business of your life — your Money – you also need a practice of self-care. This is about giving loving attention to your Financial Well-Being.

For me, I set aside two hours in my week that I calendar to do the following:

- Post my bank statement in the software to reconcile my accounts
- Review the numbers to see if I've stayed on track with my Monthly Spending Plan

- Review other statements like credit cards (if you have them) and investment accounts (better to have these!)
- Catch up on anything that is behind, like bill payment or tax preparation.

Sounds kind of strange to think of reviewing bank statements like getting enough sleep, but the reality is that both can reduce your anxiety, increase your Well-Being, and encourage healthy living.

Your Financial Well-Being depends on running your life like a business and making a profit at the end of the year. To do this you will need to set aside time and be on top of your financial matters.

What do you need to do to stay current with your Money matters? Get your calendar out now and schedule this time to complete the work. (Really!)

Financial Stability Formula #10: Live like 'Money isn't your whole life'

Remind yourself that Money is not your whole life. Your true joy and happiness comes from other places, such as people, particularly your Circle of Love, the beauty of nature, deeply knowing yourself, and helping others — whatever it may be for you.

I recently had the wonderful experience of going to Ethiopia. And I was shocked at what I learned. It was the perfect lesson for me. When I embarked on my journey, I was really afraid that poverty would depress me in Ethiopia. When I got there, I saw joy and happiness in this land where people had very little. They had a community spirit and generosity for one another. I saw more joy and smiles on the faces of people in Ethiopia than I saw on the faces of people in Silicon Valley, one of the highest net-worth places on the planet. What actually depressed me was the state of emotional poverty I saw in America upon my return.

In America, our culture has made Money a central theme of our happiness. We live in a world where people want to buy things and have the latest and greatest. Yet we live in fear that Money Madness can topple our whole lives.

You see, before I went to Ethiopia, I had so much of the joy of my life tied to Money. I felt that if I had Money, I could be happy; and if I didn't, I was sad. I learned that Money can impact some of my life, but there is more to life than Money.

You have the opportunity to celebrate the richness of your life, those things that are not tied to Money. So much of the really good stuff is free: the blue sky, a walk in nature, the smile on a child's face, a swim in the lake, a hug — you know. Got your journal? List your joys that are More Valuable than Money to enumerate all that is good. It will keep you free from being overly identified with Money as the sole source of your happiness.

There you have it. That was all 10 points of the Financial Stability Formula - the simple method to Create your Financial Stability.

Your progress and transformation on the Path of The Heroine's Journey mandate solidifying this fourth Cornerstone of Financial. Post this formula as a reminder of how to help yourself.

I get it, and I can strengthen who I am, who I have become, and how beautiful I am — just by practicing Financial Well-Being. Here's the thing. *The truth:* If you have money in your checkbook and investment accounts when you get to be a woman-of-age — that will do more to remove the wrinkles on your face than a facelift!

The Heroine smiles from within, knowing that she has successfully gone Step by Step to choose her Beliefs, take care of her Physical Well-Being, pick supportive People, and get her Financial life rocking!

If you follow the 10-Point Financial Stability Formula, you won't ever have the Bag Lady Blues – you'll be flying high in blue skies. Go for it, Heroine!

PS....

I posted the Financial Stability Formula right next to my computer. And, I revisit it often because circumstances and opportunities change in my life.

Now, I can easily tweak my plans and actions to accommodate the ebbs and flows. I do this now as I am refining my Journey.

But in the beginning, when I was in the early stages of my Heroine's Journey, I had to be stuck like glue to align my Financial Well-Being carefully. Protecting myself from living in ways that could take me off the Path and growing my Financial Stability had my daily attention.

You have the creation of your Financial Stability in your hands, and you are so much richer with the understanding, tools and practices you have acquired here. You are on The Heroine's Journey, thinking, acting, and becoming your magnificent Best-Self. In your hands is your care and fostering of Money in your life, and how you handle it will either speed up or slow down your Journey. Govern your Financial Well-Being; there's so much more to come when you do this!

As Dr. Seuss says in his fun and poignant book, *Oh, The Places You Will Go:*

"And will you succeed? Yes! You will, indeed! (98 and ½ percent guaranteed). Kid, you'll move mountains!"

~ Dr. Seuss

Free Resources

Gotch-ya! Go now to get your copy of 'The Financial Stability Formula'— and stick it on your bulletin board too...

www.HeroinesBook.com/Free-Resources.

7

Celebrate Your Stability

Stability as a Way of Life

The Heroine's Action Plan

I Am A Heroine

Rewriting Your Heroine's Story

Heroine's Journal

STABILITY AS A WAY OF LIFE

Congratulations, *Heroine!*...Here we are in the concluding Chapter of this Book: The Heroine's Journey, The Art of Becoming The Heroine of Your Own Life.

In order to get this far, you've given so much loving attention to your life's progress and your perceptive understanding of yourself. Thus far, you've traveled the Path of mastering the first seven Steps on your Heroine's Journey. You have walked the Path to Create your Stability by knowing how you actively build your firm foundation upon the Four Cornerstones.

You've delved into all of these Cornerstones as key components. Now, let's integrate them all together to serve as rocket fuel for your flight.

Integrating all Four Cornerstones

We've described throughout this Book mastering specific Tasks for each of the Four Cornerstones. You met the tests of these Tasks, you learned new skills, and you formed the foundation to Create Stability. Working one at a time, you built Courage and Strength that will allow you to weather the unexpected twists and turns on the Journey ahead.

Let's celebrate the Strength each of your Cornerstones brings to you:

> *Beliefs* — I have Uplifting *Beliefs*; I filter what I say to myself and what I choose to receive from others so that these messages support and encourage my Self-Worth on a daily basis.
>
> *Physical* — I experience *Physical* Well-Being; I Implement the best ways to live in my body and my environment so that my Life-Force is supported and encouraged daily.
>
> *People* — I love Green People! I choose carefully to create my Circle of Love around me to support and encourage me daily.
>
> *Financial* — I possess *Financial* fortitude; I live within my Means with the peace of mind to support, encourage and uplift me daily.

Living according to the wisdom of each Cornerstone individually is powerfully transformative. But what happens when you architect your life with each of these Cornerstones in place, in a coordinated and balanced way? Do you know, it's BIG?...

You shift from Survival to Thrival!

This life of joy and freedom happens when you integrate all of the Four Cornerstones together to form a new up-leveled paradigm for your thinking and your actions.

Once you fundamentally integrate the wisdom of *all four* of the Cornerstones into the deepest part of your being, it's time to celebrate the creation of your Stability. You have strategically positioned yourself with a solid foundation for an expanded life. Your life is ready to be lived more fully and bring you more opportunity, more abundance, more serendipitous moments, and more love.

Welcome to this new place of being!

Weighing Your Decisions for Stability

You are flying! *The key to remaining aloft is to always weigh the various decisions in your life by the Stability they create for you.* See the importance?

Ask yourself again and again, 'Does this choice support my Stability?'

- Does it make me feel good about myself?
- Does it increase my Life-Force energy and grounding?
- Does it foster healthy connections with Green people?
- Does it allow me to live in a financially positive way?

By asking this over and over, you'll have a mantra that fosters your Strength and energetic ability to live in freedom. Remain aligned with what enhances your Well-Being and brings you life. This is the way of the Heroine.

Maintaining Your Stability

We've arrived at the place where you are using your Cornerstones tactically and holistically. However, there's this thing about being human. There are times when you will fall out of bed on one or two of the Cornerstones.

Yikes, that can happen!

And, if you find that one of these areas is lacking for you — for instance you find yourself saying something negative about yourself — then be quick to delete this program and align yourself in a way that supports and encourages you. To stay on the Heroine's Journey and your joyful Path, it's essential to right yourself quickly.

When you maintain your Stability, you have hope, flexibility, enjoyment in the present moment and the basis for creating a happy and productive future. You have the means to Journey onward. This is where a Heroine lives daily.

Once you are here and have strengthened your foundation with all four of the Cornerstones life looks very different, but there is always maintenance support to do. For the rest of your blessed life, keep your focus on the balance of your Stability to sustain your flight.

But what happens if your Stability falters? Think of it this way. . .

You are on your way to the Market. You are pulling a wooden-flower-like cart behind you. You know the kind with the wooden side slats? In the bed of this cart (like a full array of colorful blooming flowers) are your many skills, gifts and talents carefully loaded. The wheels are what help you roll along. The front wheels of your cart are your *Beliefs* and *Physical Well-Being*, the back wheels are *People* and *Financial*. The four wheels are your Cornerstones.

As you are tooling along down the Path, suddenly you notice that your cart starts to wobble. Oppps…you look at your back left wheel and see that it is coming loose. Not so good. Can you feel that your cart is unsteady with each roll of the wheels when this happens? Thump-thump!

Oppps…now you look back and "Oh, My"!…yikes…the back right back wheel has gotten loose. Then splat, as both wheels fall off the cart. Now, my goodness…the whole back side of your cart is dragging on the ground! This is really not good!

"How will you ever get to Market to show your skills, gifts and talents this way", you're thinking? And if you can't get to Market with your stuff, how will you profit?

If you fail to pay attention…this can happen…one or more of your wheels can get jumbled — and you'll surely get stuck or drive right off your Heroine's Journey Path — and risk landing in the gutter. Stuck, you'll lose time and also you'll miss the opportunities that lie ahead.

Story: The Wheels Are Wobbling

This happened to Liz. When I met her, her situation was out-of-control. As I talked to her, the first thing that I noticed was that she was flailing and whining as she described her life. When I applied the four Cornerstones, it was easy to identify that all four wheels were coming off her cart. She was in trouble and feeling the pain and frustration big time. That's not fun.

- She was sabotaging herself with her *Beliefs*. She was saying very cruel things about herself, things that made her feel like a victim and helpless.
- Her *Physical* Well-Being was compromised. She was losing her house due to divorce and was reluctant to find a place where she would be safe from the abuse she had experienced.
- She had *People* around her that were hard on her and told her that they were fed up with her. She was being undermined by others.
- She was in *Financial* lack. She was not thinking about how to use her skills to earn some Money.

As I talked with Liz, she appeared to want to sit in the muck for a while. She was derailed. Unfortunately, Liz was not my client. If she had been, my commitment to her would have been that we solidly establish her Four Cornerstones. I reached out and offered to help her (at no charge even, to get her on her way), but she was unwilling to hoist her wings on at this time. I am so glad that you are here now, and will not suffer as I saw Liz doing.

Get Your Wheels Back On

As we know, getting knocked flat is part of the start of the Heroine's Journey. This tough time can show up quite naturally as part of the Journey. The question is: how much time do you waste before you get your wheels back on? The measure of a Heroine is how readily you secure your wheels in proper place and roll forward! Journey onward!

To get down the road, all four wheels have to be rolling on your cart. So you've got to regularly do a maintenance check on all of your wheels for proper alignment. Frequently ask yourself: "how's it going?" Where do I need to tighten up my wheels so I can maintain my momentum?

Here are some tips for ensuring that you maintain your Stability, and get your wheels in place when your cart starts to wobble. I call it the 'Stability Maintenance Protocol'.

Here are the steps:

Stability Maintenance Protocol

1. Don't ignore the messages that warn you that one of the wheels of your cart needs to be secured.
2. Go back and read this Book for a refresher.
3. Check in with your Accountability Partner for help, no need to go it alone!
4. Use the Practices and Protocols from this Book.
5. Be quick to tighten up the loose wheel(s).
6. Check in with your Circle of Love, they believe in you.
7. Check in with the Stability Circle on Facebook, for Sisterly wisdom.
8. Remember that there's a Heroine in the driver's seat - YOU!

Heroines Who Got Their Wheels On

Here are some quick vignettes of Heroines who had to tighten their wheels.

1. Meet Janie. She was working with her *Beliefs & Self Worth*. She was casual about how she applied herself to life. Because, "After all," her victim self kept asserting, "I'm not that important."

Once she embarked on her Journey as a Heroine, she changed her Belief to: "I am worthy of doing something significant in my life." With this, she got focused and contributed her gifts and talents in meaningful ways. Now she is a doula and helps women in the birthing process. She feels profoundly fulfilled.

2. And then there is Karen who was needing to strengthen *People and Love* in her life. I shared with her the same wisdom my mentor shared with me, "You are like a garbage ship. You collect it and take it all around the world with you." This caused Karen to think. She realized that 'Orange and Red' people were bringing her all kinds of drama and pain and this was filling her life up with garbage. She cleaned house. Now her Heroine-Self is opening her heart and she is surrounding herself with her Circle of Love. Life feels so much better to her.

3. Pam was very challenged in her *Physical Well-Being*. She constantly felt depressed. Her therapist asked her if she's felt this way her whole life? Pam reflected, maybe she had. Then, he declared, "You need to be medicated for the rest of your life." Pam's Heroine awoke from her slumber. Whoa! countered Pam: 'Whatever it is, I'm going to address it, deal with it, and learn from it. I will not be drugged into numbness and miss out on living my life!' Now Pam is using her tools to bolster her Well-Being as a Heroine. She even teaches classes on yoga for depression. Now she stays the Journey to live in joy.

4. Susan was consumed by *Money* issues. She was flat broke and wondering how she was even going to do the basics, like buy milk. Her career had suddenly been interrupted and she couldn't make money the way she had in the past. "That is all I know how to do", she thought. Then a new friend at a workshop suggested to her that she could step off one stage of life and onto another. This totally transformed her view. Her inner Heroine realized she could use her skills and talents in new ways to create income. She became a real estate agent under her new friend. Now she makes more money than ever before, all because of a shift in thinking. Now she's back in the Money — and freedom!

5. Sarah had a hard time sorting out which of her wheels was coming loose. She was an army nurse in the middle of a divorce. What consumed her attention was the panic that she didn't have enough Money to maintain her lifestyle with him gone. But as we worked together we uncovered the truth. Her financial life was actually stable.

    There were two other wheels that were loose. Her husband was the sum total of her world of *People,* and she had designed her physical life in a very masculine way due to the nature of life in the Army. Her inner spirit was crying for more connection with People, and her feminine nature wanted to be expressed in the design of her *Physical* environment.

    By invoking her inner Heroine she actively engaged in balancing all of her Stability Cornerstones. She has cultivated new loving people that support and encourage her in her life. She also redecorated her bedroom with a new bedspread, candles, a picture with beautiful flowers so that when she crawls into bed she feels her feminine and nurtured self. Now she wakes up feeling happy, connected and secure.

All of these women got into action. They assessed their Stability, made changes, and found new opportunities for joy, prosperity and freedom. What I love is that they didn't stay stalled, they navigated, and course corrected when necessary and got on with loving their lives.

Retake the Creating Your Stability Questionnaire (found in the Resource Section of this Book)

You've come a 'long way, Baby'! Now that you have done the Tasks for each of the 4 Cornerstones and consciously traveled on your Heroine's Journey Step-by-Step, it's time to re-evaluate your Stability, from a new far more empowered place.

Retake the Creating Your Stability Questionnaire that you first took in Chapter 1. Remember that one? It may feel very different to you now as you ask yourself the same questions again from the point of view of your Heroine-Self.

There are two valuable purposes for this process:

1. Celebrating how far you've come
2. Identifying where you still need support to establish all four of the Stability Cornerstones

As you retake the Questionnaire, you will be ranking your progress on the very same statements that you did at the beginning of this Book. Now that you have expanded your understanding of how to truly create Stability for yourself, you can expect that many of your responses have changed.

When you view your new responses, you may jump up with joy and celebrate how far you have come. And, in some cases you may also clearly see where you still need strengthening in one or more of the areas of Stability.

Let's address ways you may need improvement or support in The Heroine's Action Plan. Understanding the results of your questionnaire will jumpstart the focus of your Action Plan.

Keep in mind, no matter how far or successfully we journey, my loving band of Heroines, we are always revisiting these Cornerstones to access our Stability - each day of our lives, with each decision we make. We do this so we fully love our experience of life!

Now you see that the creation of your Stability is indeed the way of a good life. Maintaining your Stability is the secret to ever-evolving to greater and greater heights. It is fundamental to becoming your Best-Self. I want to see you fly high, take in many vistas, and go for new opportunities, experiences and fulfilling dreams.

Let's put your Heroine's mojo into action…this is where you create your Heroine's Action Plan, the tactical blueprint to ensure you always maintain your Stability. Your Heroine will activate some serious momentum!

THE HEROINE'S ACTION PLAN

"It takes as much energy to wish as it does to plan."

~ Eleanor Roosevelt (American First Lady)

Embodying Stability feels like a more effortless place of beingness. . . once we arrive there. But it takes some pretty clear and tactical action to navigate ourselves to this happy place and ultimately home to our True Wealth.

As you arrive at Step 7 on the Journey — the seven Steps of the Thirteen Steps of the full Heroine's Journey — realize that all along the way we have had to put in some pretty strategic effort in to get this far. Now, we arrive fully at Step #8 Taking Empowered Action.

Taking Empowered Action

Look from the vista of how far you've come. You are flying the distance. What does this take? *Flap* furiously. What is all this flapping about? It is getting - (shit) your stuff, ha-ha! — done!!! This is Step #8:

Taking Empowered Action.

Here is how we describe it:

Step #8: Taking Empowered Action

Spread your wings and fly.

Conscious to calm your fear, you thrust yourself into critical action from a new empowered place. You release the past in preparation for something new. You ask, "What do I truly want my life to look like?" Consider all good options and make strategic moves to shore up your foundation. You master new skills, tools and talents. Standing on the cliff, you spread your wings and lift into the clear blue sky. You flap furiously. The hardest part of the flight is the first few moments, and you maintain your Courage and Strength. You don't look back because you are focused on the future. New miracles are showing up in your life now.

Taking Empowered Action is the engine that gets you moving and keeps you moving on the Path. Without it we would simply sit wherever we happen to be hoping that the vista will change, wondering why life is passing us by. This will never get us home to True Wealth.

The Power Of Action

I have known many women who have gone through extraordinary circumstances. And, they found their way through simply by doing what needed to be done each day. It sounds simple, but really it is heroic!

Do you recall Liz Gilbert's comment about Joseph Campbell, that we spoke about at the beginning of this Book? You'll remember that he was the father of defining the Hero's Journey. The Journey that men are said to take to mature into their full selves.

Liz related that Joseph Campbell claimed that women don't have a process of growing through a Heroine's Journey. Instead, they just stay home and cry. *Wow* — triple *Wow*!

So not true! As women we are confronted, shaped and born into our True Self. We have a profound Journey. We take heroic action to move along the pathway as we face Challenges and Crises, and overcome obstacles.

Action is what makes the difference. Action turns the Tasks of the Journey into the gifts!

The Tasks, the action steps along the way that we encountered in each Cornerstone, are presented to transform you, to lead you out of the turmoil that has plagued you. They refine your character for new outcomes and a better you. They are the means for you to engage, grow, and prosper. See these as gifts given to you because ultimately they show you the way home.

The opposite of taking action is being paralyzed in fear. Even though you may be tempted to succumb, a Heroine digs deep to access her Fierce Feminine. She acts in her own best interest to shore up her Stability and prepare for the Journey ahead.

Even if life feels overwhelming and some Tasks feel monumental, just do something. Anything to get started. Start the momentum. Eventually you will pick up speed.

Without action you will get no momentum toward your True Self.

Introducing Your Heroine's Action Plan

Hurrah, it's time to take empowered Action and this requires a well laid plan. So here you are going to write your very own Heroine's Action Plan. It's your flight plan. It's your checklist of what to do and when to do it.

Remember that you had One Defining Moment in Step #4 of the Journey: Character Revelation? You realized your Heroine's Proclamation. You experienced a big-bang powerful internal resolve that you are not going to be stuck in how life showed up — you have every intention of soaring high.

Your rebel yell proclaimed that you will do what it takes to create the life that you want. Your Heroine's Action Plan is where you lay out exactly what it will take to create your desired life and get it rolling!

There is a quote from Napoleon Hill, author of *Think and Grow Rich*, the most respected work on designing your life. He says:

"Create a definite plan for carrying out your desire and begin at once, whether you are ready or not, to put this plan into action."

~ Napoleon Hill

Yep, it's off into the wild to go. A Heroine doesn't sit around and wait for all the unicorns to line up perfectly under the rainbow. She does what she needs to do with Strength and Courage knowing that she's purposefully moving forward.

Through writing and executing your Heroine's Action Plan, you will secure and fortify your Stability like Fort Knox. If you don't have a plan your energy will go towards chaos. When you adhere to a plan, your energy is directed toward the creation of your Stability.

Your Action Items

We said that your Heroine's Action Plan is where you lay out exactly *what* it will take to create your desired life and then you get it done. The *'what it will take'* gets clearly defined as your Action Items. These Action Items are the myriad of things you gotta do to critically respond to what life is throwing at you, right now. Flap your wings and get stuff done. No excuses.

It is time to get responsible — or, more clearly said: *'response - able.'* The Heroine is able to respond to what's in front of her. Step-by-Step, tactically executing these Action Items leads you to complete your Tasks from the Universe . . . and ultimately your Stability.

Get resourceful and creative to achieve what's *necessary*. You can no longer do things the old way. You will most likely need to master new skills, tools and talents and make big life changes that can better position you to fly. Our Heroine's community is here to support you through this process.

You are going to feel uncomfortable at first exerting all this tactical energy. It's just part of the process. However when you come from the perspective of *'I am a Heroine'* you will prevail.

Your Heroine's Action Plan prevents that internal panic of overwhelm from swallowing you by breaking the whole hairy enchilada down into bite size pieces, your Action Items. This will encourage your psyche to stay present under pressure, rather than go into fight, flight or freeze mode. Remember the objective of creating Stability in your life is to assure you are safe and secure. This Plan is the powerful force with which you remove the obstacles in your Path.

Once you have your Heroine's Action Plan written, you don't have to think about what steps you are taking each day. You just get your Action

Items done. If it's in your Plan, don't philosophize about it, panic over it, or avoid it. Step in and step up. Just get it done. This is your way to stay response-able.

So for those of you (myself included) who get just a little bit daunted by the prospect of having to figure out a way to do what seems to be the impossible, let me tell you a story about my friend Nancy Nunke, a true Heroine who inspired me with her ability to get into action.

Story: Cowgirl Up, Sister!

Nancy created Hearts & Hands Animal Rescue in Ramona, California, a nonprofit that rescues big animals, like horses, zonkeys, donkeys, zebras and camels. When I first went to the Ranch, I wondered, "If you are a camel and you don't have a home, where do you go?"

Nancy has the answer. No matter what their circumstances — abuse, neglect, illness, starvation — Nancy's heart is open to these heart-centered giants.

Here's the story that I want to tell you because I got a big lesson for my own Heroine's Journey. The Animal Rescue receives contributions of all kinds to support the animals. One day, Nancy and I climbed into her farm truck and went off to pick up a couch and loveseat from some people who were moving to another town. Let's just say that this City-Girl, me, has a lot to learn when it comes to the tasks of Ranch life, and this day was no exception.

We went to the house, and a couple of brawny guys hoisted the furniture into the back of Nancy's truck. Easy peasy . . . for them.

We took the furniture over to some big semi-trailers where Nancy stores donated furniture. We opened the doors. *Yikes!*, the floor of the trailer was six feet off the ground. Nancy had envisioned that she and I — alone — were going to get this monster of a couch out of her truck and 6 feet up onto the floor of the storage trailer. This was way more than I bargained for.

But this was a really important task to Nancy. She's storing furniture so that it can eventually go into a house on the Ranch where kids and

PTSD-challenged veterans will come to stay for a rehabilitation program where the animals serve as the healers. Today's task is one more action item toward her vision.

I looked at the couch, then at the trailer six feet above, and winced. How were two girls ever going to hoist this heavy couch and get it into place? I wimped out and doubted my abilities. I was even so bold as to say: "Nancy, we can't do this!"

But Nancy is a Heroine, and she had a vision that was stronger than my doubt. She said: "Cowgirl Up!, Sister!, we are *going* to do this! You don't know what you can do until you do it. We *can* do this!"

She wasn't going to let my limited Belief direct the outcome. I relented, "OK, I proclaimed, we can do this!"

Resourcefully, Nancy got a rope out of the truck bed and tied it in a loop around one end of the couch. Then she leaped onto the trailer bed. She started pulling on the rope and lifted one end of the couch upward while I guided it from the ground. I hadn't envisioned this option before she did it. She explained how leverage works for us.

And damn, if we didn't hoist that heavy sucker onto the semi-trailer six feet above our heads and plop it into place. It felt so good to accomplish the impossible.

That day, I didn't know what was possible. I had to have some faith. Now so often when I'm faced with a heavy task, I say to myself, "Cowgirl Up, Sister! You don't know what you can do until you do it!" I continue to be amused by myself when I say this, and now I see that I have way more creativity and strength to bring to the task at hand — and I 'get 'er done!'

Let's "Cowgirl Up, Sisters!" You don't know yet what you can do. You have way more capability and strength than you know as you progress on your Heroine's Journey. Let's get into action and you'll surprise yourself too!

Heroine's Action Formula

So how do you create a Heroine's Action Plan that is strategic, timely *and* supports you in creating your Stability?

Here is the Heroine's Action Formula for creating your Heroine's Action Plan.

Heroine's Action Formula

1. Visualize what propels you into action: what do you desire from life and why?
2. Identify the challenges and roadblocks.
3. Write Your Heroine's Action Plan; pinpoint your Action Items.
4. Own that you cannot escape the work to be done and annihilate resistance.
5. Get Fierce Feminine in your one-pointed focus of commitment.
6. Let go of anything that is not essential to your outcome.
7. Order and calendar your Action Items.
8. Follow through with dedication.
9. Complete the Action Item on planned time and check it off.
10. Review your progress — acknowledge what's done and what's yet to be done.
11. Celebrate your achievements!

This is the formula for achieving anything in life. It's how this Book got written and into your hands. And how you will create what is important for you too.

Writing Your Heroine's Action Plan

Now we are going to apply this Heroine's Action Formula to writing *your* **Heroine's Action Plan**. This is a creative process that will engage your higher focus and empower your success.

The aim is to identify those areas of Stability that could be strengthened to become fuel for your flight.

Grab your Journal and open to a clean full page. Ready with pen? Put a cross through the page so that you have four quadrants. Label each of the quadrants - Beliefs, People, Physical and Financial.

In each quadrant you are going to write a series of Action Items that will propel your life in these 4 areas.

Start by asking yourself a key question for each Cornerstone that will engage you in the process of writing your Action Items. Here are those questions.

Beliefs
- What am I choosing to do to support my aligned Beliefs about myself and the life I will live?

People
- What opportunities am I choosing to create with specific People to ensure that I am supported and resourced?

Physical
- What am I choosing to do for Physical safety to take care of my body and optimize my physical surroundings?

Financial
- What actions am I choosing to promote my Financial life — to protect my assets, add income and cut expenditures and more to live within my Means?

You can write your Heroine's Action Plan for any duration of time. I like to do a yearly plan that keeps me visionary and motivated and also a weekly plan that keeps me tactical and moving forward. You could even do a monthly one if you like.

Action Items On The Plan

On my weekly Heroine's Action Plan I write between 3 to 6 Action Items for each Cornerstone, but on my yearly Heroine's Action Plan I allow myself to dream and I choose 10 or more bigger Action Items.

I wrote my first Heroine's Action Plan while I was still in the Crisis Phase of my Journey. By following it *religiously* it got me through a really tough week and ensured that I made progress when I really doubted I could handle my life.

Each morning, I viewed my Plan. I felt the fire in my belly which was my burning desire to get out of my current circumstances. It motivated me to fiercely grab that day and make it count. Carpe Diem! My Heroine's Proclamation was running the show and I was going to deliver. This was my Heroine's way of owning that I am response-able and proclaiming "I can and I will — Watch me!".

And it worked! I have written and followed my weekly Heroine's Action Plan ever since, and it has propelled me into achievements and happiness that is the Heroine version of my life.

Rituals On The Plan

You would noticed that on my Heroine's Action Plan, at the bottom of each quadrant, there is a section labeled 'Rituals'.

So what is the difference between an Action Item and a Ritual? An action item is a 'to do' that gets completed in a certain timeframe to clear your Path forward. Whereas, a Ritual is an ongoing practice to bolster your Well-Being and overall progress.

Doing Rituals transforms me, day-by-day, into a greater version of my Heroine-Self. They fuel my Fierce Feminine Life-Force energy. And they give me the stamina I need to accomplish my Action Items. My Rituals keep me in right mindset, develop my Courage and Strength, motivate me to stay on track, and support my ongoing Stability.

On your Heroine's Action Plan also choose 1-2 Rituals that support each Cornerstone. These Rituals may be some of the Practices we have recommended in this Book for maintaining Stability or they may be other habits that you want to cultivate.

Rituals may include things like:

- Go to yoga class 3 times per week at 4:15 pm
- Use the Stress Storm Relief Practice each time I wake up at night with anxiety

- Drink 64 ounces of water per day
- Schedule all business meetings between the hours of 9 - 5
- Meditate 15 minutes each morning
- Track my daily adherence to my Monthly Spending Plan
- Use the Sticker System with each new person I meet
- Consistently reframe any negative beliefs about myself into positive Beliefs
- Sleep 8 hours per night

Time to get creative, because your Heroine's Action Plan will be unique to you, your needs and where you are on your very own Heroine's Journey.

Tap Into Your Resources

To identify your Action Items and to choose Rituals that are meaningful for you, here are resources you can draw on.

1. Review the Heroine's Journey Roadmap and identify — where are you in the Heroine's Journey? What steps do you need to take in order to progress?
2. Review your Stability Assessment to identify areas where you have work to do.
3. Review the 4 Cornerstones in Chapters 3 through 6 and use that information to inspire Action Items in each of the 4 Quadrants that you are recording in your Journal.
4. Identify the Practices within each Chapter and choose the ones you most need to incorporate regularly as Rituals.
5. Have an active dialogue with your Lighthouse and record wisdom in your Journal.
6. Sit quietly and listen to the Wise Woman, the Alchemist and the Midwife.
7. Visualize your garden as you pull the weeds and plant the flowers.

8.   Review your Heroine's Proclamation and Heroine's Creed to ensure that your daily Action Items and Rituals promote your success.

All right, Heroine! Now you're resourced and ready to write your Heroine's Action Plan.

In your Journal — write two Heroine's Action Plans for yourself. First write your Yearly Heroine's Action Plan, because it gives you a sense of where you are headed and a context for your Weekly Heroine's Action Plan, which you will write next.

You are in Action! You know what you gotta do and you are doing it! That certainly guarantees progress along the Path.

And yet, there may be bumps ahead. How will you weather the next unexpected storms?

Yep a Heroine's way — next we'll explore the 'Wind Currents That Test You' in Step #9. With ease and more competency this time — you've got it!

I AM A HEROINE

Yes, that's you. A beautiful, powerful, wing-ed Heroine! Awake and alive. Convicted and resourced..here's how it goes…

You have a 'heads up' and *still* life happens…

A Heroine knows that even though you have Taken Empowered Action and no matter how well you prepare — there will be unforeseen, unplanned and sometimes unpleasant stuff that comes up as you Journey onward, it's a natural part of every woman's Journey.

And this brings us to Step #9 Wind Currents that Test You.

And, this time you will be victorious because now you hear your inner voice proclaiming: "*I am a Heroine! Watch me fly!*"

Wind Currents That Test You

Let's take a deeper look at Step #9: Wind Currents That Test You.

Step 9: Wind Currents That Test You

Navigate another challenge

In flight you have a panoramic view and life looks better. You assess how much you got through and how many successes you have had that jettison your flight. You can see the horizon in front of you. Suddenly, another Challenge comes along in the form of a big wind that whips you around, scares and imbalances you. You are tested again in some kind of unexpected or surprising manner. You wonder, "Will this take me out when I have finally come so far?" Because you have been through the narrows of Crisis and Challenge and survived, this time you hear your inner voice call out "I am a Heroine." From this awakened inner knowing you steady to navigate these challenges with your new compass pointing you to glorious horizons.

So why do we have to go through rough air yet again? It is a test, a gift. If we didn't get the test, we wouldn't know for certain that our inner Heroine is awake and in charge. Once we fully embody her wisdom and power our life is forever changed.

So how can we navigate these wind currents and find blue skies again? This time, when the turbulence hits, you are not thrown back to Crisis. You rally cry: "I am a Heroine!" This is your internal identity now and from this new place you choose new thoughts and actions.

A Heroine has vast Self-Worth. She no longer rolls over when things get tough. She stands up for herself and her best interests, because she loves and values herself.

For me, now my identity is "*I am a Heroine! I can handle whatever life brings.*"

No longer *am I Joan, the victim that thinks* "you may be right about me, I might be worthless." *No, not!* I know that I am not a Garbage ship and I never was. I have wings that propel me upward to soar onward!

Now that you have arrived at Step #9, no matter what is happening, you are able to hear the Voice of your inner Heroine guiding you back to blue skies.

The Gift Of Wind Currents

You might have more than one wind current that tests you. No matter, you don't get thrown back into earlier stages if you have set your foundation of Stability. And from this place of grounding you can look upon your Journey with some new Heroine-esque insight.

You realize that your life has become so much richer and fuller because of your adventures, even the painful ones. While you might face lack, loss, disease, or adversity at some points on your Journey, it would never be your 'destiny'. It is your teacher — you know this. And you embrace this in your core. You are guided and improved by your experiences. And, all experiences serve to hone you.

In a casual conversation, a friend of mine, Lyn Gianni, dropped a truth firecracker before me that lit up brightly in magnificent color. It set the picture of my entire life before me.

She said: *"It's in her struggle that the butterfly learns to fly."* — Lyn Gianni.

So, true! But for the struggle, the wind currents that test us, would we all just sit on the couch and eat bon-boons in our Status Quo? Would we miss the adventure, and stay home? Not a Heroine.

I can't pretend that I welcomed with open wings the difficult times of 'struggle' in my life. But, as I look back over it, I absolutely would not choose to magically remove them. Because of what they taught me, I am more of '*me*' now. After each struggle, I've come to dramatically know myself better, like myself more, and feel greater humility and compassion for all that is life.

Now that I have my Heroine identity intact, I believe that I can handle stuff. And, that there is more adventure to live. I see that this Strength can lead me to making a meaningful impact. Can you relate to gifts that your Journey has brought you so far? We're not all in the same place, but perhaps my reflections on my Journey can inspire yours.

From Step #9 Wind Currents that Test You, you meet the struggles with Courage and Strength and clarity, realizing these conditions show up as strategically placed hurdles that grow the power of your wings.

With incredibly valuable insight into your life and the useful practices we've outlined in this Book, you are equipped with the Resources you need to fully live in the boon of Stability.

Your Heroine's Inner Voice

So the key to thriving through Step #9 is that now you know in your heart that you are a Heroine. And as such you have powerful and beautiful wings that have the strength to lift you high above the storms.

As a Heroine, you live as '***Worthy***' in your very being. You hold yourself here. You know who you are. Nothing takes the inner jewel of your Self-Worth away. It is your most precious asset and you guard it with Fierce Feminine. Read that again…

That critical inner voice that was once ill informed by negative beliefs and low self worth has been replaced by the resonating harmony of your Heroine's Voice. Ask it to speak up. It gives you confidence. With this song in your heart, you navigate the quality and direction of your life all the way to True Wealth.

What does your Heroine's Inner Voice tell you?

Here's what my Heroine's Inner Voice tells me to help me navigate into my Best-Self:

- I enter every conversation with an open heart.
- I hold myself in high regard.
- I harbor an attitude of gratitude for my gifts and talents.
- I live life with Courage and Strength.
- I check in with my own feeling experience in any situation.
- I am present.
- I protect my confidence at all times.
- I practice compassion.
- I choose to feel good.
- I speak my truth.
- I honor my greatness.
- I am at peace with the outcomes in my life.

- Love is my natural state of being.

Just for a moment, listen to your Heroine's Inner Voice. . .

Now you are speaking to yourself like a Heroine, imagine what you can accomplish. There is a new beauty in a woman who embodies her inner Heroine. It is seductive and magnetically attracts opportunities and people to her.

Now, You have an attitude of altitude! You are flying high!

I Am A Heroine Poem

We (me and Ivri) wrote a little poem as a reminder to all of our Sisters, that they are indeed Heroines. Put this where you will see it each morning and evening. Let this poem inspire you to joyful days and Best-Self.

Be reminded, *I Am a Heroine.*

I am a Heroine.
I am Worthy.
I am on the Journey.
I put my wings on . . . and fly.
I go with Courage and Strength.
I see that life brings me the right lessons.
I am safe in my Circle of Love.
I give and receive abundance.
I express my soul's purpose with Love.
I live into something larger than myself.
I am free.
I am a Heroine.

Heroine's Stability Creed

You are a Heroine! This is a moment of powerful manifestation. It is where you draw your line in the sand. "You proclaim your Stability, and so it is!"

You make the decision that Stability is your Heroine's way of life. You will only embrace that which shows up to affirm your Stability. You are worth it!...and you decide this!

Wouldn't it be great to have a homing device to ensure that your navigation is always pointed toward Creating Your Stability? Wouldn't you like to stay on course?

Drum roll . . . Introducing Your Heroine's Stability Creed. This creed is your declaration for how you will honor and integrate the 4 Cornerstones in your life. It is designed to remind you how to stay awake and free in the face of wind currents. This edict is essential for your thrival as Heroine.

Heroine's Stability Creed Process

Grab your trusty Journal again.

Here is the framework for writing your own Heroine's Stability Creed. Use your Journal once again. As you write, use your Heroine's Voice.

Heroine's Stability Creed Process:

1. I believe about myself that I . . . {insert your declaration}
2. I choose green people and my circle of love includes . . . {insert your declaration}
3. I take care of my inner and outer Physical Well-Being by . . . {insert your declaration}
4. I live within my Means by . . . {insert your declaration}

I'd like to share with you my own Heroine's Stability Creed. It's inspired and directed my Journey.

1. *I believe about myself that I . . . am a precious child of God, who has a great purpose to fulfill.*
2. *I choose green people and my circle of love includes . . . Angels who truly love and support me into my highest and Best-Self.*

3. *I take care of my inner and outer Physical Well-Being by . . . dedicating myself to nurturing and strengthening my body each day and creating a home that nourishes me.*
4. *I live within my means by . . . ensuring I have multiple income streams that fulfill my lifestyle money requirements and grow my assets.*

Tell me — did you *feel* your Courage and Strength as you wrote out your Creed? *Put it someplace that you'll see it daily — next to your computer, in lipstick on your bathroom mirror, at the front of your Journal, or framed at your bedside. This is your work of your creation.*

While we probably haven't yet met personally, I know you are a beautifully embodied Heroine now! Simply because you have awoken to your essential nature, you are walking the Path with such grace.

So how does your Heroine's Journey Story read now? Finally it is becoming a tale of a true Heroine! It must be a fascinating narrative of adventure and opportunity.

It's time to *re-write* your Heroine's Journey Story using your Heroine's Voice. It will be the greatest tale ever told, your own life's Story filled with love and wholeness!

Adventure awaits.

REWRITING YOUR HEROINE'S JOURNEY STORY

Here we are, my adventurous, Sister.

I soooo love this quote:

"She remembered who she was and the game changed."

~ Lalah Delia

Now that you have awakened to your Heroine nature, the game of life certainly has changed. You no longer see the Journey as fraught with misfortune and powerlessness. You now approach life as a Heroine and you reach Step #10 Crescendo. You are lifted into freedom. This is the final Step in this Book.

The one that anchors in your Stability and prepares you for the truly amazing life that is ahead of you.

The old Journey Story that you told in Chapter 1, before you realized your power and perspective as a Heroine, is no longer sufficient to help you navigate to True Wealth. Now, as you experience the power of Crescendo, you have the freedom to rewrite your Story from a Heroine's perspective — one of wisdom, gratitude, perseverance, Courage and Strength and Hope.

It is time to rewrite your Story and create your new Destiny!

Reaching Crescendo

Now with your Stability fueling your flight, you've reached a new altitude. You are soaring freely in blue skies, the moment of Crescendo! Your wings flap in smooth rhythm and you level off in the endless ethers. With a glorious vantage point of the world around you, you navigate to new horizons.

We describe Step #10 Crescendo this way:

Step #10: Crescendo

You are lifted into freedom

Finally the air currents around you become stable. When the wind currents of flight lift you, they lift you fast. You are out of survival and struggle mode, and into the freedom of soaring through the air. You are strengthened within. This journey brought you the gift of wisdom that roots you deeply in your power as a woman.

This is the moment where you've fully created Stability. You are no longer wrapped in fear, broke without resources, numbed to your sense of what is good for you, neglectful of your inner voice, lead by your former impaired beliefs, tied to external things for your security, wedded to familiarity, impaired by rules of what to be, or armored in your heart.

Now, you got it going on! Your heart is open, and you see love in yourself and in the world. You have conviction, determination, and focus. You see through the illusions of fear and separation. Your power is in your wholeness. You proclaim your Stability, and so it is!

Crescendo is the pinnacle of Stability. From this vantage point you are gifted with the ability to see your life in whole new ways. The horizon is in front of you, and magnificent vistas are there for your taking. This is your time!

Becoming The Heroine of Your Story

You have arrived at your moment of glory! Now as a free spirit, you have the perspective to tell your Story with all of its 'ups' and 'downs' from an empowered place. Lessons learned, perspective gained, Strength and Courage built, obstacles overcome, negative beliefs that you didn't let shape you, people transcended, disappointments turned to gifts, serendipitous moments — all of it. And, how you live well. Glorious.

Living well is the way of the Heroine. It comes together magically when your Heroine writes the Story. But you may notice that in the past, elements of your Story were narrated as laments. In order to stay aloft, you must let that old Story go.

By telling the same old Story, you will get the same old results. The definition of insanity is repeating the same thing over and over in your life and expecting something different to happen. It's a groove you want to get out of.

If you don't transform your Story, you'll just stew in your own mess. You will get stuck in the Crisis and Challenges phases of your Heroine's Journey and be unable to sustain the liberating Crescendo.

The purpose of life is to live in love, joy and freedom. Sometimes on the Journey you can fall out of this knowing. When you take yourself out of this state of being, you diminish your experience of life and what you are able to give.

When you finally decide to become the Heroine of your own Story, you allow yourself to receive the inherent love, joy and freedom of life. You remain in a state of hope and trust that your life will move forward in good ways. You receive love, you have faith in yourself and others, you face what you need to face, and you choose to fly.

No matter where you are on the Heroine's Journey, you can re-write your entire narrative. It is a dramatic shift in your thinking, that moment when you chose to move from Victim-being to Heroine-being. *Welcome to Heroine-land*!

Transforming The Victim

Yes, you are indeed a Heroine! And yet, the inner Voice of the Victim can be all too well remembered. When you wrote your Heroine's Journey Story for the first time in Chapter 1, it was her voice that probably did a good portion of the narrating. What would happen if you never allowed your Heroine to have her full Voice, to be the narrator of your Story?

Victim status is a rotten place to live life. When life is all over and you wonder, "did I live?" As a victim you would never have accelerated into your freedom.

When you see life as 'doing it to you', rather than seeing yourself as 'doing life', then you are confined to the viewpoint of 'victim'.

If you see yourself as a victim and are impacted by an experience which closes your heart, it will be *you* who loses. Choosing to close out pain, also closes out other juicy, yummy experiences.

If you blame, complain, assert that it was someone else's wrong doing toward you, then oops, you'll get stuck. And, stuck is yuck!… Messy muck!

So how do you get out of blame? In what regard should you hold people that have caused you pain? It's simple, but not always easy.

People come into and out of your life to jolt you into new thinking and new growth. Sometimes it's painful. But these people are just actors on the stage of your life who were assigned this role to facilitate your development.

Rather than holding a grudge and judging people in ways that make it painful for you as 'they are so bad', allow your Heroine-Self to recognize that they galvanized you into some new awareness that may be essential to guiding you to your Happily Ever After Place.

I'm not saying that you forgive and forget, I'm saying that you forgive and refocus — to live your life joyfully as a Heroine.

The Importance Of Rewriting Your Story

As every news reporter knows, you can write the same story from different angles. My question to you is: which angle helps you live a happier, freer and ready-for-new-stuff angle? Your Heroine can answer this for you.

Are you ready to release the parts of your current narrative that are holding you back or perpetuating undesirable results? Are you willing to entertain the possibility that there is something greater in store for you? Are you willing to stand in confidence of that higher vision?

It is so important to rewrite your Story, not from the victim's point of view, but from a purposeful and intentional point of view: the view of the *Heroine*. When you transform your Story and let the *Voice of the Heroine* be your narrator, you claim the freedom to soar into your magnificent, limitless life.

As you rewrite, take into consideration that each Step of the Heroine's Journey is a unique and purposeful event to strengthen your wings. Your greatest gifts come from taking challenging situations and responding as a Heroine. Your confidence, Courage and Strength get built in the process. And, there is something new that appears. Your story becomes a narrative about each progressive passage that ultimately leads you to a bigger life! Hoorah!

Now as you look back on what you thought were the biggest disasters of your life, you get to reframe them as the biggest blessings. In this version of your Story, you get to celebrate life's lessons as perfectly designed to put you on the course of your joy and purpose — your very own Heroine's Journey!

Story: From Victim To Heroine

I once wrote my Journey Story about losing everything material in my life as a Victim story. I said that getting divorced and losing my wealth was such a *disaster*. And guess what, as long as I continued to tell that version of the Story I felt lost and broken.

As I got to Step # 4 Character Revelation, here was my Heroine's Proclamation: "I am not going to be defined by my fall, I am going to be measured by my rise." This worked deeply within to align me with my inner Heroine's Voice.

Suddenly I awoke to the truth that the sad and desperate narrative I had been telling myself, and anyone else who would listen, was completely incongruent with who I truly am. It was keeping me stuck. I have so much more power than the character I was portraying myself to be in that old worn out Story.

Shifting my Story to that of the Heroine's Voice in the narrator, now I receive the full magnitude of the gifts that came from this Crisis. It freed me to move to a new location, start a new business, and find what inspires me. I am no longer narrating that something bad was done to me, that it was the disaster of my life. Frankly, it got me up and moving and I embrace the fortuitous changes, even though these gifts came wrapped in sandpaper!

I was happy to re-write that Story from the perspective of the capable, energetic and resourceful woman that I am. My Heroine showed me what I had learned, how much Strength and Courage I had developed and that my Path had taken me to a much more fruitful place in life.

It's so true! *It's in her struggle that the butterfly learns to fly*! We're all learning to fly, and freedom is found in the high altitude of the clear blue sky!

Reframe Framework

Let's get to it, you will be called to rewrite your Story, starring *you*, the Heroine of your own life. This is the critical turning point.

In preparing to rewrite your own Heroine's Journey Story from Steps 1 through 10, I'm sharing with you the bones of how this works, transforming from victim to Heroine.

This is just a rough framework. Hear it as we go through the Steps. First I will be highlighting the Step from the Victim's point-of-view, and then Eureka! Hear it as the narrative is transformed into the Heroine's point-of-view.

This will help you identify areas in your Heroine's Journey Story that could use some Heroine wisdom rethink/redo....

1. Step 1: Status Quo—

Victim: Life is nice and tidy.
Heroine: I needed to be rocked out of my Comfort Zone.

2. Step 2: Crisis—

Victim: This is the Worst Thing Ever.
Heroine: Ok, change is on the horizon.

3. Step 3: Challenge—

Victim: I'm wrecked and going to die from this.
Heroine: I'm going to live and grow from this.

4. Step 4: Crusade—

Victim: I can't do this.
Heroine: I have the Courage and Strength to do this.

5. Step 5: Angels Show Up—

Victim: I'm all alone in this.
Heroine: I'm connected and others come to help.

6. Step 6: Character Revelation—

Victim: I'm a failure.
Heroine: I have what it takes.

7. Step 7: Gathering Your Provisions—

Victim: I don't have enough to survive.
Heroine: I am responsible to acquire what I require.

8. Step 8: Taking Empowered Action—

Victim: It's someone else's fault.
Heroine: I tactically create my own Stability.

9. Step 9: Wind Currents That Test You—

Victim: This is more proof that the world is against me.
Heroine: This is just another test to prove to me that I am a Heroine and I have wings to fly.

10. Step 10: Crescendo—

Victim: I fall on the rocks below and my life is destroyed.
Heroine: I rise into the sky and do aerial maneuvers!

So how did that feel, the difference between Victim and Heroine? Two versions of the same movie. It's all in who you decide to be.

I know you have chosen to be a Heroine! Great! Then tell your Story that way.

You first wrote your Story for the first time in Chapter 1 called 'Write Your Heroine's Journey.' No matter what you wrote back then, it was perfect.

Now that you have journeyed through this Book, and you are so much wiser, it is time to rewrite your Heroine's Journey Story. In this new version you'll extract the voice of the Victim and herald your narrative as a Heroine.

Let's begin this process by doing a Visualization before you sit down to write.

This will get you into the spirit of the Heroine and remind you of the steps on the Journey so that you can rewrite your Story with power.

Visualization: Your Heroine's Story

Sit comfortably as you read this.

Imagine the place in which you feel most safe and nourished. This may be the beach, your own bed, under an oak tree or in your childhood home. Just read into this with an easy heart and an open mind.

Take a long deep breath in . . . and exhale slowly.

Again . . . breathe in . . . breathe out.

Feel yourself settle into your body comfortably.

Place your right hand over your heart . . . place your left hand over your belly.

Breathe in . . . breathe out.

We are going to visit each of the 10 Steps to Stability on The Heroine's Journey. Just let the words guide you, as you relax.

Feel yourself full of the Courage and Strength of the Heroine. As you feel her arise within you, she will come forth as your power. She is the Voice of your Freedom.

Listen as you hear her Voice as your own, guiding you.

The first step is . . .

1. *Status Quo*:

This is when you are:

> Living in your comfort zone. Life was good enough on the outside, even if it felt empty on the inside.

From within, your Heroine wakes up and reasons:

> "I am not looking back with envy and glory on my Comfort Zone. I look at its limitations honestly and shed this skin willingly. There is a purposeful reason it is no longer the circumstances in which I live."

Then . . .

2. *Crisis Appears*:

> The unthinkable happens. You've been knocked flat.

> Your Heroine digs into acceptance . . .

> "This Crisis is the catalyst of my transformation. I trust that this situation is aiding my growth, no matter how painful it may be in the moment."

> Along comes the . . .

3. *Challenge:*

> This is your darkest moment. You're confronted with your choice to fall on the rocks below or to power yourself to rise into the sky. You feel fear. You wonder: "Can I make it? Could I be ruined, die here, fall off the planet?"

> Your Heroine aligns herself . . .

> "I am not going to give up on life! It's up to me now. I have to surrender what is no longer working. I am being purified."

> So begins . . .

4. *The Crusade*:

> The circumstances are dire. You muster up Courage and Strength for a Journey into the wild. You face new realities.

Your Heroine fiercely lays claim . . .

"I don't have to suffer. I feel the fire in my belly and I know I have Courage. Life is messy, but I have faith in new possibilities."

Blessedly the . . .

5. *Angels Show Up*:

People that you never expected come to help like some universal energy called them to your aid. You feel their love and they bring hope.

The Heroine surrenders to receive . . .

"I embrace the humility that I can't do it all by myself. I am willing to be vulnerable and seen for who I truly am."

Your Aha moment illuminates in . . . .

6. *Character Revelation*:

Your inner Voice speaks a truth to you and reveals your essential character. You realize what you are made of which is far more than what you had thought.

The Heroine proclaims her Self-Worth . . .

"I am vast in my capabilities and my potential. I have the Strength to move forward. I can, and I will."

You get resourceful in….

7. *Gathering Your Provisions*:

You draw in Life-Force energy and all of the resources you require to sustain yourself on the Journey.

The Heroine owns it . . .

"I am savvy and responsible to generate what I need to fuel my flight"

You blaze into . . .

8. *Taking Empowered Action*:

You force yourself into critical action from a new empowered place in order to navigate the wilds. And you lift off. You flap your wings wildly and keep your eye on the horizon.

Your Heroine lasers in. "I get to design the Story of my life any way I want it. I master new skills, tools, and talents. They strengthen my wings and I fly."

Unexpectedly, it happens, the . . .

9. *Wind Currents that Test You*:

Suddenly, another Challenge comes along in the form of a big wind that whips you around, scares and imbalances you. You wonder, "Will this take me out when I have finally come so far?"

Wait a minute, *I am a Heroine*! I have strong wings.

"I keep the faith when it gets bumpy again. Another level of refinement for my highest good is underway. I won't get worn down. I choose to show up with confidence to navigate another adversity. This points me to glorious horizons."

You soar in . . .

10. *Crescendo*:

This is the quickening. Finally, the air currents around you become stable. You are out of survival and struggle mode, and into the freedom of soaring through the air. Your power is in your wholeness.

Your Heroine revels in the Journey . . .

"I am lifted into freedom! I have finally created Stability and this is my way of life. I have transformed my experience on my Heroine's Journey from the worst thing that ever happened to the best thing that ever happened to me. My Journey is meaningful and I am thankful for how it has purposely and eternally transformed me."

Now,

Feel into this moment of internal freedom. . .
Feel your Strength and Courage . . .
Feel your heart expanded . . .
Feel the hope you have for your life now . . .
Feel your spirit soaring . . .
This is your natural state of being. . .

Take a snapshot in your mind's eye of this image of you as the Heroine soaring in joy, prosperity and freedom.
Keep this image of your Heroine soaring in your heart . . . .
Now you are ready to rewrite your Heroine's Story from power and Self-Worth.
Now, with Journal and Plume (that's a pen!) — Begin.

Re-write your Heroine's Journey Story from the point of view of the Heroine being prompted by each one of the Journey Steps. Become that powerful narrator who consciously transforms her life through the Steps of the Journey.
Stop here to write your Story. You can get a full description of each Journey Step in the Free Resources: Chapter 1 at www.HeroinesBook.com/Free-Resources. Ready, set — Go for it!

Tell your Story from your Heroine — who claims her Self-Worth and her Voice:

Step 1: Status Quo
Step 2: Crisis Appears

Step 3: Challenge
Step 4: The Crusade
Step 5: Angels Show Up
Step 6: Character Revelation
Step 7: Gathering Your Provisions
Step 8: Taking Empowered Action
Step 9: Wind Currents that Test You
Step 10: Crescendo

Pick up again when your Story is complete — and you've written your new picture in your Journal.

You have a new Story now, the one of the Heroine. With this new Story, you know who you are and you know you are on the right Path. You are connected and supported by all of Life. And your Story will have a happy ending. You are traveling home to True Wealth.

Wooo hooo, you've come a long way, Baby! You've shown up, dug deep, pushed through resistance and taken a stand even when it wasn't easy. You've done the work. Now your Journal reflects the magic of your transformations.

Here is the beauty of life, when you step in and contribute, life turns toward you and gives you something back.

This finishes *your* work in The Heroine's Journey to True Wealth: Creating Your Stability Book.

YOUR HEROINE'S JOURNAL

The value of your Heroine's Journal — and the internal work that you've done to align your life! — Keep working in your Journal to tell your Heroine Story.

Here it is, your Journal…

- Proclaims you as the Heroine of your own life.
- Serves as the complete blueprint for creating your Stability.

- Outlines your Heroine's Journey and shows you where you are now.
- Reframes your challenges into opportunities.
- Highlights your intentions and commitments.
- Keeps you accountable.
- Inspires and Empowers you, when you need it most.
- Directs you to a life of joy and happiness, on your Heroine's Journey to True Wealth.

This Journal is your manifesto as the Heroine of your own Life. You get to go out into the world and be this *BIG*, possessing all of the security, resources, Strength and Courage that you need for your Journey ahead. Your Journey to Stability sets the stage so that you can be ready for your ever-expanding adventure into the next Steps of your Heroine's Journey.

With this firm foundation of Stability in place, you will blossom into your Authenticity, then, Expression and then, Contribution - Steps 11, 12 and 13 on the Heroine's Journey RoadMap. You'll be ready for how juicy and powerful life is as a fully embodied Heroine!

Now, with your Journal in hand, from a place of receptivity, carve out a quiet hour or so and read back through it thoughtfully and with gratitude, to remind yourself of all that you covered in this Book. As you read the truth of your own soul, something magical will happen.

Fly free, my Sister! Fly high!

YOUR SUCCESS AS A HEROINE

Wait, this is not the end of the Journey! There is more adventure ahead.

A profound opportunity is coming your way to deeply connect with your community of Heroines, get support and stay in the energy of the Heroine's Journey.

Don't flap around on your own. It is so much better when the Journey is guided and shared — faster, easier and so much more fun.

So please continue to Chapter 8, a short Epilogue that offers a big surprise.

Stay with us and Journey into the Horizon - the technicolor beauty of your fully purposeful life.

"A Heroine Claims Her Self-Worth and Her Voice" — Victory!

~ Joan Perry

8
The Heroine of Your Own Life

Going Forward

Free Resources

Bonus

Join Us

Glossary

GOING FORWARD

"If you change the way you tell your own Story, you can change the color and create a life in technicolor."

— Isabel Allende (Chilean Writer)

And Being The Heroine of Your Own Life *is* rewriting your Story. Does it feel good to read your Story as a Heroine — with hope, Strength, Courage, and a full claim on your Self-Worth? Living your Heroine-Self is your 'thing' now — from now on! And you know how to do this with your Four Cornerstones in place. Congratulations on this powerful work that you have done for yourself for your joy, prosperity and freedom!

And hold on!…there is more to come. Your Journey is rolling now, and I want to inspire and encourage you with more to come. In order to Journey Onward, stay in the middle of the Path, and fly your highest —

to be truly successful and uplifted in your life — you must stay awake, engaged and committed. Yep, this is an ongoing practice. I know this because my Circle of Love Heroines remind me when I forget.

If I resort to a victim comment — they say "Cowgirl Up, Joan"! Yep, they call me to remember who I am. They pony me up to own my Self-Worth to speak my Truth. It's a magical place to live — and my life is enormously better with this encouragement.

These Heroines pull me forward to my Heroine-Self and cheer me on to go forth with more of all the juicy stuff. It's about love and support — and most importantly staying accountable to my Tasks and foundational Cornerstones.

The Path Ahead

Remember that 'Stability' is only the first ten Steps on The Heroine's Journey. Creating 'Stability' is only what prepares you for the rest of the expansive Journey ahead. As a Heroine, you evolve into your full blossoming Step-by-Step, taking you from preparation to liberation!

First you Create Your Stability — getting your Stability in place. Stability is a work in process. Work that you are doing right now. We've covered so much here in this Book, wisdom that I touch back into every day of my life. And, it may take some time for you to incorporate into your life all that you've learned here . . . be patient and consistently up-level your life.

When you are ready, it will be time to roll your momentum forward into the next Steps of the Journey. There are thirteen Steps to be explored on The Heroine's Journey. The three remaining Steps are huge, each in themselves. So big that more learning is offered for each one of them! These include:

Step 11: Awaken Your Authenticity

It's about becoming your Authentic Self — owning your Self-Worth and Voice — in what you say and do,

Step 12: Light Up Your Expression

This one is about how you recognize and monetize your Gifts.

Step 13: Make Your Contribution

This last Step is about how you serve by fulfilling your Life Purpose. This brings you home to True Wealth.

Pretty exciting, right? This is a life fully lived — this is the Path of The Heroine's Journey.

As our Heroine's Community grows, we will embark on the next level of this life's work as we grow together. Expect 'Authenticity' to be as juicy and impact-filled as this Book has been for 'Create Your Stability'. You'll be soaring high and expanding into this new level once you have the solid foundation of your Stability. The Journey still has so much more to offer.

This is the big picture. But let's not get ahead of ourselves at this point. You have reached new vistas in flight, let's admire the landscape as we fly onward. Let's enjoy the Journey, honor what we've traveled through, what we've overcome and the gains made — and celebrate our blossoming into our Best-Selves. There are more gifts to be offered right here and right now.

FREE RESOURCES

Did you get all of your Free Resources at: www.HeroinesBook.com/ Free-Resources?

We've made them for you so that you can put to work The Heroine's Journey in your own life. Chances are you found some of your Cornerstones needing some work, and we want to help you. I know for me, when life gets a little out of kilter, rocky or more unsettling — the first thing that I do is review the Cornerstones, and ask myself what is up in each one of them — and where I need to narrow in to align things again.

I call them 'Pop' quizzes — when you think that you've got it and the wheels of your cart are rolling along just fine. Then oooppppssss! Something shows up. This happened to me recently in a big way!

I won't go into all of the details here. But I can tell you that it was more than really important that I could review my Cornerstone — get Fierce Feminine about my Self-Worth — and carry on as best I could until I could move on to get free of the circumstances. It was a 'Pop' quiz test of my Self-Worth, and my understanding of the dynamics that I was confined to for a period of time. Yiiiippppeeee, I walked away 'head held high'.

Because of this, I didn't waste a minute of getting on with my joyful, freedom-seeking, prosperity-driven life. I wish this for you too!

So, go now — get all of your Resources, and Heroine-On!

BONUS:

And we've got you.

Because you're committed and you've worked all the way through the Book — we have a *Bonus* for you! We have a deep discount for you for The Heroine's Journey: Create Your Stability Course. Yes, here you can apply what you've learned to the reality of your own life. And, we'll tell you about our Coaching programs. We are all about Heroining-Up — so you grow to your Best-Self and live the life of your dreams.

Carry on with us.

You'll find more on this at: www.HeroinesBook.com/Free-Resources

Did you know that we have a Podcast? You'll find us on your favorite streaming platform — The Heroine's Journey Podcast with Joan Perry.

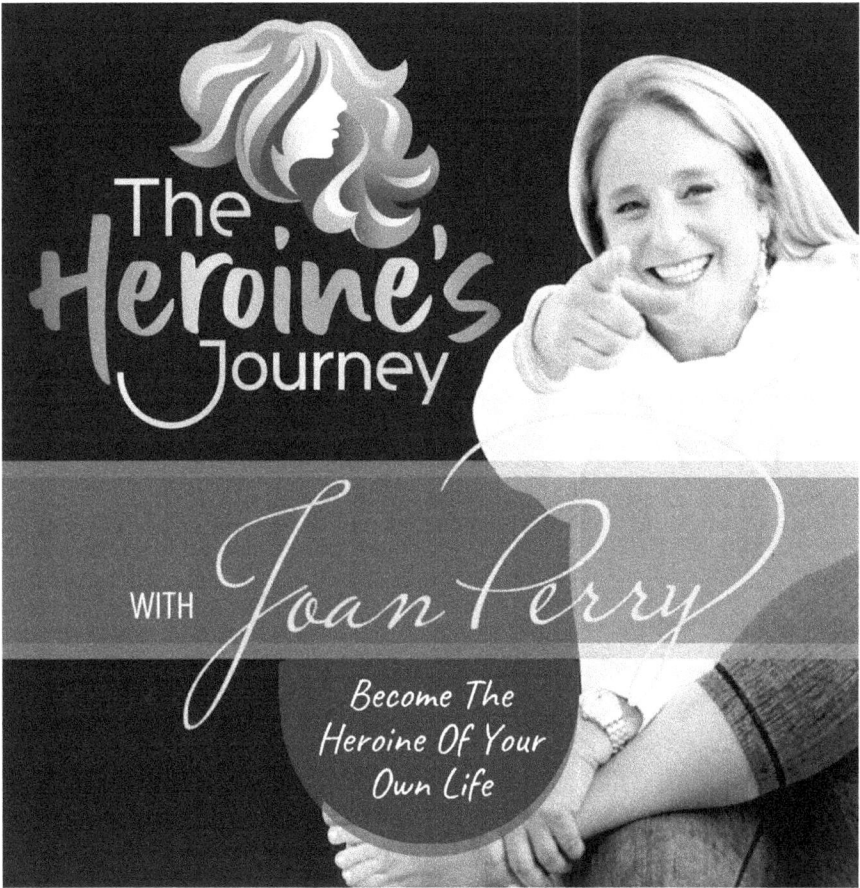

Tune into our Podcast at:
The Heroine's Journey
With Joan Perry

And we'd love to hear from you on our Facebook page and Linked-In at:
The Heroine's Journey with Joan Perry.

Check out our website at: www.WalkTheJourney.com

JOIN US!

We don't want you to feel like you are taking the Journey alone. Remember, our Stories are different, but the Path of the Journey is universal. In the Community, women share their Journeys and camaraderie lights the way. Here are some of the benefits:

Keeps you in the good energy you've created in this Book
Reminds you to think like a Heroine
Reminds you that you now live in your Self-Worth
Brings new insights and discussion

Just sayin, your Heroine will thank you for giving her what she needs to Thrive, and she *does* want to Thrive!

Journey Onward!!

Glossary

The Heroine's Journey:

The Heroine's Journey is a dynamic adventure that every woman must take to become her True Self. As she progresses through all 13 steps on her unique path, through the Challenges and Celebrations, she fortifies her Courage and Strength. This is her calling to blossom into a life of purpose and fulfillment, her True Wealth.

Heroine:

A woman who consciously cultivates an inner state of invincible knowingness of her own Self-Worth and is enraptured by her connectedness to the origin of all life. With perseverance, she aligns her outer actions to first serve her own Well-Being so that she can activate her purpose for the greater good.

One Defining Moment:

Your One Defining Moment is the moment your inner Heroine awakes! She said, 'I am Heroine, watch me fly!' It's the moment you choose to be the Heroine of your own Journey. This is a universal passage of transformation on your Path. It is so strong that it serves to navigate your decisions and actions from this moment forward. You are forever changed.

Heroine's Proclamation:

Your Heroine's Proclamation is born from your One Defining Moment. It's your rebel yell, the specific words that burst forth from your soul.

Words that empower who you are and how you will live. It's the Fierce Feminine rising, the rally cry that delivers you into utilizing the inherent power that is within you.

True Wealth:

True Wealth is the power to cultivate all the love, money, meaning and impact you can dream of while being fully in alignment with the values of your True Self. It's consciously developing all aspects of abundance, including: money, assets, people, lifestyle, physical energy and Self-Worth. It is about creating sustenance, security, and most of all, the freedom to live your full expression.

True-Self:

Your True-Self is the purest part of you, where your wisdom and power reside. In this place, you are clear and stable. Driven by a deep sense of Truth and connectedness, you act from Love.

Stability:

Stability takes root in your life when you dedicate yourself to developing the skills, tools and support systems to create a solid foundation. This brings what you need to feel supported in this world. This engenders a feeling of security and comfort that sustains you through life's challenges. Stability is the first destination to reach in the Heroine's Journey. It is the gatekeeper to designing the rich and purposeful life that you desire.

Self-Worth:

Self-Worth is your inner sense of knowing that you are a magnificent expression of Creation. This is not your ego speaking; it's your bigger, better self that lives within you. It's your Heroine-Self. This Self is what guides you on the Path of the Heroine's Journey to living the life that you truly want.

Life-Force:

Your Life-Force is the natural and spiritual energy that animates you with vitality and strength. It is the unique essence of you, that dynamic force, that runs through you to activate your power. It is your Life-Force that propels you through the entire Heroine's Journey.

Circle of Love:

A Circle of Love is 8 to 10 people who love and support you unconditionally with whom you have consciously cultivated a vulnerable and strengthening relationship that is reciprocal. Your Circle of Love people are there to lend a hand, give you a balanced outside perspective, contribute skills and knowledge, send positive energy and love, and hold you accountable. You can share vulnerably and ask for help. They truly care about you. When life gets challenging you won't feel alone. Your Circle of Love offers Hero- and Heroine-level support for your Stability.

Money:

Money is energy. It is a means of exchange that helps you acquire the earthly resources that you need for the Journey for yourself, and to contribute to others.

Financial Stability:

Financial Stability is about making money in alignment with your True-Self, gathering what you need, living within your means, keeping your money safe, and being a woman who can support herself throughout her lifetime.

The Heroine's Journey

"I don't know what the counterpart would be in the woman's case . . .

There is a feminine counterpart to the trials and the difficulties, but it certainly is in a different mode.

I don't know the counterpart--the real counterpart, not the woman pretending to be male, but the normal feminine archetypology of this experience.

I wouldn't know what that would be.

Women will have to tell us the way a woman experiences the journey, if it is the same journey."

Joseph Campbell
Archive audio L1184, Big Sur, CA, 11/8/83

www.ingramcontent.com/pod-product-compliance
Lightning Source LLC
Chambersburg PA
CBHW062201270326
41930CB00009B/1610